Iran's Nuclear Ambitions

Shahram Chubin

CARNEGIE ENDOWMENT FOR INTERNATIONAL PEACE
Washington, D.C.

Carnegie Endowment for International Peace
1779 Massachusetts Avenue, N.W., Washington, D.C. 20036
202-483-7600, Fax 202-483-1840
www.CarnegieEndowment.org

The Carnegie Endowment for International Peace normally does not take institutional positions on public policy issues; the views and recommendations presented in this publication do not necessarily represent the views of the Carnegie Endowment, its officers, staff, or trustees.

To order, contact:
Hopkins Fulfillment Service
P.O. Box 50370, Baltimore, MD 21211-4370
1-800-537-5487 or 1-410-516-6956
Fax 1-410-516-6998

Composition by Oakland Street Publishing
Printed by Edwards Brothers, Inc.

Library of Congress Cataloging-in-Publication data
Chubin, Shahram.
  Iran's nuclear ambitions / Shahram Chubin.
     p. cm.
  Summary: "Iranian-born Shahram Chubin narrates the recent history of Iran's nuclear program and diplomacy, and argues that the central problem is not nuclear technology but rather Iran's behavior as a revolutionary state with ambitions that collide with the interests of its neighbors and the West"—Provided by publisher.
  Includes bibliographical references and index.
  ISBN-13: 978-0-87003-230-1 (pbk.)
  ISBN-10: 0-87003-230-5 (pbk.)
  ISBN-13: 978-0-87003-231-8 (cloth)
  ISBN-10: 0-87003-231-3 (cloth)
  1. Nuclear weapons—Iran. 2. Iran—Military policy. 3. Nuclear arms control—Iran.
I. Title.

  UA853.I7C497 2006
  355.02'170955–dc22   2006018183

11 10 09 08 07 06   1 2 3 4 5   1st Printing 2006

For Nasrin and Nanaz

Contents

Foreword

Iran's nuclear program looms ever larger among international threats. Were Iran to acquire a nuclear weapon, it could menace Israel, whose existence Iran does not recognize, blackmail smaller neighboring states, and possibly deter the United States from fulfilling security guarantees to regional states or projecting power throughout the Persian Gulf. A nuclear Iran could be emboldened to foment political unrest throughout the Middle East, especially in countries with large Shiite minorities. Moreover, if Iran were to succeed in continuing to defy IAEA and, perhaps, UN Security Council demands to come back into compliance with its non-proliferation obligations, the effectiveness of the non-proliferation regime would be gravely undermined. The international community, particularly the UN Security Council, would be exposed as unwilling or unable to enforce vital global rules. The world would appear ever more disordered.

While Iranian leaders insist their intentions are entirely peaceful, three years of intensive investigation by the International Atomic Energy Agency (chronicled in twelve agency reports) have failed to resolve the issues arising from nearly two decades of Iranian violations of its safeguard commitments. These violations and ongoing Iranian resistance to transparency measures demanded by the IAEA's board of governors heighten fears that Iran does seek the capability to build nuclear weapons.

Decision making works by elite consensus in Iran but the elite is not monolithic—it is as segmented as the rest of the society. While its members believe Iran should develop nuclear technology as other major powers do, opinions differ on the manner in which the technology has been pursued and the wisdom of confronting the international community and defying the Security Council. The elite are divided more broadly on their willingness to engage the United States, to seek a "grand bargain," and to embrace globalization and act as a "normal," non-revolutionary state. That is, they are divided on the conditions under which they would give up the drive for fuel cycle capabilities that would give Iran a nuclear weapon option.

While the international implications of Iran's nuclear activities have been widely analyzed, the domestic factors that determine who makes decisions in Iran and why have largely been ignored in the West. Iran remains a country of unique complexity and contradictions. It has a quasi-representative government, claiming popular support, but also suffering legitimacy and economic problems. Iranians are fiercely independent and proudly nationalistic, united in resisting foreign dictation. But they are not as one in believing that the nuclear issue is the most important issue for the country—most citizens have other priorities.

Subterranean tensions within Iran have intensified since the June 2005 election of Mahmoud Ahmadinejad as President. A populist and fundamentalist, Ahmadinejad harked back to the original principles of the revolution. His brand of revolutionary rhetoric and hypernationalism combined with calls for more social justice resonated with a neglected constituency in the country. In fusing two features of contemporary Iran, militant nationalism and revolutionary defiance, Ahmadinejad reduces Iran's room for maneuver and makes a difficult issue more intractable.

Shahram Chubin's analysis is the most trenchant English-language treatment to date of how Iran's domestic dynamics, regional interests, and worldview shape the country's decision making regarding nuclear technology. *Iran's Nuclear Ambitions* integrates this comprehensive analysis with an assessment of the international community's attempts to bring Iran into compliance with its nonproliferation obligations. The result is a uniquely well-rounded treatment of the Iranian nuclear challenge.

Chubin adeptly describes the ambivalence of Western policy that, reflecting differences between the United States and France, Germany, and the United Kingdom, has been torn between promoting "critical dialogue," constructive engagement, and inducement, on one side, and containment, sanctions, and regime change on the other. He argues forcefully that Iran will be unmoved as long as the international community does not employ a more balanced policy that both neutralizes Iran's threat and provides incentives for evolution and accommodation. To achieve such a balance, the European states and Russia and China must demonstrate a greater willingness to exert stringent political and economic pressure on Iran in cooperation with the United States, while the United States must show that it is genuinely prepared to establish positive relations with the constitutional government of Iran. The countries negotiating with Iran cannot find the proper mix of isolation and cooperation, pressure and reward, if they do not take into account the divisions within Iran and the divergent interests they reflect.

Chubin argues that the distinction between engaging with Iran and seeking to change its government is false and therefore part of the problem. In his view, engagement is not an alternative to regime change but a precursor and stimulant to it, in the sense of evolutionary change driven by domestic forces. Opening up Iran by embracing it, he argues, will liberate pent-up dynamics for change. It is this element that the Iranian elite fears and resists, preferring embattlement and isolation in order to keep their hold on power. Focusing on the Iranian people and their welfare and human rights is therefore an important ingredient of a successful non-proliferation policy. Understanding this proposition suggests a substantial broadening of Western policy concerns.

This work is a welcome new baseline from which policy makers, scholars, journalists, and students can acquire deeper understanding and better ideas for addressing the interests of the Iranian people as well as the international community. Iran will not be bullied into submitting to policies that do not fit the country's history, self-image, and interests. At the same time, the international community's legitimate interest in preventing Iran from acquiring nuclear weapons is enormous and must be vigorously—and intelligently—pursued. *Iran's Nuclear Ambitions* offers insights into how this can be done. It is a model blend of historical knowledge, contemporary analysis, and policy prescription.

Jessica T. Mathews
President
Carnegie Endowment for International Peace

Acknowledgments

I am indebted to many colleagues for discussions on this issue over the past years. They are too numerous to mention but include Tony Cordesman, Joseph Cirincione, Thérèse Delpech, Bob Einhorn, Ariel Levite, Harald Muller, Vladimir Orlov, John Simpson, Scott Sagan, Paul Stares, and Pal Sidhu. For their encouragement I would especially single out Geoff Kemp, Rob Litwak, and Gary Samore. I am grateful to George Perkovich, who improved the draft with suggestions to make it more readable and guided it to publication, which he has made possible. The team at Carnegie who edited and tightened the manuscript also have helped the author immeasurably. Finally, I am grateful to Paul Clark and especially to Katya Shadrina, who have helped with indispensable research assistance, facilitating the completion of the book. To all of the above, I express my appreciation for making a difficult job more bearable. None is responsible for any errors or shortcomings.

Acronyms

AP	Additional Protocol
AEO	Atomic Energy Organization of Iran
EU	European Union
EU-3	Grouping consisting of Great Britain, France, and Germany
FAS	Federation of Atomic Scientists
G-8	Grouping of top industrialized nations of the world: United States, Japan, UK, Germany, France, Italy, Canada, and Russia (also known as the G7+1).
GCC	Gulf Cooperation Council
GPS	Global positioning system
IAEA	International Atomic Energy Agency
ILSA	Iran and Libya Sanctions Act
IRI	Islamic Republic of Iran
IRGC	Iranian Revolutionary Guards Corps (or Pasdaran)
IISS	International Institute for Strategic Studies
MOK	Mujahideen i-Khalq, Iranian opposition group
NAM	Non-Aligned Movement
NATO	North Atlantic Treaty Organization
NFZ	Nuclear-free zone
NMD	National Missile Defense
NNWS	Non-nuclear-weapons-state

NPT	Treaty on the Non-Proliferation of Nuclear Weapons
NW	Nuclear weapon
NWS	Nuclear weapons state
P-5	Permanent five members of the United Nations Security Council
PSI	Proliferation Security Initiative
SCO	Shanghai Cooperation Organization
SCIRI	Supreme Council for the Islamic Republic of Iraq
SCUD	Ballistic missile, derived from the German World War II V-2 rocket
SNSC	Supreme National Security Council
UCF	Uranium Conversion Facility
UN	United Nations
UNSC	United Nations Security Council
UNSCOM	United Nations Special Commission
WMD	Weapons of mass destruction
WMDFZ	Weapons of mass destruction free zone
WTO	World Trade Organization

Iranian Nuclear Chronology

2002

August 14   Alireza Jafarzadeh of the National Council of Resistance of Iran (NCRI) reveals to IAEA that Tehran not only possesses its declared nuclear power plant at Bushire but also two undisclosed nuclear facilities: a uranium enrichment facility at Natanz and a heavy water plant at Arak.

September 1   Russian technicians start construction of nuclear reactor at Bushire, amid strong U.S. objections. Iran notifies the IAEA that it is building new facilities as a step toward developing a nuclear fuel cycle.

December 13   U.S. State Department spokesman Richard Boucher concludes that Iran is "actively working to develop nuclear-weapons capability," releasing satellite images of sites at Natanz and Arak.

December 18   Iran's President Mohammad Khatami states that "Iran is working under the supervision of the International Atomic Energy Agency, and Iran is a signatory to the [nuclear] Non-proliferation Treaty and does not seek nuclear arms," rejecting U.S. allegations of Iran aspiring to develop a nuclear weapons capability.

2003

January 10   North Korea withdraws from the Treaty on the Non-Proliferation of Nuclear Weapons (NPT).

| February 9 | President Khatami announces Iran's intent to exploit uranium mines in Savand region, with ambitions for a complete nuclear fuel cycle, despite agreement for Russia to provide all necessary uranium fuel for lifetime of Bushire reactor. Plants are to be set up at Isfahan and Kashan for this purpose. |

February 13 U.S. Secretary of State Colin Powell warns Congress to be prepared for a "fairly long-term commitment" in Iraq.

February 25 IAEA Director-General Mohammad Al Baradei inspects Natanz and Arak, following several postponements of such a visit by the Iranians. Inspection team detects breach of NPT. Al Baradei reports being "taken aback" by the advanced state of Iran's program. Iran agrees to discuss additional protocols in future negotiations.

March 11 Iran's Atomic Energy Organization (AEO) Deputy Director Assadollah Saburi announces Iran's opposition to signing Additional Protocols to the NPT that would allow unannounced inspections due to already imposed sanctions. A readiness to sign if sanctions are dropped is expressed.

March 20 U.S. invasion of Iraq commences.

April 24 Al Baradei urges Iran to sign Additional Protocol allowing inspections of undeclared suspected nuclear sites. Khatami asks: "Why do countries possessing such [civilian atomic energy] technology not respect the principles of the nonproliferation treaty by not helping us acquire it?"

June 6 IAEA issues report to thirty-five member countries on nuclear safeguards in Iran, in preparation for the IAEA Board of Governors meeting in Vienna, describing breaches of NPT on several accounts by Iran. Iran issues a report about construction of a heavy water production plant at Arak.

June 19 IAEA reports that "Iran has failed to meet its obligations under the Safeguards Agreement with respect to the reporting of nuclear material, the subsequent processing and use of the material and the declaration of facilities where the material was stored and processed," although it stops short of referring Iran to the UN Security Council. IAEA requires Iran to produce a report divulging all nuclear and nuclear-related capabilities and technology with a complete chronology. IAEA report mentions several finds of highly enriched uranium in Iranian centrifuges at various sites. Iran, although admitting to uranium conversion experiments in the 1990s, suggests it must have acquired contaminated centrifuge components from abroad, sparking new investigations into Iran's foreign connections.

September 12   IAEA resolution calls for Iran's full cooperation with IAEA investigations, transparency, and cessation of uranium enrichment–related activities by October 31. United States announces that this resolution is Iran's last chance before referral to UN Security Council.

October 10   Hasan Rowhani is officially appointed as head of Iranian nuclear "dossier."

October 21   France, Great Britain, and Germany (EU-3) broker deal with Iran to suspend uranium enrichment, albeit temporarily. Iran also agrees to "address and resolve ... all requirements and outstanding [IAEA] issues," as well as sign and ratify additional protocols (known as Tehran agreement).

November 10   IAEA report issued suggesting that despite clear breaches to its obligations according to the safeguard agreements, there is no evidence of an Iranian nuclear weapons program following Iranian nuclear confessions. United States disagrees, calling IAEA conclusion "impossible to believe."

November 21   Iran proposes signing the Additional Protocol to the NPT, allowing for unannounced inspections, which is welcomed by the IAEA.

November 26   IAEA Board of Governors resolution adopted "strongly deploring Iran's past failures and breaches of its obligation to comply with the provisions of its Safeguards Agreement." Resolution includes trigger mechanism for immediate IAEA meeting if "any further serious Iranian failures come to light." U.S. Secretary of State Colin Powell is "very satisfied" with the resolution.

November 29   Iran has "voluntarily and temporarily" suspended uranium enrichment program, according to Hasan Rowhani, Secretary General of Iran's Supreme National Secretary Council. He adds that the program was "not in question and never has been, nor will be."

December 18   Iran signs the Additional Protocol to NPT, although its parliament needs to ratify the protocol before it enters into legal force.

2004

February 12   Previously undisclosed centrifuge designs found by IAEA. Pakistan suspected of providing both centrifuge and nuclear weapon designs to Iran, following AQ Kahn admissions about proliferation ring on February 4.

February 13   Hamid Reza Asefi, Iran's foreign ministry spokesman, clarifies that Iranian advances toward nuclear fuel cycle technology were an attempt to overcome U.S. sanctions, ensuring self-sufficiency. He adds that Iran is in favor of banning WMDs.

February 24   Al Baradei issues report noting Iran's continuing failure to resolve IAEA's concerns about its nuclear program.

March 9   NCRI's former spokesman Alireza Jafarzadeh alleges that Iranian leaders have recently ruled on acquiring nuclear weapons "at all costs," by the end of 2005 at the latest.

March 13   Iran bans inspectors in protest of IAEA resolution condemning Iranian failure to disclose all its nuclear activities.

April 6   Al Baradei and Iran agree on joint plan to resolve IAEA concerns by disclosing information about its centrifuge program by the end of April.

May 10   Nuclear site at Lavizan that was under investigation by the IAEA is destroyed by Tehran.

June 18   IAEA resolution adopted condemning Iran's failure to comply with inspectors, urging a more forthcoming approach by Iran. Iranian chief nuclear negotiator Hasan Rowhani responds by informing the IAEA that in the following days, Iran would decide on whether to resume its uranium enrichment program. He accuses the EU-3 of violating the October 2003 agreement.

June 24   Iran informs the EU-3 of its intention to resume its uranium enrichment program, effectively canceling the October 2003 agreement.

August 17   U.S. Under Secretary of State John Bolton claims that Iran admitted to the EU-3 that it was able to enrich enough uranium within a year to produce a nuclear weapon.

August 31   Iranian Information Minister Ali Younesi announces the arrest of several Mujahideen i-Khalq (MOK) members for "transferring Iran's nuclear information (out of the country)."

September 20   IAEA requests suspension of Iranian uranium enrichment program at the IAEA's 48th General Conference.

November 15   Iran agrees to the "Paris agreement," suspending uranium enrichment and related activities following talks with the EU-3. According to Hasan Rowhani, this is done "to improve relations with the West." Al Baradei reports to the IAEA that all known Iranian nuclear material has been accounted for but added that the IAEA cannot rule out any undeclared material.

2005

January 6   Iran agrees to allow IAEA visit to Parchin military site, following transparency issues. Visit limited to one of four areas identified to be of interest.

February 9   According to President Khatami, Iran will never give up its rights to peaceful nuclear technology.

February 10   North Korea admits to having nuclear weapons.

March 1   Al Baradei expresses concern about Iran not fully cooperating with inspections, although highlights that no new evidence of illicit activities has come forth. Iran is reported to still be in compliance with the Paris agreement.

March 12   Bush backs EU negotiations with Iran, offering to lift U.S. block on Iranian World Trade Organization membership as an incentive for Iran to comply.

April 30   President Khatami states that a complete halt of uranium enrichment is unacceptable, although he is willing to negotiate or compromise.

May 24   EU-3 officials meet with Iranian counterparts in Geneva, pending Iranian intentions of recommencing uranium processing at Isfahan. Iran is warned of being referred to the Security Council if this occurs. Iranians agree to suspend uranium processing in lieu of new European proposal due at the end of July.

July 26   President Khatami issues statement declaring Iran's intent to resume part of its nuclear fuel cycle program, regardless of European proposals.

August 2   President Khatami steps down. Mahmoud Ahmadinejad elected to succeed him.

August 3   Official U.S. study puts Iranian nuclear capability a decade away.

August 5	Europe proposes economic and political cooperation if Tehran relinquishes nuclear fuel aspirations.
August 6	Iran rejects European proposal, stating it does not meet Iran's minimum expectations. Europe cancels further negotiations.
August 8	Isfahan facility resumes uranium processing.
August 11	IAEA adopts resolution expressing concern over Iran's August 1 notification to the IAEA of resumed uranium conversion at Isfahan.
August 15	President Ahmadinejad appoints Ali Larijani to replace Hasan Rowhani as head of Iran's Supreme National Security Council.
August 23	Independent research reveals that weapons-grade uranium found mid-2003 was due to contaminated equipment from Pakistan, not Iranian activities. The United States dismisses this report.
August 27	Larijani states that Iran respects its commitment to the NPT.
September 2	IAEA Board of Governors reports progress over Iranian nuclear issue but calls for improved transparency and cooperation from Iran. Agency reiterates it cannot be sure there are no undeclared sites.
September 6	International Institute for Strategic Studies (IISS) dossier on Iran estimates Iran is several years away from a nuclear capability, given technical problems.
September 15	President Ahmadinejad reaffirms Iran's right to nuclear energy at a speech held at the UN 60th Session.
September 20	North Korea agrees to give up its "existing nuclear weapons" and return to the NPT after talks with the United States. North Korea announces plans to commence a peaceful nuclear energy program.
September 24	IAEA resolution warning Iran of referral to the UN Security Council, unless measures are taken to increase transparency measure, reestablish suspension of enrichment-related activity, and reconsider heavy water research reactor.
September 25	Iran rejects IAEA resolution.
October 13	Iran agrees to resume talks with EU-3.
October 26	Iranian President Ahmadinejad declares in a speech that Israel should be "wiped off the map."
November 24	IAEA Board of Governors' meeting addresses verification of Iran's nuclear program.

2006

January 3	Iran informs IAEA of its intent to resume research and development of peaceful nuclear technology.
January 10	Iran removes IAEA seals at enrichment sites.
January 16	P-5 (permanent five members of the UN Security Council) meets in London to discuss the Iranian nuclear crisis.
January 18	IAEA decides to hold a special meeting on Iran on February 2.
January 25	Hamas wins Palestinian parliamentary election.
February 2	IAEA Board of Governors meets to consider a draft resolution calling for Iran to be referred to the Security Council (supported by EU-3, Russia, China, and the United States).
February 4	Resolution adopted by IAEA Board of Governors, calling for IAEA Director-General to refer Iran to the UN Security Council with a 27 to 3 majority (5 abstentions).
February 9	U.S. Secretary of State Condoleezza Rice accuses Iran and Syria of inciting violence over the Mohammad cartoon controversy.
February 17	Iranian foreign minister calls for the United Kingdom to leave Iraq.
March 1	Negotiations on Russian proposal begin in Moscow.
March 8	IAEA submits report on Iran's nuclear program to the UN Security Council.

Introduction

In its twenty-seventh year, it is not clear whether the government of the Islamic Republic of Iran (IRI) still rejects the international system and seeks to overturn it, or is striving to improve its position within the system. This question is posed starkly with respect to Iran's quest for a nuclear capability. Important as it is to keep the Treaty on the Non-Proliferation of Nuclear Weapons (NPT) intact, it appears doubly so when faced by the threat of a revolutionary Iran seeking a nuclear capability. Given the nature of the Iranian regime and its past behavior, Iran's nuclear aspirations appear incompatible with the maintenance of the current regional system. The Middle East in particular and the global order more generally are thus challenged by Iran's quest for nuclear status.

Iran's drive for specific nuclear technology that could be used for weapons purposes raises a number of questions for the international community. The more specific issues relate to Iran's particular case as a revolutionary state, accused of sponsoring terrorism and located in a sensitive geopolitical zone that has seen three wars in the past decade and a half. The stakes are compounded because since September 11, 2001, the relationship between terrorism and proliferation—and rogue states and weapons of mass destruction (WMD)—has become the foremost security issue. In the U.S. view at least, the wars in Afghanistan and Iraq attest to the fact that proliferation, terrorism, and the role of rogue states constitute threats that must be dealt with urgently and firmly. In this view, the "nexus of extremism and technology" suggests massive-scale danger from actors that may not be deterrable. Particularly in the Middle East, the U.S. response has been forward defense, preemption, and regime change.

The broader issues include the possible breakdown of the nonproliferation regime through further proliferation and recognition that the NPT may allow a state to get perilously close to acquiring nuclear weapons. The need to plug gaps in the treaty and to strengthen enforcement poses enormous political problems in the international system.

Global Context

The 9/11 attacks on the United States changed U.S. strategic priorities. In the 1990s non-proliferation and its link to rogue states had been identified as a priority in the post–Cold War era. These same states sponsored terrorism as well, but at this juncture terrorism was still seen as largely a law enforcement issue rather than a priority—a nuisance rather than a strategic threat. After 9/11, terrorism was transformed into a major threat, but the possibility that it might be married to WMD elevated it to a priority consistent with the risks it posed as an existential threat. Now the outlaw states became potential enablers of terrorist groups and potential suppliers of WMD to those who sought to inflict the maximum destruction on the United States. These states, dubbed the "axis of evil" in January 2002, were now clearly assimilated into the War on Terrorism. The United States' dark view of the world, based on the trauma of 9/11, was followed by a determination to prepare against any future surprise.

It soon became apparent that the rogue states had indeed cooperated in the area of WMD. North Korea and Pakistan *had* exchanged expertise on nuclear and missile technology and weapons plans. North Korea and Iran *had* cooperated in the development of missile and possibly nuclear technology as well. Pakistan *had* provided, albeit unofficially through the AQ Khan network, technology and weapons designs to Libya and Iran.[1] What was referred to as a "nuclear Wal-Mart" reflected the global diffusion of technology and the porousness of borders in a globalized world.[2] Now nonstate actors, whether motivated by profit or ideology, could further proliferation unconstrained by the legal instruments that had been devised for states.

The United States reacted by hardening its policy. It saw no need to get permission from others to see to its own defense or to require weak and elusive multilateral consensus in order to act. The United States thus moved away from the reciprocal obligation that had been the core of the WMD order in the Cold War era toward a hegemonic order based on coercion rather than consensus.[3] This move away from a rules-based global order underlies the deeper crisis of legitimacy the NPT regime faces.[4]

Therefore, while the threat posed by nuclear proliferation has increased because of its possible link with terrorism and because of the diffusion of technologies and knowledge, the political context has become less conducive to effective and legitimate (that is, collective) responses. Iran has played on these divisions to cover its programs. And it is this current malaise that has led to the invocation of the image of a cascade of proliferation if current trends persist.[5]

In dealing actively with the proliferation threat posed by Iraq in 2003, the United States has gone from a high point of regional power to a position in which its credibility is damaged and it is embroiled in an internal conflict whose outcome looks, at best, unsure. The regional context has therefore improved for Iran since 2003.

As the military threat has passed, Iran has challenged the United States' creation of a new regional order. Buttressed by record oil revenues and leverage afforded it by a tight oil market, Iran has acted more confidently. In Iraq it has become a clear influence, and in the IAEA it has used the nonaligned states' sympathy to slip out of constraints imposed by the EU-3 (Great Britain, France, and Germany) negotiations. Since August 2005 Tehran has moved to consolidate its mastery of the fuel cycle, confident in its ability to deflect or manage a referral to the UN Security Council (UNSC).

The United States has yet to adopt a formal policy toward Iran. Despite concern about terrorism and non-proliferation and fulminations about the nature of the regime in Tehran, Washington has an attitude rather than a considered, measured policy. Lukewarm support for European diplomacy, insistence on referral to the Security Council (without a strategy once there), and brandishing a military option (but refusing direct involvement) does not amount to a policy.

The key issue concerning Iran's nuclear ambitions is Tehran's quest for the full fuel cycle, which would put it within months (if not days) of a weapons capability. The United States and the EU-3 seek to constrain Iran's access to this technology or to induce it to forgo it in exchange for privileged access to less sensitive technology. But Iran insists on full fuel cycle autonomy. Negotiations have revolved around this issue, with incomplete results. The basic issue is one of trust: The West does not trust Iran with the technology, and Iran refuses to relinquish it. Negotiations have focused on what would constitute reassurance for the West and still enable Iran to access the technology. Given Iran's past record of nondeclaration of activities and dissimulation and the accompanying distrust of Iran's intentions, the West has concluded that it cannot give Iran the benefit of the doubt.

Assuming that Iran's technical capabilities remain limited in the next five years, the issue will remain whether Iran will persist in its attempt to acquire a nuclear capability by stages. Iran has sought to appeal to the developing states by depicting pressures on it as discriminatory and a denial of its rights under the NPT. By formally, if selectively, cooperating with the IAEA, avoiding major provocations, and gearing its acts to limited measures insufficient to justify a major punitive response, Iran has sought to minimize its exposure to concerted international pressure. Iran also encourages and cultivates divisions among the major powers to continue on its course. Tehran counts on U.S. distraction (Iraq, Afghanistan, energy prices, Hurricane Katrina, and elections) and EU divisions and preoccupations (elections, terrorism, immigration and economies, EU referenda) to derail any momentum for sanctions. In the absence of a smoking gun and its expressions of willingness to negotiate, Iran expects the incentives for referral to the Security Council to be reduced for two reasons: first, it believes that the outcome of such a referral is uncertain; and second, its threats to react strongly if the matter is referred to the Security Council have raised the stakes considerably. By demonstrating division the Security Council would signal its impotence but a united council might only be possible by showing a different form of weakness— watering down its demands. It remains unclear what cost the major powers are willing to impose on a suspect proliferant and what price that state, Iran, is willing to pay to get close to a nuclear weapons capability.

The difficulty posed by states seeking technology that brings them close to a bomb is not simply one of evil outlaw states. The NPT was always Janus-faced, at once promoting nuclear technology (Article IV) and non-proliferation of nuclear weapons. The problem, as Albert Wohlstetter remarked in the 1970s, is that the technologies are essentially the same. The spread of nuclear technology, legitimate and even encouraged by NPT rules, can bring states close to a weapons capability. Without diversion and "without plainly violating their agreement," states "can come within hours of a bomb."[6] It is no wonder that thirty years later President Bush can remark that "we must therefore close the loopholes that allow states to produce nuclear materials that can be used to build bombs under cover of civilian nuclear programs."[7] This sentiment was echoed by U.S. officials in the 2005 NPT review conference with specific reference to Iran: "Some countries, such as Iran, are seeking these facilities (uranium enrichment or plutonium reprocessing plants), either secretly or with explanations that cannot withstand scrutiny. We dare not look the other way.... We must close the loopholes in the Treaty that allow the unnecessary spread of such technologies."[8]

The problem is that tightening the treaty without renegotiating it will be difficult, not least in light of the discontent with the treaty on the part of many non-nuclear-weapons states. If ad hoc approaches are taken, there is the issue of drawing the line: Who is to decide where the line on such technologies is drawn, who is included and who excluded, and on what criteria?[9] The problem is compounded by the possibility of future energy crises and environmental concerns about global warming, which may indicate the revival of nuclear power. Increased interest in nuclear power would make controlling technologies more controversial politically.

Iran's ambiguous quest for nuclear technology thus unfolds at a time and place of great sensitivity. By seeking this technology—while claiming formal adherence to the treaty, using diplomacy, and adopting the language of a victimized non-nuclear-weapons-state simply seeking its due under Article IV of the treaty—Iran tests both the treaty and its supporters.

A policy to deal with Iran's specific motives and circumstances should not entail rewarding proliferation or derogating from the provisions of the NPT. However, devising an effective policy requires understanding Iran's ambitions and perspectives. Iran's achievement of a nuclear capability would increase its confidence and reinforce its tendency to block Western initiatives and seek a more prominent regional role.

The purpose of this study is first to assess the motivations driving Iran toward a nuclear capability all but indistinguishable from nuclear weapons. I discuss reasons why this should be of concern for the international community and assess Iran's tactics in the current negotiations and its intentions, as well as analyze international responses. I am principally concerned with what Iran is doing, what its motivations are, how it is going about it, and what it hopes to achieve. Necessarily the study is based on analysis and inference involving a discussion, for example, of negotiating style and tactics. I assume this issue will not be neatly solved in the near future and that a good understanding of motivations, arguments, and tactics will continue to be essential, whatever new developments may occur in the next few years.

Setting the Stage: The Background to Iran's Nuclear Program

After explicitly targeting and criticizing the Shah's nuclear program as an example of the monarchy's corrupt taste for megaprojects, the Islamic Republic of Iran rediscovered an interest in nuclear power in the midst of the Iran–Iraq war (1986). Despite the fact that the unfinished Bushire reactor had been abandoned by German technicians and bombed by Iraq, Tehran sought to revive the project. The argument for this at that time was based on the costs already sunk in the project. When Germany, at the behest of the United States, declined to resume construction and finish the project, Iran turned to the Soviet Union. The untested idea was to try to marry Soviet technology and nuclear core to the existing German-built foundations. Reliance on Soviet and later Chinese assistance became features of Iran's nuclear program in the 1990s. By this time Iran had articulated a new and ambitious long-term program for nuclear power plants, with the stated rationale of energy self-sufficiency. It is now known that already in the 1980s Iran had been in contact with the AQ Khan network to give its sputtering program new impetus.

With declining oil income (in real terms after 1986), a rapidly increasing population, and extensive war and reconstruction expenses, Iran could not give the program the highest priority. The program hitherto had therefore been characterized by persistence and incrementalism. This changed after 1999, however, when the nuclear effort was intensified.[10] The accelerated drive came at a time when Iraq was tightly contained, when reformists were in office in Iran, and when the Clinton administration was making overtures for normalization to Tehran.

Iran's view of nuclear weapons was influenced by the lessons of its war with Iraq, especially with regard to self-reliance and preparedness (hedging against surprise). Close observation of the international reaction to the North Korean case in 1994 yielded yet another lesson. Nothing in the Security Council response to that crisis suggested inordinate risks associated with developing nuclear weapons or any inevitability about a united front in that chamber. Throughout the 1990s Iran's insistence that U.S. accusations about its nuclear program stemmed from a bilateral feud with Tehran appeared plausible to some. U.S. efforts to halt the transfer of technology to Iran's allegedly civil nuclear program met with only mixed receptivity in Moscow and Beijing.

This brief synopsis of Iran's nuclear program suggests the following. Reactivated in the midst of war under adverse conditions, Iran's nuclear program was initially influenced by security issues. But Saddam Hussein's nuclear threat had essentially been eliminated or contained by 1991, well before Iran's program took off. The continuing impulse for that program stemmed from a prudent though vague desire to hedge against an uncertain future. In the 1990s, as the Islamic revolution lost its luster for its supporters at home and abroad, the nuclear option appeared to offer a way out, a point around which to rally nationalist opinion and to legitimate the regime. In a sense the nuclear program was in search of a rationale, which evolved from insurance against Iraq to energy independence and from regional status to deterrence against the United States. And along the way it picked up domestic interest groups.

Iran accelerated its nuclear program in 1999. The undeclared drive for enrichment or a nuclear capability or option within the treaty was upset by the revelations of mid-2002, which showed that Iran had built undeclared fuel cycle facilities, whose economic rationale was debatable and whose value for producing nuclear weapons was great.

Iran had sought to create a *fait accompli* on the Korean model but was derailed by the public revelations of its undeclared activities in mid-2002. Put on the defensive by these revelations (occurring when the United States was planning the Iraq war), Tehran sought an accommodation with the EU-3, which included constraints on its activities. It took two years before Tehran regained its confidence to break free from the constraints it had accepted in September 2003. Iran thus moved away from reassuring the international community on its program to a defiant assertion of its rights. In the two years between September 2003 and August 2005, Iran's negotiations with the EU-3 (and through them the international community and IAEA) proved counterproductive. Intended to find a balance between the necessity of reassuring others of the peaceful nature of its activities and its ambitions for a nuclear program, the negotiations succeeded only in exacerbating suspicions. Iran acted as if it were a victim rather than a state found in flagrant dereliction of its commitments. The additional distrust created by the negotiations themselves were a result of Iran's negotiating style and tactics.

The sketch that follows underscores the negotiations' principal stages and results (see chronology for a complete list of key events in the timeline). Revelations of Iran's activities saw the IAEA energized and its Director-General Mohammad Al Baradei visit Tehran in February 2003. Inspections followed. In September the IAEA's Board of Governors called on Iran to ensure full compliance with the safeguard agreement by taking all necessary acts by the end of October 2003. Iran was told to suspend all further enrichment activities and to ratify and implement the Additional Protocol (AP) for enhanced inspections. Under pressure and the threat of referral (and possible U.S. military action), Iran accepted an agreement with the EU-3 in Tehran, suspending enrichment (for the duration of negotiations) and signing and implementing the AP. In return, Tehran sought to have its relations with the agency normalized and its nuclear file speedily dropped. Iran cooperated with the agency but remained adamant about resuming enrichment and maintaining opacity about some aspects of its program. When Iran sought to define its rights to include enrichment-related activities deemed suspended by its negotiating partners, the Tehran agreement of September 2003 was followed by the Paris agreement of November 2004, which closed any loopholes about enrichment-related activities. In June 2005 Iran served notice of its intention to resume conversion activities. It rejected a broad incentives package proposed by the European states and resumed its activities in August of that year. Moreover, the new Iranian government adopted a more belligerent tone. Shrugging off progressively stronger resolutions from the IAEA threatening referral to the UNSC in the autumn, Iran resumed enrichment research in January 2006. The agency decided to refer Iran's case to the Security Council in March 2006, where it is now being considered.

Iranian Challenge

An Iranian nuclear capability is primarily an issue about Iran and the Middle East regional order, notwithstanding the enormous impact on the NPT regime. The nature of the regime in Iran and its behavior animate special concern about Iran's nuclear ambitions. A nuclear capability would give Iran the confidence to obstruct and challenge U.S. power and Western influence in the Middle East. A nuclear capability would also be an immediate guarantee against forcible regime change. This study argues that it is not Iran's acquisition of sensitive technologies per se that is of special concern, but the nature of the regime in Tehran and its behavior and orientation that give the threat a world-historical dimension. A nuclear Iran would be a dangerous, destabilizing competitor in a sensitive geopolitical area. The conjunction of a nuclear-capable Iran and a weakened, disintegrating Iraq under Iranian influence would compound the problem, dramatically destabilizing the region.

Therefore, the focus on Iran's nuclear capabilities should not obscure the primary concern: Iran's regional policies. A different Iran, or an Iran pursuing more moderate goals in the region, would not be perceived the same way as Tehran is today. An Iran less hostile to the West, less aggressive toward Israel, and less bent on creating a different regional order would certainly be less threatening. A different regime, a secular democratic one, would be the object of less concern, even if it were pursuing the same nuclear capabilities.[11]

This means that the discussion regarding Iran's nuclear ambitions is at times a discussion of the nature of the Iranian regime and raises the question of whether that regime is likely either to be replaced soon or to change its behavior to an appreciable extent. Iran has not yet had to choose between regime maintenance and its regional policies. Tehran sees the extension of its influence as an integral part of the regime's legitimacy, but *in extremis* it has no hesitancy in tempering its ambitions (as in 2002–2003).

Iran uses discontent with the NPT and anti-Americanism in the Middle East to pursue its goals, thus generalizing its case and strengthening its diplomacy. Iran is without a significant strategic partner or dependable ally. It is thus obliged to pursue its goals alone, which suits its particular brand of assertive defiance and opportunism. Tehran can rely on Russian, Chinese, and Indian interest and indulgence in respect to some of its ambitions (though not necessarily to its preferred spoiler role). Iran's size and weight make it a more formidable rival than other states identified as proliferants. Blocking Iran's access to technology, mobilizing diplomatic coalitions for sanctions, and countering its regional initiatives are thus much harder than in the case of countries like North Korea (or Libya). And as a major oil and gas supplier located at the crossroads of the Caspian and the Persian Gulf and the Arab and Asian subcontinent, Iran is not without potential assets.

Iran has invested in its nuclear infrastructure for nearly two decades. The program has been marked by persistence and incrementalism, by determination rather than urgency. As the absence of a crash program would suggest, the motives for investing in a nuclear option stem more from political than security imperatives. While the security rationale has been shifting, the political motive has remained unvarying and fixed. The impulse behind the program has been persistent, even if its aims have been unclear.[12]

Iran seeks technology related to nuclear weapons and, assuming the absence of a large-scale clandestine program, still has not made a definitive or irreversible decision to acquire nuclear weapons as opposed to an option. This is important in practical terms because it signals that Iran seeks to stay *within* the treaty—as much for the technical cooperation it needs as for the vindication of its image as a respectable (as opposed to rogue) state. There is thus still time for an effective international reaction before Iran reaches the technological point of no return of self-sufficiency in its nuclear program.

Iran's quest for a nuclear capability (for "nonweaponized deterrence") can be understood by reference to certain key goals: a deterrent (regime maintenance), an instrument for regional influence, a nationalist card for regime legitimation, and a bargaining card.

The formative experience of the IRI with international politics was in the immediate aftermath of the establishment of the Islamic Republic when it was challenged by Iraq. The lessons it learned from that hard and bitter war, together with what have become enshrined as semisacrosanct "principles of the revolution," inform its nuclear policy as well as its public discourse: independence, equality, and nondiscrimination. The nuclear question is particularly notable for raising all of these issues in terms of access to technology, dependence on foreign suppliers, equality of treatment, and so on. Above all, the nuclear issue is one of symbolism, reflecting Iran's coming of age as an important power. The Iranians see it—and the issue of trust and confidence—as a two-way street of reciprocity and respect.

Iran's quest for a nuclear capability by stealth is not surprising in a region where transparency is not a part of the culture and where opacity and dissimulation are the norm. Disentangling fact from claim and argument from artifice is not easy. Grappling with Iran's aims needs a reconstruction of motives, experiences, and worldviews, while intentions are harder to assess. It is easier to argue that Iran seeks a capability than to assert that this decision has been made definitively, no matter what the cost. It is also difficult to be sure whether the nuclear program has become self-sufficient, whether there exist significant clandestine facilities, and what time frame this implies. Finally it is difficult to be certain whether the decision has been made to acquire nuclear weapons or an "option" short of that. The argument presented here is that while

Iran has been persistent, it has also been "playing it by ear," with no irreversible decisions taken and these sensitive to the costs associated with proceeding. In addition there is no strategic urgency arguing for a nuclear weapon as opposed to an option. However, the program is pursued according to what the traffic will bear. Iran's leaders have antennas very sensitive to the relative balance of power and what they can get away with. They see the regional balance of power since 2004 and the diplomatic balance of power since 2005 as having increasingly turned in their favor. Iran's relations with the IAEA and negotiations with the EU-3 since the 2003–2005 period can be characterized as defensive and thereafter as self-confident and assertive.

As Iran pursues its drive for a nuclear capability, the motives impelling it to do so and the implications of its achievement become more important; these questions will be addressed throughout this volume.

1

The View from Tehran

realist perspective

Revolutionary states see the world as a hostile place and tend to act to make it so. A fundamental ambivalence characterizes such states. They alternately feel impelled to spread their message but feel surrounded by hostile states; they veer between overconfidence and insecurity. In Iran's case, the default position in its foreign policy has been one of obstructionism, due as much to its worldview as to its response to the strategic environment. Normalization and routinization of foreign policy necessitates jettisoning revolutionary claims, which are believed to be an intrinsic part of the regime's legitimacy. The revolutionary reflex competes with a detached pragmatism and often subverts it. Iran's sense of frustration at being blocked regionally stems as much from its sense of "status discrepancy" as from objective conditions.[1]

Since September 2001, Iran has exchanged a relatively tolerable strategic environment, in which Saddam's Iraq was contained and Taliban Afghanistan was marginalized, for a new context in which Iran is literally encircled by its old nemesis, the United States. The United States figures centrally in Iran's threat perceptions because Iranians believe that the United States has never reconciled itself to revolutionary Islamic Iran and misses no opportunity to deny it its rightful role and to weaken it.[2]

14

Iran lies at a natural crossroads between the Caspian and the Gulf and the Arab world and the subcontinent, but it has been unable to translate its geopolitical assets into political advantage. As a non-Arab Shiite state, Iran lacks a natural constituency, either regionally or in the wider Muslim world (Shiites are a minority in Islam). Iran also lacks dependable friends or strategic partners, as the relationship with Syria underlines. Nor is Iran in any significant multilateral regional institution such as the Gulf Cooperation Council (GCC). Iran made a Faustian bargain with the Soviet Union (and its successor, Russia) that has held: In exchange for Iranian restraint and stabilization of the Caucasus and Central Asia, Tehran would gain access to Russian technology and arms. Moscow considers Iran an important state and strategic partner, and cooperation in Tajikistan, Afghanistan under the Taliban, and Nagorny Karabakh is evidence of this. Both states seek to keep the United States and the North Atlantic Treaty Organization (NATO) from establishing a presence in the broader region and are committed to reversing it. This tacit opposition to the West gives Iran a certain weight in Russian calculations, but it does not extend to encouraging Tehran in the direction of nuclear weapons, nor does it outweigh Russia's continuing imperative of maintaining good working relations with the United States.

Iran's regional relations are otherwise unremarkable, posing no threat to Iran even if they are not characterized by uniform warmth and close cooperation. With Turkey and Pakistan, Iran retains normal relations without any acute bilateral sources of dispute. Iran sees India and China as "rising Asia" and part of its strategy of looking east as a counterweight to offset dependence on Europe and the United States. Iran's relations with these states are growing, especially in the area of energy, and they are set to become more important strategically in the next decade. Like Russia, however, neither state wishes to see Iran acquire nuclear weapons or to have to choose between relations with Tehran and Washington.[3] How far Iran can play on resentment of U.S. policies to encourage a new multipolarity remains to be seen.[4]

With the Arab states of the peninsula, Iran has formally mended fences, but relations are not infused with trust.[5] If anything, Iran's neighbors feel threatened, not the reverse. Further afield, Iran has yet to normalize diplomatic relations with Egypt, which remains suspicious of Iran's ambitions. Iran depicts Israel as illegitimate, venomously directing its revolutionary rhetoric at it. But absent Iranian hostility, Israel poses no threat to the Islamic Republic.

The world viewed from Tehran then is mixed, with threat and opportunity in equal measure. The principal threat arises from the possibility that the U.S. presence may become permanent, which would translate into an environment that leaves Iran beleaguered, without friends or influence. This scenario will hinge on the outcome of the current struggle in Iraq. An alternative scenario would arise from a U.S. withdrawal with its reputation compromised and inclination to pursue forward defense reduced. But with this benign scenario from Tehran's perspective would come problems—the risk of Iraq's disintegration, civil war, and competitive intervention by regional states. The opportunity to benefit from a U.S. retreat would be not without risks.

Iran's regional ambitions are clear enough. Iran seeks to become the indispensable power, without which no regional policy can be implemented.[6] It seeks to do so from a position of strength and by exploiting its leverage in the region.[7] Therefore, the reverse side of U.S. encirclement in the region is U.S. entanglement, which provides Iran with opportunities. As former defense minister Ali Shamkhani observed: "Wherever they [that is, Americans] are, we are also ... and wherever they can hit us we can hit them harder."[8]

To conclude, Iran's strategic environment does not create the insecurity driving Iran's nuclear program, which is driven more by frustration over status and the ambition to be taken more seriously and to play a larger, more global role. The one exception—U.S. threats of regime change since 2002—does not account for the start of the nuclear program or its persistence, although it may be the reason why Iran continues to insist on it in the face of international opposition.

Iran's Revolutionary Values and Non-proliferation

Some have suggested that Iran may be the key proliferation tipping point in the unraveling of the NPT.[9] Iran takes the current prolonged crisis about the scope and limits of its nuclear program seriously. The Iranian leadership has characterized it as the "most difficult case in the entire history of the country," comparable to the acceptance of the United Nations (UN) resolution ending the war with Iraq (SC 598) and even to the oil nationalization crisis of 1953.[10] Iranian officials admit that the crisis around their nuclear program came with revelations of secret activities in August 2002. Since 2003 the level of military alert has been raised.[11] A senior official, justifying the negotiations with the EU-3, has observed that "being a revolutionary does not mean that we must discard everything and put ourselves on the road to confrontation with the rest of the world...." Rather, Iran through interaction could maintain its national security and protect its interests and nuclear technology.[12] Iranian officials deny any resemblance of Iran's situation to that of Libya or North Korea. They see Libya as a case of total capitulation, and North Korea as an inappropriate model as well because it claims to have nuclear weapons, which Iran does not. Nor do they see Iraq as a model, because its approach "was to drip feed information, and show resistance and reluctance, in order to be able to maintain some facilities and activities ... and in the end (Saddam's regime) was toppled."[13] Conversely, Iran professes a willingness to be transparent to disprove claims that it seeks nuclear weapons.

Since 2002 when the nuclear issue became widely publicized internationally, the justification for the program has been given intense domestic coverage. Iranian leaders have sold the nuclear program as an inalienable right under the NPT, as a means of diversifying energy sources and as cutting-edge technology necessary to enter the ranks of scientifically advanced states. Iranian officials have depicted the issue in terms of rights on the one hand and denial of technology to keep Iran backward on the other. In playing the nationalist card Tehran has unleashed forces more intransigent than its negotiators. Iranian officials have had to justify Iran's policies, such as agreements to negotiate with the EU-3 in 2003 and 2004, as necessary prudent measures to avoid giving Iran's enemies pretexts to attack it: "Iran (thus) has its own model and it means that we want to develop nuclear technology in Iran and at the same time gain the trust of the world."[14] Iran's approach therefore has been to reassure the international community by being sensitive to its concerns. For example, it signed the Additional Protocol in October 2003 under international pressure, stating: "gradually we reached the conclusion that each and every industrial country that had trade ties with Iran wanted us to sign the Additional Protocol."[15]

Iran's willingness to bow to the cumulative pressure from countries with which it desired to maintain relations differentiates it from other proliferators: It does not see itself, or want others to see it, as an international pariah. There is, nonetheless, a less accommodating side to Iran's interaction with other countries; the nuclear question symbolizes the values and aims of the revolution, above all the defiant assertion of independence: "Iran has made a Revolution in order not to be the obedient servant of any country and to act on the basis of its own national interests. Even if this has some costs ... we are prepared to pay these costs."[16]

These values and the worldview they reflect, together with the lessons learned over the past quarter century, are strong conditioners of Iran's nuclear program as well as its diplomacy. They merit extended examination precisely because they are intrinsic features of the discourse and politics of the Islamic Republic of Iran and as such will influence Iran's strategy and any possible negotiated agreement.

The long and costly war with Iraq early in the life of the IRI has been the principal conditioner of Iran's approach to national security ever since.[17] The war in retrospect is seen as confirming the hostility of the outside world toward the Islamic revolution. The revolution was forged through martyrdom and unity during the war, so it is seen as a golden period marking an epic that should inform all subsequent policies. The war with Iraq served as both warning and lesson.[18] Surprised by Iraq's attack, Iranians resolved never to be caught unprepared again. A clear and overriding lesson surely was that reliance on conventional forces for deterrence was less effective than reliance on nuclear weapons. With nuclear weapons, even the most dedicated or better armed foe would surely be deterred, whereas conventional deterrence was more liable to fail. These lessons have now been incorporated into what might be called the revolution's values. (Official Iranian statements, however, concentrate on the inadmissibility of the use of nuclear weapons.)

In summary, these values can be expressed as independence, equality, and respect. They reflect an extreme sensitivity to any appearance of dependence, dictation, or domination by others as well as a desire to be taken seriously, treated without discrimination, and accorded the status that Iran's importance in the world merits. Although tempered over the past quarter century, Iranian leaders still believe that Iran constitutes a role model for others in creating an Islamic revolution and siding with the oppressed against global arrogance and an unjust international order.[19] Iran's quest for international status is a major element in its outlook, a nationalist glue that unites hard-liners and reformists, secularists and religious conservatives.[20]

The lessons of Iran's war with Iraq and the values of the revolution reinforce each other. They militate toward self-sufficiency in arms production; hedge against technological surprises (such as Saddam's use of surface to surface missiles, which caught Iran without equivalent weapons); and do not rely on the international rules or community for any favors during crises.[21] Iran believes that it is now—or should be—a major regional power and that no policy in the region should be implemented without taking into account its views.[22]

This defiance plays out in the issue of Iran's nuclear energy program and the U.S. opposition to it. International efforts to constrain Iran's nuclear activities are seen as technology denial and dictation intended to keep Iran backward and subordinate.[23] It also plays into the issue of discrimination or "nuclear apartheid" voiced by President Ahmadinejad at the United Nations in September 2005.

This outlook and its war with Iraq led toward its current emphasis on missiles and the cultivation of options to avoid surprises. Both Iran and Iraq attributed more importance to the role of missiles (and chemical weapons) in the outcome of the war than was warranted.[24] As a result both countries, wary of another round in the future, continued an arms race and emphasized these programs. As the unloved victim of chemical weapons, Iran felt even more aggrieved and justified to seek insurance against a future attack.[25] The experience with Iraq consequently encouraged Iran to seek self-sufficiency through the establishment of a domestic missile industry (in part to substitute for aircraft) and to maintain a certain ambiguity about its chemical, biological, and nuclear programs.[26]

Iran's thinking was influenced by other developments as well. The rapid U.S. victory in Iraq in 1991 contrasted with Iran's eight-year inconclusive war, underscoring the vast military disparity in conventional power between Tehran and Washington. Indian General Krishnaswamy Sundarji's comment—that if you wish to confront the United States, it would be wise to have nuclear weapons—seemed especially relevant to the Iranians. Iraq's enforced disarmament through the UN Special Commission (UNSCOM) after Desert Storm underlined how advanced Iraq's nuclear program had been (between six months and two years from realization) and how it had been underestimated. Later, North Korea's Agreed Framework with the United States in 1994 suggested that nuclear weapons might serve as a bargaining chip for technology and need not result in automatic sanctions or attack. Nuclear tests in India and Pakistan in 1998 passed relatively unscathed by international sanctions and in a short time became accepted as each became U.S. partners or allies. Finally, the U.S. attack on Iraq in April 2003 justified by reference to suspected weapons of mass destruction (WMD) programs contrasted with the restraint and caution shown toward North Korea, a self-confessed nuclear power, which appeared to underscore Sundarji's comment about the deterrent effects of nuclear weapons.[27]

Iran therefore has reasons, based on its own direct experience, its worldview, and its reading of events, to consider whether nuclear weapons would add to its security. Additional incentives came with the change in U.S. policy from dual containment in the 1990s to regime change after 2001.

Iran's initial reaction to 9/11 mixed sympathy with wariness. The war in Afghanistan was indicative of this: Hostility toward the Taliban was matched by a reluctance to see the United States entrenched nearby. Iranian leaders saw the War on Terrorism as a pretext for a foreign regional presence.[28] Already in mid-2002 a top Iranian official correctly predicted a U.S. war against Iraq, stating that "even if Saddam lets the weapon inspectors in, the U.S. will attack."[29] In both cases Iran formally opposed the acts but remained neutral. The war with Iraq was preceded by a further deterioration in relations between Washington and Tehran. The Bush administration's identification of Iran as a terrorist state and with an "axis of evil" (January 2002) and the announcement of a future strategy of preemption and regime change where necessary increased Iran's perceptions of threat. This environment may have reinforced Iran's motivation to pursue its nuclear program, even after Saddam's demise.

After the 2003 war with Iraq, the United States became both a *regional* state (a neighbor on two sides of Iran) and a *revolutionary* state, supporting democratic change in the region rather than the status quo at all costs. Iran saw this regional presence as a threat to its interests.[30] Initially Iran was concerned that the new U.S. policy would target it next. Iran's response has been to show that it is not vulnerable to regime change and to demonstrate a linkage between Tehran's influence—for good or ill—in Iraq and Afghanistan and U.S. policy toward Tehran, especially on the nuclear issue.

Iranian officials were surprised by the U.S. administration's new policies. They understood the discussion about a new draft nuclear posture review as an implicit threat to make nuclear weapons more usable against potential (nonnuclear) adversaries. Washington's interest in smaller nuclear weapons (mini-nukes) made the threat of nuclear use against alleged proliferators more worrisome to Tehran.[31] The appropriation of U.S. funds to support the Iranian opposition in mid-2003, together with the initial stunning military success of the United States in Iraq, gave Iran's leadership pause: Regime change had become a real threat. Iranian reformists might have been emboldened by the U.S. proximity and encouragement to call on external assistance. Always sensitive to power realities, Tehran's response was to seek an accommodation. Already in mid-2002, Hashemi Rafsanjani, Chairman of the Expediency Discernment Council of Iran, had offered Iran's cooperation with the United States, as it had in Afghanistan, if it were treated as an equal.[32] By mid-2003, Washington terminated discussions between Iran and the United States in Geneva upon learning of Tehran's provision of sanctuary to Al Qaeda elements involved with terrorism in Saudi Arabia. However, as the United States became more entangled in Iraq in 2003, with the prospect of a rapid political victory fading, Iran regained its confidence. Iranian leaders now talked of the failure of regime change and the fact that the United States was now bogged down in Iraq as well as Afghanistan.[33]

When the possibility of a U.S. military strike against Iranian nuclear facilities became topical in 2004, Iranian officials responded by dismissing the reports as part of a psychological campaign, pointing out the political repercussions, given lack of support for this in Europe or elsewhere.[34] In addition Iran has justified building its uranium enrichment plant at Natanz underground by reference to the threat of a U.S. attack.[35] Iran also threatened retaliation and in numerous statements suggested that an attack on Iran would not be considered limited or elicit a limited response, that such a response would target U.S. forces in the region, that a response would not be limited to the region, that Iran would itself consider preemption, and that the United States could ill afford the subsequent regional instability.[36]

To prevent a possible resort to force by the United States, Iran also pursued a complicated regional diplomacy. Although Iran's interests in Afghanistan and Iraq are largely similar to those of the United States, the U.S. military presence, especially over the long term, is considered a threat. Moreover, that the United States is now militarily stretched by its commitments in these two countries gives Iran breathing space to delay or blunt what might otherwise be a credible military threat on its nuclear facilities.[37]

Iran's response to the enhanced U.S. military presence in the region has been to treat the United States as a potential hostage, to keep it entangled, and thus to prevent a speedy success and withdrawal that would enable the United States to concentrate on the next issue: nuclear Iran. This response has entailed playing a spoiling role to assure at least a delay in the stabilization of Iraq (and the cultivation of local actors as possible conduits for policy, which has parallels in Afghanistan as well).

The implicit linkage between Iran's regional policy and Tehran's relations with the United States is clear enough. As the United States has looked to establish a base structure around Iran (including Central Asia), Iran has stepped up its spoiling strategy.[38] The question of whether the United States is willing to compromise on Iran's nuclear ambitions in exchange for assistance regionally has not been definitively answered—in part because the evolution of events in Iraq remains unpredictable and in part because the implications of nuclear Iran are so serious as to make such a tacit exchange a losing proposition in the longer term.[39]

2

Nuclear Energy Rationale, Domestic Politics, and Decision Making

Energy Diversification and Self-Sufficiency

Iran argues that it is developing nuclear energy to generate electricity and to master the fuel cycle to become a supplier of nuclear fuel in the future. Its arguments in support of this claim are both economic and strategic. Iran is a major producer of oil and soon gas, and it justifies its interest in nuclear technology by reference to the need to diversify its energy sources and keep abreast of a technology that it identifies as modern and synonymous with being an advanced scientific state. Initially cancelled by the Islamic Republic, the Iranian nuclear program was restarted in the mid-1980s. The rationale was that the partially built Bushire reactor represented a "sunk cost" that should be recouped. The argument for nuclear energy was then strengthened by the prudent need for diversifying energy sources. As Mohsen Rezai, Secretary of the Expediency Discernment Council, put it, "The important issue is that Iran's energy basket must be a mixture of all kinds of energy. Abandoning the nuclear program will harm our national interests."[1]

The argument is further reinforced by the fact that Iran's rapid population growth and domestic oil consumption are reducing Iran's oil export revenues.[2] Iran currently envisages the production of 7,000 megawatts of electricity from nuclear energy and initial construction of ten nuclear reactors.[3] This program implies "self sufficiency in all aspects of using the peaceful use of nuclear energy" from extraction through enrichment.[4]

Therein lies the problem: By insisting on acquiring the full fuel cycle, including facilities for uranium enrichment and plutonium reprocessing, Iran would acquire the ability to fabricate the materials necessary for nuclear weapons with little difficulty. Much of the world questions Iranian arguments on the need for self-sufficiency in all aspects of the fuel cycle and on the energy justification for the scale of the program. That Iran emphasizes enrichment (Natanz) and a heavy water plant (Arak) at this early phase in its program when not a single reactor is yet functioning rings alarm bells. Furthermore most countries with reactors do not go into enrichment. Indeed, most have not sought such a capability because it is not economical. The Iranians insist, however, that the nuclear issue is not just a question of energy but of science and technology and self-sufficiency, and as such an issue of great practical and symbolic significance.[5] Iran is thus determined to avoid dependency on others for its future fuel supply and wants to be among the top fuel producers and suppliers within the next fifteen years. In the meantime, Iran will buy fuel. According to one expert, it will take Iran ten years before it will be able to generate good quality reactor fuel domestically.[6] Iranians are proud of their efforts, claiming that "all parts of the centrifuges used in the Natanz complex are manufactured by Iranian experts" and that it has broken into the "monopolized nuclear fuel market."[7]

Iranian leaders are unapologetic about their goals: "We want to have enrichment and all other parts of nuclear technology to use this valuable science for the good of our people and the country. And we will do this at any cost."[8] Because there are doubts whether these constitute Iran's real goals, Iran is being tested by the international response.

The Iranian arguments for energy diversification are more plausible than those justifying the program on grounds of self-sufficiency. There are several reasons why the self-sufficiency argument is problematic. First, even states like Sweden, which has ten reactors, do not feel the need for enrichment facilities and instead buy their fuel on the open market, which is less expensive. Second, even with possessing the full fuel cycle, Iran will remain dependent on imports of uranium because it lacks adequate indigenous supplies. Third, with reference to increased domestic energy consumption, the problem for Iran is the growing demand for gasoline, not electricity. Iran's domestic consumption of heavily subsidized and thus wasted gasoline is costly and growing in line with the population. Therefore, nuclear power generation plants, which only produce electricity, will not begin to address this demand. (Iran's vast indigenous gas reserves are discounted from the equation.)

Nuclear Power and Nuclear Status

Iran's depiction of its accession to the ranks of states mastering nuclear technology as enormously significant has two functions: First, it legitimates the regime domestically and, second, gives Iran greater weight internationally. The regime's depiction of Iran's achievement is vague at best and deliberately distorted at worst. Science, technology, and power are equated, and peaceful nuclear power is said to give Iran entry into an "exclusive club."[9]

The nuclear issue has thus, according to some, become a rallying point around which all can agree, like the "sacred defense" of the country against Iraq. As reported in the Iranian press,

Atomic energy has become the glue that has reinforced the solidarity of the nation.... Just imagine, if we could link the glories of the sacred defense with the people's national solidarity in the area of the inalienable right we are entitled to regarding atomic energy, what immense power would be forged and what a great epic it would create, so majestic and glorifying.[10]

Ambiguities about the nature of Iran's programs and ambitions are underscored by these claims. Iran, it is said, "has advanced nuclear technology" including enrichment and "this is very important in the world." The West's stance against Iran "indicates that Iran has access to this very exclusive and sensitive technology." Supreme Leader Ali Khamenei, in an address to prayer leaders, stated that "the bullies of this world know full well that we do not have nuclear weapons. However what has made them anxious is the Iranian nation's access to nuclear technology."[11] Iranian pride in its "amazing" progress in technology is palpable and attributed to the regime. Iranian scientists, one leader insisted, have now made the world admit that Iran is a scientific and technological power.[12] The United States and Europe, in this mind-set, are united in pressuring Iran to abandon enrichment "because enrichment is a way forward to scientific advancement and if a country is able to succeed in doing so, the efforts of the world of arrogance will lose their effect."[13]

Iranian officials suggest that nuclear technology has enhanced Iran's power, "guarantee[ing] the Islamic republic's presence in the international scene" and giving the Europeans pause as they "realize they could not embark on force when talking to Iran."[14] In short, Iranian leaders attribute a great deal more significance to the attainment of an enrichment capability than potential energy self-sufficiency.

Domestic Politics

While the nuclear issue is depicted by the Iranian leadership as a burning national issue, the reality is different. Foreign policy, including the nuclear question, is generally far from the mind of the ordinary Iranian, who is more concerned about employment, inflation, and prospects for self-betterment. While most Iranians favor an Iran that is independent and has status, it is questionable whether they would seek the nuclear fuel cycle at the cost of confrontation with the international community, referral to the UN

Security Council, and sanctions. When the new government adopted a more confrontational course in August 2005, Iranian stock and real estate markets plummeted, and questions began to be raised domestically about its course.[15]

How has domestic politics influenced Iran's nuclear program? Is there, as the regime insists, national unity on Iran's right to enrichment, which precludes any policy adjustment?

Domestic Nuclear Debate

Iran's principal motive for developing nuclear technology appears to be domestic legitimation of the regime.[16] By tapping into and exploiting nationalist sentiment, the regime hopes to reinforce itself. It has certainly oversold the notion that possessing the full fuel cycle reflects cutting-edge technology that no self-respecting nation can afford to forgo. This national consensus, which has been selectively invoked, has left the regime with less room for compromise. Even so, a broad spectrum of views on the nuclear program exists; flexibility is possible but requires determined leadership. The nuclear issue is only partly about technology and status. As mentioned earlier, it is more importantly a surrogate for a broader debate about the country's future—about what model Iran should adopt and how it should interact with the wider world. The nuclear issue is a metaphor for Iran's quest for greater respect and a wider regional and global role. The June 2005 presidential elections reflected this broader debate.

Polls consistently show some 80 percent of the population supporting Iran's access to nuclear technology as a right that reflects and contributes to Iran's advanced scientific status. Iranian leaders consequently invoke national demand in their international negotiations.[17] In reality, however, the nuclear debate in Iran is more complicated. Although no one supports technology denial as such, Iranians are not duped by the way the issue has been depicted. The debate has been manipulated by the regime, which has failed to open up the facts or issues to public scrutiny, framing the issue in terms of denial, rights, equality, and respect.[18] When the debate is framed differently, the results change. Iranians do not want to pay a high price for the program given their domestic economic needs. They wish to avoid confrontation and international isolation. The extreme case was well put by one forty-five-year-old Iranian man who preferred to remain anonymous: "If the result would be similar to North Korea, where the people have a low standard of living but are making the atomic bomb, then we don't want that."[19]

One difficulty in analyzing the Iranian debate is the fact that Iran denies having intentions to acquire nuclear weapons, so officials do not discuss the strategic or other rationales for seeking the capability to make or use them. Some conservatives openly argue for leaving the NPT and seeking nuclear arms, whereas reformists emphasize political deterrence (democracy and unity) and peaceful technology.[20] This muted debate over the value of nuclear weapons extends to the regime itself and is reflected in its uncertainty about whether to continue to seek sensitive technology in the face of U.S. and European Union (EU) objections, whatever the price, or to settle for less controversial technology and improve relations with the international community.[21] In the broader context of political flux and change in Iran, current differences on the nuclear issue today are emblematic of different views on the way Iran ought to develop and engage internationally. Self-sufficiency versus interdependence, isolation versus engagement, ideology versus pragmatism—all are at play in Iran today.[22]

Differences do not fall strictly along factional lines but nearly so. Certainly the nuclear issue figures into politics and factions seek to use it politically. In the recent presidential elections, international affairs were linked to domestic issues for the first time.[23] Iranians see that their priorities concerning jobs, investment, and normalization internationally are connected to the struggle between their government and the international community over the nuclear program. The reformist candidate (Mostafa Moin) took the clear position that if seeking enrichment poisoned relations with the international community, Iran should forgo it. The conservative (former military) candidates (notably Ali Larijani and Mohsen Rezai) were equally clear: They favored acquisition of the full fuel cycle, depicting it as an issue of self-respect and scientific necessity.[24] More interesting was the position of another strong candidate with a security background, Brigadier General Mohammad Bager Qalibaf, who presented the issue as the need to balance between Iran's rights and the people's desire to avoid hostilities and avoid disturbing the peace, concluding that continued diplomacy offered the best hope of developing technology and building confidence with others.[25] This theme was echoed by former president and candidate Hashemi Rafsanjani, widely admired as a wily politician who might be able to actually deliver what more admirable candidates (like Moin) could only promise. Hasan Rowhani, the chief nuclear negotiator, encouraged Rafsanjani's candidacy, arguing that without Rafsanjani the conservatives would certainly win.[26] Rafsanjani, reborn as a reformer, also promised more diplomacy on the nuclear issue. More significantly, he invoked his special relationship with Supreme Leader Khamenei for being able to achieve results. Strikingly, it was not what he said on the nuclear issue but what he said on Iran's international relations that was significant. His discourse reflected the broad shift away from the conservative view of the world: He embraced globalization enthusiastically and pledged "positive and constructive interaction with the international arena: renewing bonds and links with the rest of the world in order to remedy the country's vulnerabilities on the international stage and speeding up the process of foreign investment in Iran."[27] In response, conservatives ran a "stop Rafsanjani" campaign, calling into question his ties with Khamenei and casting aspersions on his foreign support.[28] In the election Rafsanjani lost to the hard-liners. Mahmoud Ahmadinejad's populist victory was a triumph for what he promised domestically: less corruption and more attention to social equality. His indifference to international affairs and opinion reflected his constituency, the rural and urban disadvantaged.

Outsiders find it difficult to distinguish among Iranians or to identify significant differences among them on the nuclear issue.

And it is true that this issue has become a litmus test of national-ism from which there are few dissenters. Most Iranians accept the proposition that the nuclear issue reflects a general discrimination, involving not just nuclear, but all advanced technology.[29] Some see the issue as symbolic of "the way that world powers view the nature of Iran's regime."[30] One reformer suggested that the nuclear issue raised still more fundamental questions: What kind of state does Iran seek to be? What sort of role does it aspire to play? And what kind of relations does it seek with other states?[31] It is in this con-text, it could be argued, that Iran's nuclear aspirations are bound to be judged by other states.

Most Iranians support the quest for status, respect, and a broader regional role. They see advanced technology, scientific progress, and independence as linked and desirable. This nation-alism, together with the resentment over discrimination, has been fanned by the regime to expand the nuclear program. The nation-alist consensus in turn has been used by negotiators to argue that domestic constraints prevent Iran from forgoing sensitive technolo-gies. While this is true up to a point, it is also very much self-imposed and vague. The Iranian public has not judged whether a nuclear weapons option is desirable on its own merits but only on the proposition that Iran should not be denied technology to which it is entitled.

Role of Conservatives in Nuclear Policy

In Iran, the political elite determines national security policies in the Supreme National Security Council (SNSC). The default setting in the council has been hard-line, with the reformists marginal-ized whatever their standing in the Iranian parliament (Majles).

The *reformists* generally support the nuclear program but see nuclear as one among several technologies, neither the Holy Grail nor a panacea. They do not wish to see its pursuit lead to Iran's estrangement from the international community and hurt relations with neighbors.[32] In practice, however, nuclear policy issues have been decided between conservatives of two types: pragmatic (like Rafsanjani and Rowhani) and ideological (like Ahmadinejad and Larijani). It is worth noting the similarities and differences among the various factions and groups.

Both types of conservatives appear to agree on the need for a nuclear weapons option but differ on means or the price to be paid to achieve this. In reality they seek different ends: The *pragmatic conservatives* seek power to be able to cut a deal and normalize relations, whereas the *ideological conservatives* shun a deal and want power to be able to impose themselves on the region and beyond. Both groups seek a larger regional role for Iran and see the United States as an obstacle to that goal.[33]

The pragmatists who controlled negotiations during the 2003–2005 period were under constant pressure from the ideological faction. They pursued a nuclear option within the NPT, were open to compromise when necessary (Tehran and Paris agreements), and sought to limit the fallout from Iran's program. Sensitive to international opinion and to the potential costs of a disruption of relations, they were willing to suspend activities (enrichment) and under pressure to accept constraints (the Additional Protocol) to keep up the appearance of reasonableness and cooperation. While seeking to enhance power they were unwilling to do so in a confrontational mode, leaving open the possibility of a "grand bargain"—an across-the-board accommodation that would see Iran's interests and security guaranteed in exchange for a normalization of relations and moderation of its behavior. For economic and strategic reasons, this faction is more open to engagement and sees globalization as an inescapable reality.

This policy stance has changed, however, since the ideologically conservative faction took control of nuclear policy in August 2005. The Ahmadinejad presidency represents a throwback to the early days of the revolution, with its emphasis on first principles (social justice, independence, and export of the revolution). A strong military and security constituency (notably the militia *Basij* and the Iranian Revolutionary Guards Corps, known as the IRGC or *Pas-*

daran) supports this administration as do some conservative clergy, notably Ayatollah Taghi Mesbahi Yazdi of the Haggani seminary at Qom.[34] The world, in the view of this group, is a Hobbesian one of unremitting struggle, where predatory powers lurk to dictate and dominate and where the only currency is military power. Power, in this view, is the indispensable element for survival and for the extension of the regime's values beyond its borders. What is known by Ahmadinejad as active diplomacy describes a policy that seeks to increase power not just to survive but to impose Iran on the international community.[35] Power and military strength thus ensure the regime's survival, values, and influence and must not be bartered away, any more than they can be acquired through negotiation. Negotiations, in this mind-set, reflect and ratify the balance of power but add nothing to it. The best articulation of this view comes from Larijani, who observes that to resist U.S. pressure Iran has to use its "prominent geopolitical position.... You have to find a way to be able to take the country's level and status to a point so as to automatically solve your national security problem, other-

‑‑‑ this pressure factor will always weigh upon you." What he has
‑‑‑ ‑‑‑ mes atomic Iran, no longer will any-
‑‑‑ ‑‑‑ se they would have to pay too high a
‑‑‑ ‑‑‑ gested that foreign sensitivity toward
‑‑‑ ‑‑‑ partly because of Iran's geopolitical sit-
‑‑‑ ‑‑‑ ion."[36] This perspective translates into
‑‑‑ ‑‑‑ hat aims at acquiring technology, not
‑‑‑ ‑‑‑ ers of security guarantees as demean-
‑‑‑ ‑‑‑ se kinds of condescending guarantees
‑‑‑ ‑‑‑ ecting itself." Iran in this view does not
‑‑‑ ‑‑‑ atus conferred on it: It is prepared to
‑‑‑ ‑‑‑ s.[37] Larijani sees North Korea's impla-
‑‑‑ ‑‑‑ sooner or later, he believes, the West
‑‑‑ ‑‑‑ uclear status, as it has North Korea's.[38]
‑‑‑ ‑‑‑ nfrontation, the ideological conserva-
‑‑‑ ‑‑‑ reasons. First, they see Iran's geopolit-
‑‑‑ ‑‑‑ ber of important cards to play. Second,

Iran's increased oil income serves as a buffer against possible sanctions. Third, this approach will successfully divide the West from the nonaligned states, Russia, and China. Indifference to costs, isolation, and sanctions differentiates the ideological from the pragmatic conservatives. Where the pragmatists seek eventual normalization, their ideological counterparts welcome the opportunity to purify the regime and society by limiting contamination from the outside and asserting the revolution's values of self-reliance and authenticity.

Despite the fact that the ideological and pragmatic conservatives are agreed on the goal of increasing Iran's power and influence and using nuclear technology to do it, they have very different visions of the role Iran should play and the kind of relations Iran should have with the world. Of the two, the ideological faction, largely self-absorbed and insular, is the more prone to overestimate Iran's power and centrality and misjudge the external world.[39] Ahmadinejad's comments on Israel (and the Holocaust) are indicative. They did him no harm on the "Arab street" that sees its governments as too timorous or corrupt to defend Palestinian rights. In the Iranian political context, Ahmadinejad only voiced what the most extreme elements in the regime had long felt. As much as a deliberate provocation, the statements reflected the new president's complete and studied indifference to and contempt for international opinion.

The pragmatic conservatives have sought to put a brake on this approach. Rafsanjani has called for serious prudence and sensitivity, and Rowhani noted that in a matter of months the new government had already provoked serious discussions of referral to the Security Council on two occasions and had once been the object of a critical Security Council statement.[40]

In the wake of the Ahmadinejad team's confrontational tactics and rhetoric and the International Atomic Energy Agency (IAEA) vote on September 24 that put Iran on notice of referral to the UNSC, Rafsanjani led the rebuking voices. He argued against slogans and for the more difficult task of delicate diplomacy: "Our main task is to prove that we are not the sort of people to utilize nuclear weapons" and to prove to Iran's opponents that "Iran will not use the technology for military purposes."[41]

Critics of the Ahmadinejad mind-set face self-imposed limits; however, these limits have more to do with domestic political-economic issues than nuclear strategy. The critical issue remains the domestic power struggle for control over finances and sources of income. The pragmatists are fighting a rearguard action to maintain their control over lucrative areas of the economy such as energy and banking. They are thus unwilling to push an issue that could put them at a disadvantage in terms of nationalist opinion. For example, Ahmadinejad charged that critics of his foreign policy are attempting to create a diversion to continue their corrupt domestic practices.[42] The pragmatists are unwilling to risk division, polarization, and destabilization of the regime, least of all on this issue. They therefore have sought a practical accommodation on domestic issues with their ideological counterparts. However, if the costs of the crisis increase appreciably for Iran with the involvement of the Security Council, the pragmatists will be in a position to point to the ineptitude of the ideological faction and the need for less haste in the program.[43]

Supreme Leader Khamenei, who prefers consensus, has been unwilling to take sides on the nuclear issue and appears, if anything, closer to the ideologists on it. Thus, Larijani and Ahmadinejad feel they have a free hand in their approach to the nuclear issue, with no domestic force acting as a constraint. They continue to see the benefits of brinksmanship, especially as the other side appears uncertain, divided, or resigned. So far their approach has gained benefits (for example, resumption of conversion and research) without paying a tangible price. This outcome apparently vindicates their approach, which seems set to continue. Whether this will change as the costs of this approach increase is a critical question, but it appears unlikely, in part because the leadership has painted itself into a corner from which it will be difficult to exit.

In sum, then, the broad consensus on the nuclear issue obscures very real differences that exist among the elite on overall foreign policy. There is little dispute on making Iran a more important power, if possible by acquiring a nuclear capability, on seeking independence, and on taking an independent position in international affairs. Differences exist, however, on *how* to pursue these goals and whether Iran should not adjust its aims in exchange for the achievement of some of them. In essence, the basic division in foreign policy is between those who seek an accommodation with the West from a position of strength (Rafsanjani, Khatami, Rowhani) and those who wish to challenge it by adopting the course of the Islamic Republic circa 1979 (Ahmadinejad, Larijani, Ayatollah Taghi Mesbahi Yazdi). This division corresponds to those who are willing to consider a grand bargain with the United States and to adjust their regional policies in exchange for recognition and security guarantees and those who reject compromise in favor of pursuit of regional hegemony and self-reliance. Thus, if one group sees capabilities and policies as bargaining chips, then the other seeks the determined pursuit of goals without reference to the costs or consequences. In nuclear policy this translates into a division between those who emphasize confidence building and are willing to compromise and those for whom a nuclear capability is indispensable and compromise unthinkable. The contrast between the two is captured in the differences in the diplomacy of Rowhani and Larijani described below. President Ahmadinejad's election has given voice to a harder, more belligerent element, which has aggravated these differences and given rise to what amounts to a struggle for power between these two tendencies. The Supreme Leader will find it harder to paper over these differences in a continuing ambiguous consensus and may need, for once, to take sides.

Decision Making

Policy reflects politics as well as narrower institutional considerations. The broad political context and climate necessarily affect decisions. Hard-line newspapers such as *Keyhan* have quasi-official

status and more leeway than their dwindling reformist counterparts, which sets the tone for—as well as skews—the public debate.
Figures 1 and 2 schematically and approximately reflect the nuclear
decision-making structure in Iran. Iran's nuclear decisions reflect
institutional inputs and interest group biases, with policies emerging that are not a product of a unitary system. In addition to the
decision-making structure diagrammed in Figure 1, one could note
the Supreme Leader's soundings among his clerical network (in
Qom and elsewhere) and the primacy of informal networks.[44] Recognizing that these informal contacts and procedures are as influential as the formal organograms, decisions taken by the Supreme
Leader reflect a rough-and-ready consensus. Among the inputs into
decisions are interested parties such as the Atomic Energy Organization, which looks to its institutional interests and strongly supports the nuclear program. It can argue in terms of sunk costs,
experience acquired, and the costs of a long suspension of activities in terms of morale and attrition of scientific personnel. The Foreign Ministry and SNSC can argue the costs of estrangement and
confrontation with Europe and the IAEA and international obligations. The SNSC is not monolithic and reflects all tendencies; therefore, the appointment of Hasan Rowhani, the long-standing
secretary and pragmatist as chief nuclear negotiator, in 2003 was in
itself a significant choice. Decisions reached in the SNSC provide
the leadership with a sort of consensus safety net, enabling it to
avoid taking the heat for controversial decisions. Since August
2005, the composition of the leadership of the SNSC has changed,
as Ali Larijani has now replaced the pragmatic Hasan Rowhani as
principal negotiator (see Figure 2).

Effects of Domestic Politics on Negotiations

Iranian negotiators' and politicians' insistence on a national consensus behind the nuclear program serves two functions: one, to give
leverage to the negotiators who will have "to answer to the people"

Nuclear Decision Making: Institutions and Key Players

Iran's nuclear program in the 1990s was split into two parallel streams: a civilian program under the AEO; and a military program under the Revolutionary Guards. The two streams were consolidated in early 2000. Decision making on nuclear issues in Iran has traditionally been confined to three institutions coordinated by the leadership. The AEO has dealt with technical issues, the Foreign Ministry with their foreign ramifications, and special units of the Revolutionary Guards with the security of facilities.

After September 2003, nuclear "czar" Hasan Rowhani, Secretary of the Supreme National Security Council (SNSC), coordinated nuclear issues. In August 2005 he was replaced by Ali Larijani as Secretary of the SNSC. Rowhani remained on the SNSC as the Supreme Leader's Personal Representative.

Since June 2005, President Ahmadinejad, seeking to put his own imprint on foreign policy, has significantly changed the personnel. In replacing Rowhani, Larijani has in effect become National Security Advisor. Rowhani's deputy's position (Mousavian) has been split into two: one covering international security, including the nuclear dossier (Javad Vaidi), and another covering political and foreign affairs (Ali Monfared). The nuclear negotiating team has also changed. The preceding team has been terminated, but no clearly designated replacements have been named as yet. Larijani, rather than the Foreign Minister Manuchehr Mottaki, will have principal responsibility for the nuclear issue. Akhoundzadeh serves as Ambassador to the IAEA in Vienna. The new Defense Minister replacing Shamkhani is Brigadier General Mustafa Mohammad Najjar.

Sources: Elaine Sciolino, "Iran Plans a Vast Nuclear Build Up," *International Herald Tribune*, May 15, 1995, p. 1/6; Elaine Sciolino, "Tehran Grants a Glimpse of a Nuclear Site Reborn," *International Herald Tribune*, May 20–21, 1995, p. 1/5; Chris Hedges, "Iran's Push for Nuclear Arms and a Small Airstrip in Germany," *International Herald Tribune*, March 16, 1995, p. 1/8; and *Arab Times* (Kuwait), "Iran Restarts 'Eyes' Work at N Plant," August 2, 2005.

Figure 1. Institutional Flow of Decision Making

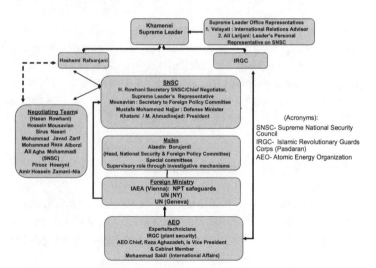

Figure 2. Key Decision Makers

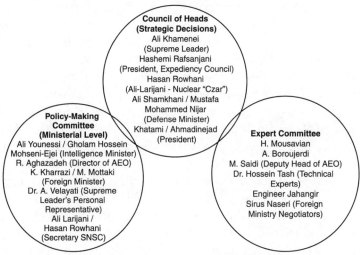

New Negotiating Team and Ministers: Changes for 2006

Ali Larijani	Replaced Rowhani as Secretary of the SNSC.
Javad Vaidi	Deputy Head of International Affairs of SNSC and Head of Delegation.
Ali Hossein Tash	Deputy Head of SNSC for Strategic Affairs
Mohammad Nahavandian	Deputy for Economic Affairs of SNSC.
Mohammad Saidi	Deputy Head of AEO for International Affairs.
Ali Asghar Soltaniyeh	Deputy Director-General for political and international Affairs, Foreign Ministry (until December 23, 2005). Then IAEA representative.
Mohammed Mehdi Akhoundzadeh	Permanent Representative to IAEA (until December 23, 2005).
Abdol Reza Rahmani-Fazli	Deputy Secretary of SNSC.
Ali Monfared	Deputy to the SNSC Secretary, replaced Mousavian.
Manuchehr Mottaki	Foreign Minister, replaced Kharrazi.
Mustafa Mohammad Najjar	Defense Minister, replaced General Ali Shamkhani (2005).

Source: Rowhani, *Keyhan* Interview, Report to President Khatami. The reconstruction with names is the author's and reflects informed guesswork.

if they are too soft in negotiations and two, to stiffen the spine of politicians who might be tempted to weaken support for the project. For example, Rowhani has said that "any Iranian government that wishes to stop uranium enrichment will fall." Hashemi Rafsanjani echoed this saying that "they are telling us blatantly that we should not acquire nuclear technology: and we, in return, tell them that we shall not abandon the peoples' right and we shall not submit to bullying."[45] However, in a system that has manipulated the issue of nuclear energy by depicting it as an issue of denial and discrimination, skepticism is in order when Iranian leaders insist that public opinion would or would not tolerate a certain path or that it forces them to do such and such.[46] Related to this is the assertion that no matter who is president, policy will remain the same.[47]

The Majles is also invoked to argue that Iranian negotiators cannot be flexible. For example, the passage of a bill by the Majles in mid-2005 calling for a resumption of the enrichment program was quickly approved by the hard-line Guardian Council, though without any legal standing. Negotiators also say that the government is under heavy pressure, with people and the media demanding results from the negotiations. This pressure is said to stem from the hard-liners who shun any compromise and want to provoke an international crisis to strengthen their own grip on power.[48] In response Iranian negotiators have sought to use this domestic pressure to pressure their European negotiating partners. The result is the kind of brinksmanship just short of rupture.[49]

Iranian negotiators feel, with reason, that by accepting a freeze on enrichment activities during negotiations with the EU-3, they entered into an asymmetrical commitment that gave the Europeans an incentive to prolong the discussions and thereby impose serious costs on Iran's nuclear program. To try to win back some of the ground it feels it lost, Iran has sought to impose deadlines and sometimes to manufacture an air of crisis about the urgency for an accord. Suspension is resisted for several reasons. The AEO opposes a freeze because of its impact on the retention and employment of scientific personnel.[50] The cost of a cessation (of a small pilot project), one expert argued, is a minimum $5 billion and the failure of fifteen years of effort. From a technical standpoint, the argument is that the elimination of one of the five phases of nuclear production "will render all other phases and the efforts of scientists in past years ineffective."[51] Hard-liners are also skeptical about where the suspension will lead. They fear that periodically rolling over the suspension will make the nuclear issue, with delay, less contentious and thus susceptible to compromise—in effect that prolonged suspension would become cessation by another name. Every effort was made to mobilize against this in the negotiations and to insist that suspension served no good purpose since Iran will not, under any conditions, relinquish its rights.[52]

The hard-liners, while not the only forces in Iran's politics, are disproportionately powerful, vehement, and vocal. Reformists' criticisms of this extremism are mild but trenchant.[53] What difference does this prevailing hard line make to decisions on the nuclear issue? Having hyped the subject domestically and put the prestige of the regime on the line, the Iranian government may find it difficult to walk away from the contest without some compensation. A decent compromise package, however, *could* be sold domestically by a determined leadership. But such a leadership would have to first sideline the extremists and then retreat under a smoke-screen of strong rhetoric.

And this does not seem to be the intent of the new Iranian government. In August it sought to depict its predecessors as "soft" in defending the "nation's rights."[54] But in their defense, the earlier team revealed that they only used the negotiations to buy time and stall while continuing with conversion as long as possible.[55] These revelations have not enhanced Western faith in Iran's *bona fides*. The nuclear issue has been used to buttress the regime's legitimacy, which has been successfully depicted as a nationalist issue around which all Iranians can rally. The issue of the right to technology has elided almost imperceptibly into the "right to the fuel cycle." In this there have been a few dissenters.[56] The hyping of the nuclear issue as a right, a symbol of modernity and independence, as well as a consensus issue on which there is little scope for disagreement may have bound Iran's hands and narrowed the scope for an eventual agreement.

At the same time the lack of trust on all sides makes a technical fix that might otherwise be an option less acceptable to all sides.[57] Because the issue is fundamentally political, not technical, and because it hinges on trust, the international negotiators insist that "none is easier to monitor than some." Specialists have concluded that it would be "difficult if not impossible to verify that Iran was *not* secretly making nuclear weapons under *any* deal that allowed Iran to enrich uranium. The inspection burden would either be unacceptable to Iran or provide inadequate assurance for the rest of the world [emphasis added]."[58]

Another possibility that looks more feasible is one in which Iran mines and processes uranium to gas (at the Isfahan facility) but then ships the uranium hexafluoride gas to Russia. Russia would then convert it into fuel rods and ship it back to the reactor in Bushire. This would enable Iran to claim that it is using uranium from Iran to power Iranian reactors, while the Europeans could claim that they stopped Iran from the enrichment process that would have given them the ability to make fissile material for nuclear weapons.[59] However, this Russian proposal is unlikely to fly as it is just another way of denying Iran enrichment. Iran insists on access to the full fuel cycle but under extreme pressure might settle for the interim acceptance of the principle of enrichment and a limited or pilot project reflecting this. Domestic politics limits Iran's ability to forgo enrichment or the dismantling of any facilities, while a freeze or the forgoing of future capabilities would be easier to swallow. Schemes that take the most sensitive parts of the fuel cycle out of Iran to Russia, for example, might be acceptable, if Iran retains the right (even limited to principle) to the full fuel cycle. Iran has objected to multinational or regional enrichment facilities or to a five- or ten-year moratorium on enrichment, proposed by Al Baradei. But both of these proposals are less objectionable than the U.S. approach, which is to limit enrichment to those countries already possessing it.[60] This constitutes, in Iran's view, another set of discriminations within the NPT, and it accounts for why Iranian officials have sought to depict Iran's nuclear know-how as irreversible and insist that Iran has already achieved the requisite capability.

Nevertheless, Iran's insistence on self-sufficiency and right to the full fuel cycle is difficult to square with the EU-3 and U.S. insistence that Iran forgo enrichment. Any formula that leaves Iran with a capability would be unacceptable to the United States and the EU-3, while any formula assuring them runs up against Iran's redlines regarding enrichment. Compromise appears difficult, exacerbated by a lack of trust on both sides. Ironically, negotiations that might have helped by buying time have only underscored the differences. In short, as discussed in chapter five, Iran's negotiating strategy with the EU-3 and its behavior with the IAEA have not enhanced its goal of gaining acceptance of its right to the full fuel cycle.

In sum, then, the regime has used the nuclear issue for domestic legitimation and is now limited by it. Although Iranian decision making reflects a broad consensus, there is leeway for choice by the leadership. This in turn depends on the leadership resisting the temptation to provoke a crisis for narrow partisan and regime reasons and on a realistic estimate of Iran's relative power and leverage. It also depends on being offered a package that can be used as a cover for compromise.

3

Fear of a Nuclear Iran

Iran is difficult to read and Iranian society is hard to categorize.[1] Iran is not a typical outlaw state in that it has at least some redeeming qualities: It is not overtly confrontational or given to wild swings in behavior or to delusional goals; it has not denounced arms control treaties to which it formally adheres; and there is evidence of pluralism and some debate within the country. Though a threat to Western interests, the nature of that threat is difficult to categorize. As was shown in Iraq, not being able to read a state's nature can lead to faulty assessments, particularly when dealing with already limited intelligence.

Iran's combination of a sense of grievance and a sense of entitlement is not reassuring. Though pragmatic, Iran has demonstrated a powerful streak of opportunism—seizing tactical openings without reference to other concerns and being unfussy about its tactical alliances to promote its interests. Related is the closed nature of the regime that is often self-absorbed to the point that it can grossly misread or ignore others' concerns, increasing the risk of miscalculation.[2] Moreover, the closed nature of the regime breeds secrecy, dissimulation, and deception. This deliberate ambiguity facilitates activities that can be disclaimed (deniability). All of these traits are evident in the areas discussed below.

Nuclear Infrastructure and Program

Iranian leaders insist that their nuclear infrastructure is intended for peaceful purposes. Whatever the merits of a large-scale nuclear program for a state well endowed with oil and gas deposits, the infrastructure being developed is itself a cause for concern. The nature, scale, and sequencing of the program suggest a weapons program.[3] Together with Iran's failure to disclose certain activities to the IAEA until they were exposed and the possibility that other such activities remain in a clandestine undeclared program, there are ample grounds for suspicion. Furthermore, there are still some troubling questions pending with the IAEA: namely, activities in Lavizan and Iran's interest in polonium, which is normally associated with a weapons program.[4] In addition there are unanswered questions about whether Iran acquired P2 centrifuge technology on offer from Pakistan. If so, these centrifuges would shorten the time needed for Iran to build a weapon. There is also the issue of organizational links and contacts between the AEO and the military, which raises questions about the exclusively peaceful and civil nature of program.[5] The pattern of Iran's clandestine procurement over the past decade has long convinced the United States in particular of Iran's weapons ambitions. To these are added the question whether Iran—like Libya—received nuclear weapon designs through the AQ Khan network.[6] Finally, the way in which revelations of Iran's sensitive facilities (the uranium enrichment plant in Natanz and the heavy water plant at Arak) surfaced and the reluctant and contradictory method in which Iran has dealt with them— through half truths, inconsistencies, undeclared activities, lies, and erection of obstacles to hinder and render inspections useless—all suggest the body language of a state with something to hide.

Iranian officials appear to delight in obfuscation, slipping from discussing nuclear technology to a weapons capability and back again:

Believe me, psychologically it is as if we have a nuclear bomb now and they (i.e. the West) treat us in accordance with that belief ... they treat us like this because they think we have such a thing. They are always worried that something may happen and they may have to deal with a nuclear Iran with nuclear weapons. We want to produce fuel. We truly want to produce fuel. It has nothing to do with us if technically the system for the production of fuel through enrichment is such that we are able to produce something else.[7]

Whether Iran is, or is close to being, self-sufficient in nuclear technology will determine how effective international pressure and sanctions will be, if the country embarks on a determined nuclear weapons program. The point of no return is reached when a country is no longer technologically dependent on other sources; it is only a matter of time until enough fissile material is amassed for a nuclear weapon. Given the uncertainties of intelligence, estimates of Iranian achievement of a nuclear capability range from five to ten years.[8]

Missiles

Alongside the nuclear infrastructure, Iran's missile program is especially troubling. The development of the missile industry in parallel with the quest for nuclear technology suggests they may be linked and that the missiles are intended as delivery systems for nuclear or other WMD warheads.[9] This may indeed be the explanation, but it is not the only one. There are both certainties and uncertainties about this program. What is clear, however, is that Iran relies on missiles and wants their development to reflect its status as a regional power. Its missile program is highly political, and much publicity and fanfare attend its various milestones.[10] Tehran has placed emphasis on missiles since 1988 and believes they will be decisive in future conflicts.[11] It initially developed missiles with assistance from North Korea (from Soviet-era SCUDs together with Korean NO DONG technology). Today its missiles take the form of the SHIHAB-3, deployed since July 2003. Similar to the SCUD-C (or Pakistan GAWRI), this missile is liquid fueled and has a range of approximately 1,000 kilometers with a one-ton warhead. So far, while largely a self-sufficient domestic industry, Iran's missile program is relatively constrained, with rather limited guidance and precision systems and several delays and failures. Iran is preparing to send a satellite into orbit, allegedly for peaceful purposes, but this would imply a multistage missile that Iran has yet to master. A multistage missile will certainly have military implications. Iran also seeks to develop the more technically demanding solid fuel propulsion for its missiles, which would increase the range of missiles and improve their accuracy and stability.[12] Guidance can also be improved through generally available technology like the global positioning system (GPS). And, finally, Iran continues to seek cruise missiles from states and on the open market.[13]

It is clear that Iran has ambitions as a missile power.[14] It attributes to missiles an almost mystical quality from the experience of the war with Iraq and seeks to make political capital from its technological breakthroughs. Iran has recently announced the testing of a ballistic missile with multiple warheads as well as high-speed underwater missiles.[15] While trumpeting the successes of its missile program, Iran has not been very sensitive to other states' concerns.[16] Israel, in particular, whose existence Iran considers illegitimate, has been the most concerned. The range of Iran's missiles (reaching Israel), together with the anti-Israel slogans painted on missiles at parades, does nothing to reassure Israel about Iranian intentions. Given the short distances and the cross-cutting alliances in the region, the introduction of more missiles could make for hair-trigger responses and mistakes. The missile culture of the region (missiles have been used in Iran, Iraq, Yemen, and Afghanistan) compounds this threat. Given limited reaction time and the narrow margin for error, Israel has to treat any incoming missile "as if it carries WMD warheads" and react accordingly.[17]

It would be imprudent to assume that Iran will lag technically indefinitely or that its missile program has no relationship to the development of a nuclear infrastructure. Both programs could have other uses, but both also constitute options or investments in what could become an integrated nuclear weapons and delivery system.[18] That said, it is important not to infer an automatic relationship between Iran's missile and nuclear programs. It would be wrong to assume any automatic *relationship* between a missile program and a nuclear program. *But it would be imprudent to assume no relationship.* In both cases, the domestic political dimension—Iran as a technologically developed state—is as important as the quest for regional status. Iran has sought to avoid reliance on outside arms suppliers since 1988 when U.S. sanctions virtually grounded its air force. Ever since, missiles have been seen as a substitute for airpower, which is costly (spare parts, avionics, pilots, and training) and creates dependency. In contrast, missiles are assured of penetration, survivable (hidden, dispersed, mobile), and cheaper over their life cycle. Never mind that they are less accurate, less flexible, and carry less payload. Unlike airpower, they decouple destructive capacity from military capability (or skill). As such, missiles can act as a crude deterrent. They are thus the ideal weapon for an ambitious and status-hungry state limited in military capacity. Unfortunately, one could make exactly the same argument in justification of a nuclear weapons program.

Closed System

The Iranian political system even after twenty-seven years still functions more like a conspiracy than a government. Decision making for national security has been concentrated in a few hands, most notably where the nuclear program is concerned.[19] This in itself is a cause for concern because it is not clear if the handful of decision makers are familiar with the lessons of the nuclear era or have given serious thought to the implications and responsibilities entailed in the possession of nuclear weapons materials. Safety of materials and integrity of command and control are areas of concern as is vetting of officials for political reliability. In a regime with radical elements, the possibility of unreliable elements passing on materials is very real. The parallels with the Pakistan experience suggest that the "insider" problem may be even more serious in Iran, where there are several factions within the ruling establishment.

The increasing role of the Revolutionary Guards in Iran's politics is another source of concern. Of 152 new members elected to the Majles in February 2004, 91 had Guards backgrounds, and a further 34 former Guards officers now hold senior-level posts in the government.[20] In the June 2005 presidential elections, besides Ahmadinejad, there were three other candidates from the Guards. The dominance of the Guards and intelligence officials could open the country to a new militarism.[21]

These elements may become a law unto themselves, having interfered twice in recent months on issues about which they felt strongly.[22] As a hard-line interest group, the Guards could have disproportionate influence on how Iran looks at nuclear weapons and behaves with them once acquired. Moreover, as custodians of Iran's most sensitive weapons sites, the Guards are in a critical position to assure safety and to prevent leakage of dangerous materials to terrorists. Yet these same Guards have been in charge of liaison, training, and running of terrorists. Because the Guards are recruited and chosen for their ideological commitment to the regime, their zealotry has certain risks. Vetted only for regime commitment (rather than psychological stability), the Guards may contain unstable elements willing to transfer sensitive nuclear or biological technology to terrorist groups. Technology transfer could be done by a freelance insider, by inadvertence through leakage from poorly secured facilities, or as a result of an institutional policy decided by the Guards leadership, perhaps unhappy with a government in a crisis. Without strong civilian control and a clear chain of command that takes very seriously the threat of leakage or transfers, the risk will continue to exist.[23] Whether the regime's penchant for secrecy is compatible with accountability is worrisome.

Besides transfer and leakage from sources within the regime, there is a more general risk from *ultranationalists*, military or civilian. This is the tenor of the discourse of the current government, which may reflect much deeper currents. The regime has played the nationalist card in the nuclear issue, so far successfully, but with one clear result: It has narrowed its own room for maneuver. Iran's grandstanding on Palestine as a Muslim issue is analogous to Arab states using it as an Arab issue—as a way of accruing domestic capital for their minority regimes deficient in political legitimacy.[24] The cultivation and exploitation of ultranationalism is a two-edged sword that leaves regimes as much a captive as a driver of the phenomenon (note the recent parallels with China and Japan). The danger here is that in crises such regimes losing control become the captive of mobs and emotions, increasing the risk of miscalculation and conflict.[25]

Terrorism

As terrorism has evolved, the aims of terrorists can no longer be assumed to be limited. Given the motivation to inflict major destruction, the limiting factor in terrorists' capacity to do so has become technological. But reliance on technology denial in an age of globalization is a thin reed on which to base security. Reliable barriers to prevent the diffusion and leakage of technology to groups determined to target states has become a strategic priority. After 9/11, a major concern has been to close off any paths by which this destructive technology might reach hostile terrorist groups.[26]

In U.S. thinking, the most likely source for WMD technology for terrorists is supply from outlaw states seeking to damage the United States by waging proxy wars through asymmetrical strategies. In this view such states by definition seek WMD and consort with terrorists: Why would they not transfer WMD to terrorists who share their animosity toward the United States? The first thought of the president after 9/11 was to wonder whether Iraq or *Iran* had something to do with the attack.[27] Since 9/11 the idea is that because of these relationships and their possible role *as enablers of terrorists' WMD ambitions*, rogue states need to be dealt with severely. Preventing proliferation to such states became a means of preventing their transfer to terrorists. As President Bush said in a 2005 speech at the National Endowment for Democracy, "We're determined to deny weapons of mass destruction to outlaw regimes and their terrorist allies who would use them without hesitation."[28]

Since 1984 Iran has been labeled a state sponsor of terrorism, and in recent years it has been promoted to being "the most active state sponsor of terrorism."[29] This record and reputation, together with its WMD ambitions and its—at best—ambiguous nuclear program, make it a potentially dangerous adversary as well as a major threat as a supplier of such weapons to terrorists groups. As Senator Richard Lugar (R-IN) put it, "The possibility of a nuclear weapons capable Iran is particularly grave because of the Iranian regime's connections to terrorists."[30] U.S. government reports estimate that "only Iran appears to have the possible future motivation to use terrorist groups in addition to its own state agent, to plot against the U.S. homeland."[31] Nuclear proliferation, a serious enough matter in itself, is doubly so when the potential proliferator has the profile of Iran.

Iran's support of terrorism is in fact a mixed record. Although it is no longer used *routinely* as an instrument of state policy, Iran has by no means dispensed with terrorism completely.[32] Such support is now focused on the Middle East in general. Iran still actively supports Hezbollah, and (allegedly) through it and on its own, supports the crossover to Sunni Hamas and Islamic Jihad.[33] Iran's continued support for Hezbollah and its militia at a time when Lebanon is in flux and Syria is in retreat also exposes Tehran to criticism as a spoiler.[34]

Characteristically, the regime in Tehran seeks to have it both ways: to show that terrorism is a thing of the past, while keeping its options open. The former foreign minister Ali Akbar Velayati has argued that even terrorism in the past was "not in the interest of the country," attributing responsibility to "those who were against balanced and active relations ... with Europe." At the same time Iran reports comments from the Secretary-General of Hezbollah saying that if Iran were attacked, U.S. interests throughout the world would be attacked and that "we can build an atom bomb and we should have [atom bombs]."[35] Hezbollah is also a political party in Lebanon with members sitting in Parliament. As a result Hezbollah has shown restraint, as well as sensitivity to Israel's capacity to retaliate and to its own position in Lebanese politics. Hezbollah is not normally considered comparable to Al Qaeda, which clearly seeks WMD, but such statements raise doubts and give credence to one analyst's observation that "there are numerous groups, from Al Qaida to Hezbollah to various doomsday cults, who would have the motive and capacity to seek out nuclear weapons."[36]

Al Qaeda and Hezbollah have had contacts and cooperated before 9/11. The most serious development, however, is Iran's provision of sanctuary to Al Qaeda elements escaping from Afghanistan in 2002–2003 and inconsistent statements about whether or not Al Qaeda elements were in Iran, which raised questions about Tehran's motivations. Iranian officials initially denied providing safe haven to Al Qaeda and later suggested that they would be repatriated on a selective basis or tried in Iran.[37] Iran gave the impression that it was holding on to Al Qaeda operatives as a bargaining card, possibly for trading against U.S. control of the Iranian opposition force, the *Mujahaddin* (Islamic guerrilla fighters), in Iraq.[38]

There is no reason to believe that Iran today, any more that Saddam Hussein earlier, would transfer WMD technology to terrorist groups like Al Qaeda or Hezbollah. Iran has used any group that can further its interests, irrespective of sectarian affiliation or political orientation, as evidenced by its link with Al Qaeda and through Hezbollah with Islamic Jihad and Hamas. Currently Iran is suspected of arming Sunni and Shiite groups in Iraq, providing them with arms, technology (through the cut-out and conduit of Hezbollah), and training. The aim is to bleed the United States and Great

Britain, signal Iran's regional leverage, and keep the United States bogged down and unwilling to consider targeting Iran. In the process Iran is abetting the diffusion of technology (such as shaped charges and infra-red bombs) in precisely the way it did from Lebanon to the West Bank and Gaza.[39]

Relations with such groups are essentially tactical, and the overlap of interest is not total. No government that wanted to survive would hand over to such groups the means and the decisions that could affect its own vital national security interests. Direct transfer, however, is only one of the ways that links with terrorists might increase dangers from proliferation. Hezbollah, for example, might feel emboldened by its sponsor's new capabilities and act in ways *expecting* support from Tehran.[40] In the past Iran has used its ties with Hezbollah (armed with Katushya missiles) as a threat to deter Israeli strikes against Iran.[41] Using ties with terrorists as deterrence against U.S. strikes in the future cannot be discounted.

This opportunistic attitude is quite consistent with Iranian operating style. Simply put, Iran has never paid a price for this involvement dating from the Marine bombing in Beirut 1983 through Al Khobar in 1996. Iranian links with Al Qaeda, together with the current policy of ambiguity toward that group, suggest either a degree of ignorance about the intensity of feeling on this issue in the United States, or an insouciance about the ability to get away with it through calculated ambiguity and indirection.[42] Neither explanation—ignorance or brinksmanship—is reassuring about Iran's use of terrorists and its likely policies once it has a nuclear capability.

Impact of a Nuclear Capability on Iran's Behavior

Would possessing a nuclear weapons capability lead to greater restraint or more aggressive policies in Iran? How would the acquisition of nuclear weapons affect Iran's goals or behavior? Even a risk-averse state might be emboldened by a new capability. Analysts differ on whether nuclear weapons would have a sobering effect on all states, irrespective of orientation, and on the degree of risk-taking states would be willing to run given the heightened stakes.[43] Broadly speaking, the threat coming from an Iranian nuclear weapons capability is multifaceted and could include the following elements:

- Iran might be tempted to support terrorist groups such as Hezbollah more openly, perhaps by seeking to *extend deterrence* to them. At the least, new capabilities might stimulate more radical elements (especially in the Guards) to argue for a more ambitious set of policies.

- A more activist belligerent Iran might seek to use its nuclear weapons to *sanctuarize* its homeland from reprisal. Iran has tended to be conscious of its own military weakness and has avoided running risks, but in light of its opportunism and given the uncertainties as to how a new major military capability might influence behavior, neither eventuality can be completely discounted.[44]

- Iran's strategic culture (its experience of Iraq's surprise attack in 1980, its decision-making culture, and its operating style) is likely to determine the command system it sets up for its nuclear capability. Given the likelihood that the Revolutionary Guards will be the custodians of this new capability and that they see WMD as offensive weapons rather than deterrents, there are grounds for concern.[45]

- Iran's track record, even without a nuclear capability, is not a model of restraint. Islamic Iran has made it a practice in crises to destabilize the region by threatening horizontal escalation, by widening the dispute by stirring regional instability, or by threatening states friendly to the United States.[46] In the current impasse between Iran and the United States and the EU-3, Iranian officials have made some characteristically veiled threats: If the United States continued its (diplomatic) pressure, Iran would have "no choice but to agitate conditions for America and to endanger its interests." Iran has indicated that a referral to the UNSC could result in regional repercussions: "The region needs stability and the smoke of any escalation in the region will hurt their own eyes."[47] In light of current and past threats to hold the region hostage, there is room for doubt about what a nuclear-capable Iran would threaten.

- Despite its far-flung borders and more than a dozen neighbors, Iran has invested heavily in missiles, domestic production of arms, and research and development of WMD, even though none of the regional threats it faces are likely to be unconventional. That Iran's conventional capabilities have remained limited and barely developed since 1988 therefore has dangerous implications.[48] Emphasis on missiles and possibly nuclear weapons might give Iranian leaders the false impression that such weapons are somehow more elastic in their uses than is warranted by the experience so far. In looking for new and novel uses to compensate for their conventional inadequacies, and in stretching their uses, Iran runs the risk of lowering the threshold of nuclear weapons use. Iran would thus leave itself with no other practical option except threat or actual use of such weapons. This threat would be reinforced domestically by a consideration of sunk costs: Of what use are these weapons if they cannot be applied practically in all contingencies? A balanced conventional force in Iran would be more reassuring to Iran's neighbors and the international community.

Nuclear Weapons or Nuclear Option?

Iran has been clearly influenced by other proliferators. In assessing the 1993–1994 North Korean case, Iran may have asked itself: "Do you get international cooperation by cooperating with safeguards or do you get cooperation by high-powered confrontation and bargaining?"[49] What is striking about the North Korean case, which may or may not be applicable to Iran, is the perceived centrality of nuclear weapons as *the* guarantor of regime security. This implies that it is not a bargaining chip but an insurance policy unlikely to be given up.[50]

There are grounds for assuming Iran's interest in nuclear weapons. Iran's quest for status and regional influence, the need for deterrence vis-à-vis the United States, and the possible political benefits domestically in shoring up the regime are all possible reasons for seeking nuclear weapons. However, a nuclear weapons *option* might meet these needs equally well without the costs associated with overt proliferation. Iran's own statements are at best contradictory and reflect the aim of exploiting ambiguity for strategic purposes.

After a rocky start in the 1980s, when Iranian officials made several statements about the necessity for WMD and specifically references to chemical weapons as "the poor man's atomic weapon," such comments have since been repudiated.[51] Periodically, however, the military in the form of the Revolutionary Guards appears to revive this thinking. In 1998 secret comments by the Guards Commander General Safavi—to the effect that Iran needed to reconsider its participation in international conventions banning WMD in light of the threat posed by Israel—were leaked and never convincingly repudiated.[52] There are also reports that the Guards and military strategists are convinced that only a nuclear Iran can assume its place as a major regional power and adequately deter a possible attack from the United States or Israel.[53] Former Guards commander Mohsen Rezai criticized the negotiators for reducing Iran's deterrent capability by cooperating with inspectors and "turning over our country's top intelligence documents," suggesting (like Saddam Hussein) that uncertainty about Iran's capabilities serves as a deterrent.[54] Some conservatives have also noted the importance of cultivating or simulating "irrationality" in bargaining and, by extension, deterrence.[55]

Iranian officials insist that they have no nuclear weapons ambitions but also note Israel's "dangerous" possession of nuclear weapons, which in their view means that "stability cannot be achieved" in the region.[56] They insist, nonetheless, that their own nuclear ambitions are peaceful. As proof of their intentions, Iranian leaders point to their refusal to countenance the development or use of chemical weapons, even when a victim of Iraq's chemical weapon attacks between 1983 and 1988. They claim that Iran opposes WMD on principle, with statements like "nuclear weapons do not solve any problems" because power comes from morale and unity.[57] They maintain that WMD have had no place in Iran's defense strategy, national security, and defense doctrines—a stance they argue is reflected in Iran's adherence to all the relevant arms control treaties.[58] They further allege that Islam forbids nuclear weapons and that Supreme Leader Khamenei has issued a *fatwa* banning them.[59] Rowhani has put the case more practically:

> Our decision not to possess weapons of mass destruction is strategic because we believe that these weapons will not provide security for Iran. On the contrary, they will create big problems. Iran exerted huge efforts during the past few years to build bridges of confidence with the states of the region. We absolutely do not want to blow up those bridges by mobilizing our resources to produce weapons of mass destruction. We are confident that our possession of these weapons will force these countries to seek the support of big powers. Consequently, regional security will worsen. This will not serve our national security.[60]

Earlier Rowhani argued that Iran's acquisition of nuclear arms would come at too high a price, not just in terms of regional influence, but also "their production would block our progress in other scientific and technological fields."[61] (Presumably this refers to the sanctions they would trigger.) Former defense minister Admiral Ali Shamkhani also opposed nuclear weapons, stating that "the problem is that we enjoy advanced technical know-how and the enemies develop a perception that we are after nuclear arms, whereas, we follow a strategy of not having such a dangerous weapon."[62]

A former representative to the IAEA, Ali Akbar Salehi, gave the most detailed argument against nuclear weapons. He argued that possession would not enhance a state's prestige, defended the NPT despite its discriminatory nature, and noted that for Iran nuclear weapons "would raise more threats against it, not assure security, by having nuclear weapons." He saw no threats on Iran's periphery necessitating nuclear weapons and believed that any such weapons Iran acquired would not be able to deal with either Russian or Israeli nuclear weapons.[63] Iranians consistently emphasize Israel as a strategic alibi, to divert accusations from Iran's own program and to defuse any potential regional criticisms. Curiously, there is little discussion about the limited value of Israel's nuclear weapons in dealing with the Arab states' conventional threat or the two intifadas, nor is there reference to the specificity of the Israeli case given the existence of an existential threat and the legacy of the Holocaust.[64]

As was discussed in chapter two, there is no public debate in Iran about the wisdom of acquiring nuclear weapons, and the little discussion that exists is characterized by an alarming degree of ignorance or oversimplification. Hard-line newspapers tend to argue for nuclear weapons on deterrence grounds, noting that Japan would not have been attacked if it had possessed nuclear weapons and that possession does not necessarily mean use.[65] Others argue that nuclear weapons are of doubtful utility: "In fact it is not clear what the value of having atomic bombs is. It seems that the only thing that atomic bombs are capable of doing is to kill innocent people and incite public opinion against the country using these weapons."[66] There is a curious absence of serious consideration of the specific costs and benefits of nuclear weapons and no discussion of the relative cheapness of nuclear weapons, given their concentrated power, or that the costs of such programs typically come in spikes with modernization cycles.[67] Nor is the utility of nuclear weapons for Iran's specific security needs post-Saddam and post-Taliban discussed. Deterrence is discussed as a catch-all rather than relational concept, as if it were easily achieved and absent associated costs. In general, the discussion appears more to be about morale and status than defense.

It makes a difference for policy whether Iran seeks nuclear weapons or just the option, and its nuclear drive has been consistent with either. Both goals would be consistent with the aims, values, and lessons of the regime. No clear distinction is possible in a country that emphasizes possessing the full fuel cycle, a missile program, and a quest for recognition as a member of the nuclear club. Even more questionable is Iran's intentional muddying of the issue of fuel supply security (which in principle is soluble with guarantees) and the issue of the fuel cycle itself. In an unhealthy dynamic, both the United States and Iran have, for their own different reasons, "exaggerated Iran's nuclear capability," making it "harder to resolve."[68]

The arguments for a nuclear option (or nonweaponized deterrence) are at least as strong as those for nuclear weapons. It appears doubtful that Iran has decided definitively in favor of nuclear weapons. In the absence of strategic urgency, the costs of getting nuclear weapons outside the treaty do not appear commensurate with the benefits for Iran. So there is no detectable grand strategy but rather a determined push to get as close to a weapons capability as possible within the treaty and then see what happens. In playing the issue by ear with no irreversible commitments, Iran hopes to avoid paying too high a price for achieving a near capability.[69] But Iran's determined incrementalism can be upset by the dynamics of interactions. Iran's own domestic politics, which has seen leaders exaggerate the program, may inhibit Tehran from appearing to halt or reverse it. And the unwillingness of Iran's interlocutors, particularly the United States, to give Iran space or cover for a retreat could further narrow options. Miscalculation on both sides is thus a real risk.

Nuclear proliferation is traditionally visualized in terms of a threshold, which once crossed, dramatically changes the status of a state. Conceptualizing it as a continuum enables one to see various stages in the process of proliferation—a spectrum of possibilities comprising elements of various capabilities. Given gradations short of a full weapons capability, change of status (nuclear/nonnuclear) is less dramatic and more shaded. The possibilities are often referred to in shorthand as models: for example, the Japan model (a full civilian capability easily converted to weapons capability within the treaty); the Iraq model (covert weapons activities within the treaty); and the Israel model (weapons capability, unassembled, outside the treaty) (see Figures 3 and 4 for details on these models).

Iranian leaders have denied even seeking a capability, claiming that they "do not want to be close to producing them [weapons]."[70] Yet insistence on the fuel cycle, which has been the focus of negotiations and the crux of the differences, ensures a close capability to produce weapons should such a decision be made. This so-called breakout option is implicit in what Iran seeks, in effect a Japanese model of a full spectrum of capabilities short of weaponization within the treaty—precisely what the EU-3 and the United States seek to deny it.[71]

Iran's attempt to position itself to acquire a nuclear option is a classic case of nuclear hedging. As Ariel Levite has noted:

> Nuclear hedging refers to a national strategy of maintaining, or at least appearing to maintain, a viable option for the relatively rapid acquisition of nuclear weapons, based on an indigenous technical capacity to produce them within a relatively short time frame ranging from several weeks to a few years. In its most advanced form, nuclear hedging involves nuclear fuel cycle facilities capable of producing fissionable materials (by way of uranium enrichment and/or plutonium separation) as well as the scientific and engineering expertise

Alternative Models

Figure 3. Pathways, Thresholds, and Positions of Selected Nuclear-Capable States

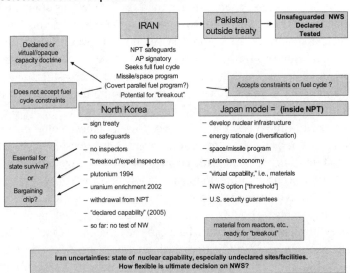

Iran uncertainties: state of nuclear capability, especially undeclared sites/facilities. How flexible is ultimate decision on NWS?

Figure 4. Motivation and Capability Contrasted

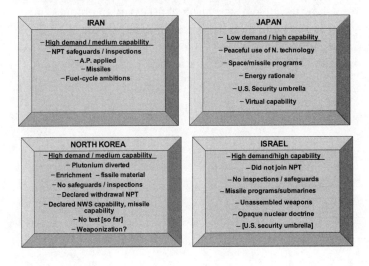

both to support them and to package their final product into a nuclear explosive charge.[72]

IAEA Director-General Mohammad Al Baradei has suggested that "countries look at know-how as a deterrent. If you have nuclear material, the weapon part is not far away." Taking the thought one step further, one U.S. intelligence official has noted that a deterrent value need not come from a successful nuclear program but from convincing others, including neighbors, of the existence of such a program.[73] The implication is that the appearance of full fuel cycle capabilities can itself achieve some of the functions or benefits of a nuclear deterrent. Iran's quest for a virtual capability is consistent with an inclination to hedge against an uncertain security future, to maximize its opportunities within the NPT, and to brag about (and exaggerate) its technological and scientific progress at home.[74] This does not preclude a willingness to meet international concerns (that is, to use its claimed capability as a bargaining card), but it does seek to drive a hard bargain that includes regime security guarantees. Alternatively, Iran can still take its time and drive closer to a fuel cycle capability by legally and gradually acquiring and building up under inspections its "nuclear know-how technology and materiel necessary to produce nuclear weapons some day if a dire strategic threat should arise."[75] The critical question, then, is how close to a weapons option Iran can prudently be allowed to get, and what can be done about it.

4

Iran's Negotiating Strategy

Iran has improvised a strategy to deal with the "outing of its nuclear facilities" undeclared to the IAEA for nearly two decades. Iran's tactics and negotiating style, far from reassuring the international community, have exacerbated the problem of trust. Thus, four years after the issue first surfaced, questions remain as to the extent and peaceful nature of Iran's nuclear program.

From Damage Limitation to Confrontation

The surprise revelation of its undeclared nuclear activities in 2002 caught Tehran unprepared. It came at a sensitive time, with victory in Afghanistan feeding a U.S. sense of confidence that was manifest in planning the next phase of the war against terrorism and proliferation of WMD in Iraq. Tehran swiftly sought to limit damage and decided to deal with the revelations and attendant inquiry from *within* the treaty, as a way of gaining time to devise a strategy.

Iran's policy has been conscious of developments elsewhere. Libya's decision to give up its WMD activities in 2003 on the one hand and North Korea's decision to withdraw from the NPT and claim possession of nuclear weapons on the other clearly contrasted with Iran's course, which is somewhere between the two. At the same time, revelations of the extent of the activities of the AQ Khan network in sales of nuclear equipment and designs to Iran put Tehran under further pressure to admit the totality of its program. Unwilling to imitate Libya or North Korea, Tehran continued to cooperate with the IAEA and the EU-3, reluctantly and partially confirming only what was uncovered, while insisting on its rights to technology as an NPT member. Iran's approach has several defining elements.

- Iran's receptivity to the EU-3 and cooperation with the IAEA has varied with Tehran's sense of vulnerability or confidence.

- Having "talked up the issue" domestically after 2002, negotiators tied their own hands in the negotiations.

- Domestic divisions also led to counterproductive grand-standing by negotiators.

- Iran saw concessions as dangerous, starting a slippery slope to more (U.S.) demands, culminating in regime change.

- Iran's negotiating style, legalistic and hair-splitting, paralleled its behavior toward the IAEA inspectors, formally correct but unhelpful. Taken together these attitudes suggested that Iran had something to hide. Iran's tendency to seek to win every round of negotiations, manufacture crises, renegotiate agreements, and redefine obligations put tactics before strategy, weakening any advantage Iran might have gained by the process of formal cooperation with the IAEA and the EU-3.

- A certain narcissism ("how am I doing?") is evident in Iran's approach to the world, leading to misjudgments about other states' likely reactions.

- In the end, negotiations reduced trust rather than built confidence.

The evolving strategic context after 2003, however, gave Iran reason for increasing self-confidence. Against the backdrop of unwelcome revelations about the AQ Khan network and Libya's capitulation came the deterioration of the U.S. position in Iraq and the resurfacing of the North Korea crisis, diverting resources away from Iran. The rise of oil prices and the geopolitical sensitivity of the region, giving Tehran the cushion of windfall revenues, also increased Iran's sense of its own leverage (not least with new consumers India and China). Having spent over a decade of diplomacy depicting the denial of technology as a North–South issue, Iran also expected support from the non-aligned countries in the UN and IAEA.[1] Iran believed that its intrinsic importance would enable it to divide the EU–U.S. and Russia through native shrewdness and skill, if necessary.

International negotiators have sought to force Iran to choose between the full fuel cycle and confrontation. So far Iran's policy has been to push the door open as far as it can, without crossing the threshold of actual conflict. Nonetheless, Iran feels more secure and confident in 2006 than it did in 2002 and is thus willing to take the initiative in rejecting a freeze on all enrichment activities and more willing to risk confrontation.

Iran and the Negotiations

Once its undeclared activities were revealed, Tehran accepted intensified inspections and signed the stiffer Additional Protocol, giving inspectors increased access to sites.[2] In acting to demonstrate its good faith, Iran was seeking to reassure the international community of its benign intentions and to "remove the pretext" for U.S. aggression. Iran's officials argued that they had only been guilty of acts of omission (a failure to report activities), not the commission of impermissible activities. In extenuation they argued that required declarations had not been made because U.S. sanctions imposed much earlier would have been extended to those entities cooperating with Iran, if such declarations had been made.[3]

To buy time to devise a strategy, Iran designated Hasan Rowhani, the Secretary of the SNSC, the principal organ on security, as the chief negotiator. This action effectively took the dossier away from the Foreign Ministry and the AEO, which had dealt with it when it had been a routine issue.[4]

Iran saw the crisis in autumn of 2003 as a possible pretext for the United States "to carry out a new Iraq in Iran."[5] Iran sought a way out and grasped the lifeline thrown by the EU-3 initiative in the Tehran agreement. The scenario repeated itself in autumn 2004, when Iran reacted again to its isolation and the ultimatum of the IAEA, this time accepting the Paris agreement with the EU-3. (This agreement essentially suspended enrichment-related activities as well as enrichment itself.) Since then Iran has been trying to balance and reconcile access to the full fuel cycle *and* avoidance of an international crisis. In not wishing to choose between the two, Iran has often acted as if it wants to cheat—to be a party to the NPT but not abide by all its rules and to claim its benefits but be ambiguous about its responsibilities. As one reformist noted, Iran should either accept or reject the NPT: "If we accept it, we should ... accept the concomitant restrictions as well."[6] To bridge the gap between its quest for technology development (that is, "not give up their rights"), and its desire to avoid a crisis with the rest of the world, Iranian negotiators accepted confidence-building measures, with only mixed success.[7]

Iranian officials defended the EU-3 negotiations domestically by noting that without them there would have been a crisis with the Board of Governors (BoG) of the IAEA and "the great contracts that Iran signed with their [IAEA] countries in the field of oil and gas would have been impossible."[8] More broadly, Iran needed to have "constructive and positive interaction" with the world for its economic development. As chief negotiator Rowhani stated, "We have no other choice. Causing other countries to have concerns means closing the paths to interaction" and hence failing in development.[9] The message was clear: Iran should not cause a crisis over the issue of enrichment that would impair its overall development prospects. As suggested earlier, this Rowhani/Rafsanjani view is not universally shared, because some in Iran would prefer a crisis, enabling them to make a point of principle and stopping interaction with others.[10]

Iran thus used the EU-3 channel to try to avoid making a stark choice between the two goals, at least postponing the crisis while probing to see what benefits it could extract in exchange for renouncing the controversial technology. Iran's leverage has been limited, consisting of threats to resume enrichment and reminding the EU-3 of their stake in a successful outcome and the dangers of a breakdown.[11] In an interview, Rowhani stated that "if the talks break down and the issue goes to the Security Council, it will be a great failure for Europe and multilateralism as a whole."[12] At the same time, Iran was aware of the constraints on Europe, which negotiated with the United States looking over its shoulder.[13] Furthermore, Iran was aware that little separated the EU-3, Russia, and the United States on these issues—only differences in approach—so there was little room for creating or exploiting division.[14]

Iranian negotiators have tried to show that their hands are tied domestically. Therefore the red line of uranium enrichment is not negotiable because it is the "national will and is the establishment's decision. Nobody can end it." This implies that Iran cannot renounce the right to it in principle and would have extreme difficulty *reducing* its current capacity (for example, dismantling facilities), although freezing it in place would be politically more feasible.[15]

By cooperating with the IAEA, Iran wanted to puncture the sense of crisis and close the special nature of the inspections and cyclical periodic reporting and accounting to the IAEA Board of Governors. These regular reports put Iran on notice, and both its cooperation and progress on answering various questions relating to its nuclear activities ensured continuous pressure on Tehran. These periodic reports (eight between mid-2002 and October

2005) ensured that Iran had to get its story straight or risk contra-diction from technical analyses, environmental swipes, and infor-mation from other sources.

In the course of these inspections, numerous anomalies, incon-sistencies, and late or partial declarations were noted. Iran did not declare Natanz enrichment, purchases from the AQ Khan network, work on laser enrichment, or the most recent on plutonium. It also left open questions about the source of highly enriched uranium, whether and when Iran obtained and used P2 centrifuge technol-ogy, and whether it bought weapons plans from the AQ Khan net-work as the same time as Libya.

But despite these inspection problems, it is possible that late declarations about activity in tunnels and air defense around Natanz might have an innocent explanation, as might the contam-ination of the imported P2 centrifuge from Pakistan. So, apart from the noncompliance with safeguard obligations, there is little (that is, no activity as such that is proscribed) with which Iran can be for-mally charged. The smoking gun remains elusive.[16]

Negotiating Style and Confidence Building

Iran's tactics have exacerbated problems of trust and reassurance. The Tehran agreement with the EU-3 in October 2003 soon became a subject of contention. With the United States embroiled in Iraq, Tehran felt freer to harden its terms. Ostensibly because of the failure of the EU-3 to close the nuclear dossier in the IAEA (an unrealistic expectation given the number of unanswered and new questions appearing almost daily), Iran threatened in March 2004 to begin testing its uranium production facility at Isfahan. Iran argued that this facility had not been covered by the Tehran agree-ment.[17] Iran later announced its intention of resuming "the manu-facture and assembly of components"[18] while affirming interest in continuing discussions for a long-term agreement with the EU-3.[19] Iran also shrugged off the IAEA's June 2004 report critical of Iran, calling for more proactive cooperation by Iran as well as asking Iran to reconsider its heavy water and uranium conversion facility (UCF) programs. Reflecting how disconnected Tehran was from international realities, Iran responded: "We are not satisfied because we believe this was the time to close the file."[20]

Iran and the EU-3 came to a new agreement in November 2004 in Paris.[21] Iran agreed to suspend all activities related to uranium enrichment pending a final agreement. This resulted in the adoption of a milder resolution in the IAEA the same month. This Paris agreement, reached during the U.S. presidential elections, looked for a more comprehensive solution, embedding the nuclear issue in the broader political, economic, and security context and implying U.S. involvement directly or indirectly.

Tehran's negotiating style was again in evidence. To improve its negotiating position, it sped up its uranium enrichment program leading up to negotiations.[22] Then, at the last minute, Iran insisted that twenty centrifuges be excluded from the suspension, a move that was rejected by the EU-3. Finally, the agreement was depicted as a big victory, in which Iran "managed to defuse the threats against [it] and to defend [its] rights."[23] Much the same pattern was repeated in 2005. Iran again sought to expand the area of permissible activity. In March it indicated it wanted to expand quality control checks and maintenance of nonessential enrichment centrifuge parts to essential centrifuge parts that had been sealed by the IAEA under the suspension agreement. By May Iranian negotiators told their EU-3 counterparts that their understanding was that conversion of uranium to gas (preenrichment) does not amount to enrichment and hence was not covered by the Paris agreement. Resumption therefore was inevitable—only the date was uncertain. This interpretation was not supported by the letter of the Paris agreement, which specifically covered enrichment-related activity. Faced with a solid EU-3 front and the threat of referral to UNSC, Iran stepped back from the brink.[24] Iran's tendency to seek a foot in the door by exempting some centrifuges or preenrichment was now becoming a stop-and-go strategy that saw periodic crises and new agreements. The danger of this was that Iran might slice away at understandings by proceeding with conversion before an international response and then agree to another suspension, in each case advancing its program further without incurring a response.[25] In essence this is what occurred after August 2005 when Tehran resumed conversion while insisting on its continued interest in negotiations.

The EU-3 concluded from this that Iran's negotiating behavior would need to be revised if progress were going to be made. Iran's negotiating style of reopening agreements, exploiting or ingeniously creating loopholes, manufacturing crises and deadlines, and making last-minute demands is tactically impressive but strategically counterproductive.[26] Together with tactics similar to those used with the IAEA (delay, inconsistencies, half-truths, and grudging corrections), Iran has done little to increase either its popularity in the UN or its credibility with its interlocutors. The result is that the EU-3 is disinclined to give Iran the benefit of the doubt and feels that Iran bears the burden of proof to assure the international community of its peaceful intentions.

Iranian behavior has not been reassuring. For example, its negotiators say, "We have one principle: for mass destruction weapons, the basis is conventions, nothing more, nothing less," or "We are not bound to put forward solutions beyond what international regulations and IAEA safeguards require from us."[27] In light of this record of obstructionism and legalistic nitpicking, Iran's insistence on reciprocity and nondiscrimination evokes little sympathy. Thus, comments made to Japan TV by Deputy Head of the AEO Mohammad Saidi come across as petulant and self-serving: "The Japanese have never shown us the pictures of their centrifuge machinery. If they do we will show you ours."[28] While Iranians argue that the objective of the negotiations was to create trust, not to suspend uranium enrichment permanently, the way these negotiations have been handled has only accentuated mistrust.[29] Iran's unwillingness to suspend work on the heavy water reactor at Arak (suggested by the IAEA) and its insistence on resuming centrifuge production in mid-2004 further eroded trust.[30] From the view of the international community, Iran has, in Javier Solana's words, "a lot of ground to make up" in building trust.[31] Director-General Al Baradei, a neutral figure, noted that the onus was on Iran: "In view of the past undeclared nature of significant aspects of Iran's nuclear program, a confidence deficit has been created, and it is therefore essential that Iran works closely with the agency in a proactive manner." Iran's restrictions on the inspections of Parchin, Kelayeh, and Lavizan fed this distrust. It "chipped away at the confidence issue" and the legalistic approach "created needless suspicions."[32] The result was that Russia joined the consensus on Iran's suspicious behavior. The French president too appeared exasperated with Iran.[33]

This question of trust, however, cuts both ways. Iran's behavior has managed to drive the EU-3, the IAEA, Russia, and many nonaligned states closer to the United States, but Iran remains convinced that compromise or weakness is self-defeating because the United States will be unwilling "to take yes for an answer."

Iran's problematic reporting raises questions about its motives. One explanation for its contradictory, grudging, and threatening behavior is that it fears a true accounting of its past activities would betray the fact that those activities breached the fundamental injunction against acquiring nonexclusively peaceful nuclear know-how and capability. Statements after the failure to give the right dates for experimentation with plutonium—to the effect that the activities were not the same as earlier reported—simply stretch credulity.[34] Iran's activities delaying access to sites (2004), razing the entire facilities at Lavizan (2004), initially barring access altogether to Parchin (2005), and then refusing to answer questions are inconsistent with any attempt to reassure the international community about its program.[35] Iran's tactics match this obstructionism. Dissatisfied with the wording of an IAEA resolution, which it considered too critical, Iran delayed a visit of the inspectors to Tehran, explicitly linking the two.[36] Later in 2004 as part of its brinksmanship with the EU on the question of suspension of enrichment and possible referral of Iran's case to the Security Council, Iranian officials threatened to remove IAEA cameras at some sites and start a series of steps commencing with the "nonratification" of the Additional Protocol that they had provisionally signed.[37] Iran also tied the timing of its ratification of the AP to the resumption of "full operations" (that is, enrichment at Natanz). It is notable that Iran uses its safeguards agreements and inspections explicitly as leverage, which implies that if pushed too far, Iran might cease cooperation and leave the international community even further in the dark about its programs and aims.

Iran's record of deceptions leaves open the possibility that there may in fact be *less* to the program than meets the eye.[38] While asserting inalienable rights and alleging conspiracies to deny it the means for development, Iran has had to balance two considerations: how to maintain (and develop) its nuclear program and how to do so *without* creating an international consensus against it.[39] This, together with domestic divisions, accounts for the schizophrenic nature of Iran's response.[40]

Iran's periodic deadlines for ending the negotiations stem from a basic asymmetry in the structure of the negotiations. Suspension of enrichment activities was tied to the duration of the negotiations, yet these were open-ended. As long as negotiations continued until July 2005, Iran's enrichment program, including conversion activities, was frozen by the Paris accords. Iran tried unsuccessfully in the 2003–2005 period to narrow the areas covered by the term *enrichment*. Another tactic was Iran's periodic deadlines for "progress" and accusations of the EU-3 "dragging out" the talks deliberately.[41] Essentially Iran could end the negotiations and be referred to the UNSC or try to resume enrichment while continuing negotiations and risk being referred to the UNSC (something the new government chose to do in August by resuming conversion activities unilaterally).

Assuming the absence of a covert program, the total freeze on enrichment proved painful. Salehi has observed that "the success of the diplomatic authorities will depend on reducing the suspension period."[42] AEO head Reza Aghazadeh noted the "imbalance in commitments," saying that negotiations might last several years and the freeze is "affecting the process of our activities."[43]

The negotiations bought time for both sides. For the EU-3, it was an opportunity to set into motion diplomacy that was lacking, given the U.S. refusal to go beyond public threat. For Iran, the EU-3 served as a buffer and intermediary. It is not to disparage the potential importance of the EU as a strategic commercial partner to note that in the final analysis, Iran would need to deal with the United States.[44] In judging success (at least until July 2005) one can agree with Rowhani that delaying the crisis is not necessarily its avoidance: "If the danger is not removed completely, then one cannot label this delay a success, of course unless in the end we sit down at the negotiations table with the first rate power [United States]."[45] The negotiations with the EU-3 were, in effect, a holding action and a substitute for direct contacts with the United States, which alone could provide the guarantees that Iran seeks.

In its negotiations with the EU-3, Iran resorted to many of the same tactics it used with the IAEA, including brinksmanship, injured pride, and threats of open-ended crises. Iran sought to establish the principle of the *right to enrichment* and to demonstrate that this right is *irreversible* in that Iran has mastered the full fuel cycle and cannot unlearn it, even if subjected to military strikes.[46] Constructive ambiguity has led to differences on precisely how enrichment is defined or what it constitutes and so enrichment has been left to the IAEA to define. For Tehran the indispensable goal has been recognition of the right to the full fuel cycle. To that end, Iran has offered to voluntarily *suspend* enrichment (with the definitional uncertainty noted) for a limited time to enhance confidence. For the EU-3 the aim has been to get Iran to commit to a permanent *cessation* of all fuel cycle activities in exchange for a package that would include proliferation-resistant nuclear technologies (light water reactors), guaranteed fuel supplies at reasonable prices, security guarantees, and trade and diplomatic incentives.

Iran has sought to depict its right to technology under Article IV of the NPT as an issue for all developing countries, who would be affected by any denial of Iran's rights, thus jeopardizing the NPT itself.[47] However, Iran's tactics have left it with few defenders among the nonaligned states.[48]

Iran has also been unsure how to treat the EU countries. It recognizes the EU link with the United States but is uncertain how to use this bridge, seeking to divide the EU-3 (and Russia) and even the United States by dangling the enticing prospects of participation in Iran's future economic and nuclear development.[49] Iranian officials have noted the EU's stake in the success of the negotiations, calling a possible failure a setback for the EU in specific and multilateralism in general. They have called on Europe to stand up more to the United States. On the success of the negotiations, they argue, hangs the future weight of Europe in international affairs.[50]

This attitude can spill over into Iran's overestimation of its position: "Politically the Europeans need us," insisted negotiator Sirus Nasseri. But there is a recognition of Iran's stake in the outcome as well. As Rowhani noted, "If we manage to succeed and finish this issue, important ties with Europe will follow."[51] At the same time, Iran threatened to go public with its own "reasonableness" in the negotiations, should they reach an impasse.[52]

One part of the negotiations after November 2004 focused on how to reassure the international community of Iran's peaceful intentions. Iran argued that this could be managed by monitors, enhanced inspections, and the like but that it would not budge from the use of the full fuel cycle. In light of their suspicions about Iran's aims, the EU-3 was convinced that the phrase *objective guarantees* (which figures in the Paris agreement of November 2004) could have only one meaning: complete abstention from the fuel cycle including the *dismantling* of existing facilities, especially at Natanz and also the heavy water plant at Arak. Although technical fixes are theoretically possible, they are not acceptable for the EU-3 in this case. The necessary level of trust does not exist, and the EU-3 is convinced that any level of activity could be used to shield a covert program. It also believes that any level of activity in any agreement would soon be the subject of reopened negotiation by Iran, which would creatively reinterpret it to its advantage. Cessation meaning *no* activity is thus much easier to monitor than *some* activity. There is little likelihood that this will be acceptable to Iran. Iran has little leeway domestically to forgo technology that has been depicted as indispensable for its development. The EU-3 backed by the United States will find it difficult to accept Iran's access to the fuel cycle without very firm assurances.

Iran's View of the U.S. Role in the Negotiations

Iran sees the United States today as an unpredictable power, "acting first and thinking later."[53] In addition, Iran sees it as seeking to internationalize its dispute with Tehran.[54] Regarding the negotiations, Iranians recognize that "the Europeans and the Agency [IAEA] are what we see on the surface. The Americans are the ones we really have to deal with" and that U.S. "help could be positive from our point of view."[55] Nevertheless, Iran is unwilling to deal with the United States because Tehran believes that entering any negotiations with the United States would be a trap in which open-ended discussions would destabilize Iranian society while U.S. manipulation of the media would make it impossible for Iran to terminate them.[56] Therefore an Iranian unwillingness to engage without upfront concessions from the United States parallels the U.S. approach. Iran sees U.S. pressure and hostility as long-standing and not exclusively or principally tied to the nuclear issue. Former foreign minister Ali Akbar Velayati articulated the slippery slope argument against *any* concessions: "They are bullying us and if we surrender and retreat in the face of blackmail, this is in effect shutting down Iran as a country."[57] Iranian leaders believe that the issue between the two countries goes beyond access to particular technology, claiming that "nuclear technology is only a pretext. If the Americans could not use this pretext, they would resort to other excuses such as support for terrorism and violation of human rights."[58] They believe that even if Iran adhered to the AP and resolved its problems with the IAEA, U.S. pressure would continue.[59] A similar view is reflected in Iran's hesitancy about giving access to military sites (not covered by the AP)—that allowing access to military sites would constitute the thin end of the wedge to open-ended inspections of all sites.[60] Army Commander Mohammed Salimi was in no doubt about U.S. aims: "The enemies of Iran are bent on changing the regime in Iran as they had in the eastern and western states."[61] Iranian diplomats insisted that negotiations could not precede a policy change by the United States: "A country that expresses an interest in negotiations can not at the same time talk of regime change."[62] Ultimately, Iran's negotiations with the EU-3 (with the United States present but not visible) hinges on trust between both Iran and the EU-3 as well as Iran and the United States. But as has been noted repeatedly, Iran's behavior and negotiating style have not been conducive to building that trust and may even have eroded it.[63] The U.S. aims in Iran remain opaque at best, giving Iran little reassurance that compromise would be rewarded or alter ultimate U.S. aims of regime change.[64]

It is clear that Iran does not want to follow the path of Libya in its relations with the United States. Rowhani observed trenchantly that the Libyan model "does not mean that they would only assemble all their centrifuges and put them on a ship and send them to Washington. The Libyan model means following the path of recognizing Israel, means [cutting] off relations with liberation movements in the world...."[65] For Iran to embrace the Libyan model then is for Iran to cease seeking to be an Islamic revolutionary role model and to relinquish its aspirations for regional leadership.

The notion of a slippery slope inhibits any Iranian concession. Tehran is convinced that granting concessions is the thin end of the wedge for the United States to multiply its demands. Given the mutual distrust and lack of flexibility, reliance on relative bargaining position and overall power is bound to take priority.

Iran's negotiating behavior changed in mid-2005. During the 2003–2004 period, Iran intended to buy time and deflect an attack by showing a cooperative spirit and using a moderate tone, but by mid-2005 Tehran had adopted a more militant and confrontational approach. A new ultranationalist government and swollen oil revenues together with Iran's sense that the United States and the EU had become distracted and weakened had turned the tide. Accordingly, Iran believed it could take a tougher line and did so by rejecting the EU-3 package offered in late July as insufficient and resuming conversion activities. Iran also stepped up its campaign to depict the U.S.–EU line on forbidding enrichment as an encroachment on the rights of NPT members—an argument that resonates with Brazil and other nonaligned states. By leveraging the tighter oil market, Iran sought to induce key states such as India and China to consider the advantages of cooperation with Iran.[66]

Iran's resumption of conversion in August 2005 ended the negotiations with the EU-3, which considered conversion termination a precondition for further discussions. Two IAEA resolutions in September did little to change Tehran's position. The second resolution (September 24, 2005) threatened eventual referral to the Security Council for "noncompliance" but gave a mixed message in that it was adopted by vote rather than consensus. Iran intensified its diplomacy especially with the nonaligned states, hoping to prevent such a referral. Iran has offered international participation in its nuclear program, but the precise meaning of this offer is unclear.[67] Tehran has sought to widen the negotiations to include the nonaligned and other members of the IAEA board rather than limit them to the EU-3. Iran also increased its cooperation with the IAEA in October by granting access to Parchin and allowing interviews with some officials. Iran indicated its willingness to resume negotiations with the EU-3 "without preconditions" (that is, without prejudice to its continuing conversion activities).

Iran's harder line reflected a new ultranationalism in Tehran among some elements, including President Ahmadinejad. This hard-line stance is evident in the tougher diplomatic policy and the more reckless rhetoric. Ahmadinejad's speech on the UN's sixtieth anniversary and his statement in Tehran on Qods (Jerusalem Day) that Israel should be "wiped off the map" reflected insensitivity to international opinion and diplomacy, going beyond a toughening of terms. It is doubtful whether either of these speeches gained Iran any new votes. Advocating the elimination of another state also did little to dampen concerns about the implications of Iran's nuclear ambitions.[68]

The IAEA Board of Governors meeting of November 24, though calmer, was another step on the road to Iran's referral to the Security Council. Iran invested hopes in divisions between Europe and the United States and the nonaligned movement (NAM). Iran also resorted to the usual threats: suspending cooperation with the agency on inspections and the "voluntary implementation" of the Additional Protocol and invoking a Majles bill requiring suspension in the event of referral. Al Baradei's report on Iran's compliance was mixed, showing some progress but pointing to continued unanswered questions. This meeting left open the next phase but showed considerable support for the resumption of negotiations with the EU-3, with the precondition of Iran halting enrichment-related activity. But Iran showed no signs of recognizing this in the December Vienna meeting with the EU-3, which was intended to discover whether there was any basis for a resumption of negotiations cut off since August. The only prospect was in the Russian proposal backed by the EU-3, but Iran's position toward this proposal appeared equivocal, neither embracing nor rejecting it, but playing for time.

On January 3, 2006, Iran announced the resumption of research on enrichment, meaning small-scale experimentation and development of a pilot project. Tehran followed this up with the repeated threat to end voluntary cooperation with the agency in the event of referral and to move to full, industrial-scale enrichment (for which there is no evidence that Iran can actually accomplish technologically).[69]

Iran sought but failed to get the Organization of Petroleum Exporting Countries (OPEC) to agree to production cuts that would increase its leverage on threats to cut off its oil supplies.[70] Playing on the IAEA's fears that Iran might leave it blind as to inspections, Iran sent a formal letter to the IAEA on February 2 noting that political pressures and threats of reporting Iran to the Security Council would lead Iran to "suspend all the voluntary measures and extra cooperation with the Agency that have so far" been in effect.

Iran was still surprised to see that the IAEA Board vote later that month on February 24 was convincingly in favor of reporting Iran to the Security Council (27:3 with 5 abstentions), leaving the precise date for decision after the Director-General's report on March 6. The threats of noncooperation and burying the Russian proposal appeared to have backfired. Iran's faith in support from Russia and China had proven to be, in Rowhani's critical assessment, a mirage.[71]

Iran pressed ahead regardless of the fact that it was digging itself a deeper hole by immediately declaring the resumption of enrichment activities and the limitation of cooperation with the agency. At the same time, its ambiguity toward the Russian proposal continued in various meetings. Iran's bottom line was encouragement of international cooperation in enrichment abroad, but not at the price of transferring enrichment out of the country. Iran's threat to move to enrichment from the current limited 164-centrifuge capability to an industrial scale appeared to be yet another bluff. Iranian officials admitted that they needed time "before 60,000 centrifuges could be operational."[72] (Al Baradei's report for the March meeting noted that Iran was testing centrifuges and had plans to begin installation of the first of 3,000 centrifuges later in 2006.) The Iranian position appeared to be in disarray as well, with the president threatening withdrawal from the NPT only to be contradicted by the Foreign Ministry.[73] A last-minute attempt to keep the diplomatic option alive came on the eve of the March Board of Governors meeting. Larijani sought, without success, to convince the Europeans to accept small-scale enrichment in Iran for an indefinite period, with a freeze on larger-scale activity for a period over which the sides would build confidence.[74]

Iran approached negotiations as a contest of wills rather than an opportunity to reach common ground through reciprocal compromise. By elevating differences into issues of principle (justice, rights, and equity), Iran made them nonnegotiable. A rhetorical emphasis on the legal nature of the dispute only served to blind Iran to the political nature of the problem and to convince it that it is, again, the victim.[75]

But true to form and Iran's particular brand of self-deception, the threat of referral did not check its rhetoric. According to one SNSC official, the referral of Iran to the Security Council is "not the end of the story but the beginning of a new chapter."[76] This tendency toward self-deception stems from Iran's rapt self-absorption and its tendency to convince only itself with its rhetoric. Self-deception accounts for its misjudgment about others' reactions, its overestimation of its own importance, and its miscalculation about the impact of its various threats. Iran has dissembled, stonewalled, and obfuscated in its dealings with the IAEA in respect to information and access. With the EU, it has cajoled and scorned, threatened and pleaded, and reopened or reinterpreted agreements. Far from reducing opacity, Tehran has played on ambiguity about its intentions and about the scope of its program. Inside and outside the negotiations Iran has shown a proclivity for brinksmanship and managed crises. Consistent with its behavior as a spoiler, Iran has threatened destabilizing linkages. In the event of referral, Iran has threatened in recent months to cut off oil supplies, to interrupt oil shipments, to aggravate regional instability, to end inspections and cooperation with the IAEA altogether (including application of the Additional Protocol), to resume enrichment, and, more ambiguously, to withdraw from the NPT itself.[77] None of this is calculated to reassure other states about Iran's behavior if it had a nuclear capability.

5

The International Response

Despite initial differences, the United States, the EU-3, and the IAEA all agree on the need to prevent the emergence of a nuclear Iran. The differences, which have been on the best way to accomplish this goal, have not posed an obstacle to policies, which have been largely mutually reinforcing. U.S. pressure has energized the IAEA, and the threat of Iran's referral to the UNSC has increased the IAEA's leverage on Tehran. The agency's prominent role as an international institution has made its medicine more palatable politically for Tehran (and Russia and China) and defused any notion that the issue is primarily a U.S.–Iran feud. The IAEA has lent its weight to buttress the EU-3 initiatives, while the latter has acted as a "good cop" to the United States' "bad cop," offering incentives and dialogue to temper U.S. threats and sanctions.

In assessing the success of the international community in the Iran arena, it is important to underline criteria for comparison and continuing uncertainties as to ultimate outcomes. The United States, critical of the IAEA's failure to quickly and unequivocally condemn Iran, showed ambivalence about the EU-3 diplomatic initiatives. The IAEA and the EU-3 in turn considered the U.S. response of quick referral to the UNSC as premature and probably counterproductive. The cases of Iraq and North Korea may be instructive about the chances of success in the approaches in Iran. Overreaction in 2003, following initial *under*estimation of Iraq's WMD program (1990-1991) has weakened the case for muscular responses divorced from international consensus. North Korea is a testimony to the ineffectuality of the UNSC in a clearcut case of noncompliance.[1] Why would Iran's more ambiguous case yield greater success in the UNSC? Would a referral, possibly followed by a condemnation and sanctions, be more successful in freezing or reversing Iran's program than the diplomatic route? And could it be contemplated realistically without first exhausting the diplomatic route?

The IAEA had its own reasons for pursuing a policy of "steady engagement and robust" inspections: to deal with the first serious case of non-proliferation after Iraq (and North Korea) and to demonstrate (and test) the value of the Additional Protocol.[2] The EU-3, too, had its own motives: to deal with an important issue of international security, to demonstrate the benefits of multilateralism and the 2003 EU security strategy in action, and to prevent a recurrence of the transatlantic rift that had appeared over Iraq.

U.S. concerns about Iran's proliferation fluctuated between an inclination to deal decisively with an emerging regional threat and the reality of military and diplomatic constraints on a unilateral solution. Reluctantly the United States supported the EU's diplomatic approach, unpersuaded that it would be successful. At the same time the U.S. position was weakened by a lack of clarity about its goals, which wavered between non-proliferation and regime change. The incoherence in U.S. policy did little to convince Russia (and by extension China) of the wisdom of following its lead.

U.S. Approach

After 9/11 the United States intensified its concentration on rogue states, which led to a change in U.S. non-proliferation policy. Priority shifted from a focus on the spread of *weapons technology* to the

identity of states seeking weapons of mass destruction (that is, proliferation now became a problem not of weapons but particular
states or regimes).[3] This shift entailed a downgrading of the importance of the NPT regime (the instrument for dealing with proliferation in general), viewing it as ill-suited for dealing with the serious
cases of proliferation. This in turn led to a diminution of the
reliance on international instruments and diplomacy and an
increased emphasis on a unilateral posture (2002-2005).

Later the emphasis shifted back to diplomacy, but the focus on
the nature of the regime in question has persisted. Secretary of State
Condoleezza Rice gave the philosophical underpinning of the
administration's policy shift, stating that "the fundamental character
of regimes matters more today than the international distribution of
power ... democracy is the only assurance of lasting peace and security between states, because it is the only guarantee of freedom and
justice within states."[4] One feature of democracies is openness, while
other systems are opaque. President Bush has emphasized this
aspect of democracy in relation to Iran, warning that "a non-
transparent society that is the world's premier sponsor of terror cannot be allowed to possess the world's most dangerous weapons."[5]

In the case of Iran, the issue is not simply confined to that state's
opaqueness and nuclear ambitions but extends to its challenge to
the U.S.-dominated regional order. Iran's quest for a nuclear capability magnifies that challenge, which seeks to substitute Iran's revolutionary Islamic model, with Iran in a dominant position, for
that of the U.S. model. U.S. officials underlined this broader context to Congress, with Rice calling Iran "destabilizing" and the
"biggest strategic challenge," observing that "no one wants to see a
Middle East that is dominated by an Iranian hegemony, particularly
one that has nuclear technology." In answer to questions on this
issue, the secretary noted that "Iran is pursuing policies in the Middle East that are, if not 180, 170 degrees counter to the kind of
Middle East that we would build."[6]

Iran uses terrorism, anti-Americanism, and instability (in Iraq
and elsewhere) to promote its preferred regional order. The nuclear

issue is thus one of several issues of contention between the two states, which necessitates that U.S. policy consider the nuclear issue in this overall context. Consistent with the belief that the regime itself as much as its policies are the problem, the United States has widened the stakes. President Bush's 2006 State of the Union address again focused on a policy of "ending tyranny in the world." In Iran's case, a specific distinction was made between nation and regime, with President Bush describing Iran as "a nation held hostage by a small clerical elite that is isolating and repressing its people." Care was taken to show respect for the Iranian people and their democratic aspirations—a distinction echoed by Vice President Richard Cheney and Under Secretary of State for Political Affairs Nicholas Burns, who both emphasized the gulf between the regime and the people.[7]

Acting on this premise, the United States has increased its investment in democracy promotion in Iran. A special office for Iranian affairs has been set up, with more broadcasting, scholarships, and support for Iranian nongovernmental organizations (NGOs) and increased funding ($75 million extra). Intended to encourage the development of an opposition within Iran, the basic policy aim is clearly regime change. Whether the funds or the means are adequate for the task, however, is another matter.[8]

In principle the United States has five broad, overlapping choices in its policy response to Iran:

1. **Prevention**, through sanctions, export controls, denial strategies, and interceptions that seek to impose a cost on the continuation of the program and to delay it.

2. **Containment** and freezing the program at a certain level, which implies living with some level of capability though limiting its growth but dealing with it through some combination of deterrence and defense.

3. **Rollback or reversal**, which implies a decision to prevent the emergence of a capability through its coercive elimination. This response could have military elements (strikes,

invasion, as in the case of Iraq in 1981 and 2003) and a political dimension, covered by the term *regime change*. Regime change may or may not lead to a reversal of policies, but policy reversals do not need regime change, as Libya in 2003 and South Africa in 1990 demonstrate.

4. **Regime change**, which entails the removal of the regime by force on the model of U.S intervention in Iraq. How effective an instrument of non-proliferation this can be over time is uncertain.

5. **Co-option**, accepting the inevitable and trying to influence safety, security of materials, doctrine, and commerce.

There are drawbacks associated with all five approaches. Prevention was the strategy attempted by the United States throughout the 1990s. But because of globalization, the seepage of knowledge and technology, the emergence of nuclear "grey markets," the cooperation among pariah states, and the reluctance of some nuclear weapons states (notably China until the late 1990s), the most that can be hoped for is delay. Eventually the question reemerges: What to do about it? Containment is similar to co-option but at a different stage of nuclear technology. Both imply acceptance of some level of capability, but containment attempts to deny a proliferator any strategic benefit from its capability and to ensure no further progress (with the possibility of a reversal in the future). Containment is a policy choice in parallel with prevention or when prevention fails. Co-option attempts to minimize the damage for future proliferation or instability (for example, living with a nuclear Iran is something that must be prepared for but not advertised).

Assessment of U.S. Response

U.S. policy has not been as coherent or as focused as the strategic stakes might dictate. U.S. policy toward Iran today consists of a combination of elements: continuing efforts at prevention, moves toward containment, and some consideration of rollback or reversal through regime change or policy change.

To this end, the United States has used multilateral institutions fitfully and erratically. Washington managed to have the UN pass a resolution requiring states to enact national legislation to implement the NPT and prevent materials from falling into the hands of terrorists. By getting states to take national responsibility for international commitments, UNSC Resolution 1540 was a landmark in dealing with the possible access to nuclear materials by terrorists.

Another success outside of the UN is the Proliferation Security Initiative (PSI) launched by the United States, with bilateral agreements now concluded with over sixty states. This initiative, facetiously labeled "an activity, not an institution," seeks to ensure enforcement of non-proliferation agreements by intercepting sensitive and illegal cargos at sea. As the number of members participating increases, the need to make it consistent with international law becomes more evident.[9] At present interceptions can only take place on the high seas (as opposed to territorial waters).

An administration that sees regimes, not weapons, as the problem tends to focus on individual states, not the multilateral mechanisms to constrain them—a point that is confirmed by the U.S. failure to use the NPT Review Conference of May 2005 effectively. The relatively low-level representation in the U.S. delegation reflected the degree of U.S. interest in the process. Instead of focusing on the lacunae in the NPT, the United States sought to brand Iran (and North Korea) as noncompliant.[10] In a speech in 2004 President Bush suggested that no *additional* states should be allowed to enrich uranium, in effective freezing the line at those who could already do so (Germany, Japan).[11] This position was aimed at Iran and North Korea but was opposed by Brazil, among others. For success, the review conference would have needed more give-and-take reflecting the NPT's "grand bargain." The United States refused to fashion its diplomacy accordingly or to define what Iran should or should not be allowed to do as encapsulating the broader challenges facing the treaty.[12] The United States failed to use the review conference to strengthen the norm against proliferation. Though it claimed to be speaking for a strong international consensus in what was generally considered a debacle of diplomacy, the United States also failed to get a tough statement from the P-5 countries that could be built on to pressure Tehran on future referral to the Security Council.[13] The United States allowed Iran to define the issue as one of technology denial rather than noncompliance.

In more restricted gatherings such as the annual G-8 meetings, U.S. diplomacy has been more effective in getting strong statements opposing Iran's deceptions and nuclear ambitions, but whether these are translated into support for strong measures in the UNSC is another matter.[14] Such declarations, however, are useful in reinforcing the international dimensions of the issues raised by Iran and continuing public exposure and pressure on Iran.[15]

In its *prevention* strategy the United States has long concentrated on unilateral (including secondary) sanctions. Since the mid-1980s sanctions were imposed for terrorism, which were increased in the late 1980s and supplemented by the 1996 Iran–Libya Sanctions Act (ILSA) that forbids foreign investment above $20 million per year in the energy sector and the Iran–Iraq Arms Non-Proliferation Act (P.L. 102-484) banning dual-use items. The United States has imposed secondary sanctions on companies and countries (including China and Russia) that trade or invest in Iran. These secondary sanctions deter most companies that trade with the United States and have certainly discouraged investment in Iran's oil sector by Japan and others. Several measures strengthening these existing measures are before the U.S. Congress, including the Ros-Lehtinen bill that would fund Iranian opposition groups.[16] In July 2005 the United States threatened to seize all U.S. assets of any foreign company that provides or attempts to provide financial, material, technological, or other support to Iran's AEO.[17]

This array of sanctions has imposed an economic cost on Iran and has clearly hurt the Iranian oil industry, which has been unable to develop or modernize with indigenous capital and technology alone. Black market prices in Iran are exorbitant, the goods lack manufacturers' guarantees, and there is a premium on deception and evasion of sanctions through front companies, false invoices, and the like. Sanctions may have delayed Iran's nuclear program as well, because they have cast a wide net with their ban on dual-use technology. However, in being forced to develop indigenous nuclear technology, Iran has nativized the technology and has come close to the mastery of the fuel cycle even in the face of two decades of U.S. and other sanctions. U.S. sanctions, therefore, might have been more effective had they been international (as was the case with Libya).[18] Largely punitive, they remain of symbolic importance today because Iran's nuclear program has nearly reached the point of no return. It is no wonder that President Bush observed in December 2004 that the United States was "all sanctioned out" in respect to Iran.[19]

The Libyan case suggests that effective sanctions may encourage regime evolution, because they cause proliferators to reconsider the costs and benefits of a particular course. For Libya, *UN sanctions* bit *over time* and affected the regime's cost calculus. In addition, the United States was willing to accept a *change in regime policy* rather than hold out for a change of regime itself.

In the case of Iran, however, the bilateral sanctions have been painful but not unbearable. Iranians have tended to see the nuclear issue as a pretext and U.S. hostility as general and open ended, with each demand likely to generate another, eventually culminating in regime change. Nor has the United States offered Iran the kind of inducements it did to Libya.

In addition, the United States has not been willing to take yes for an answer in the case of Iran, because distrust and ideology have forced the United States to an all-or-nothing approach. *Regime change* has dominated U.S. policy until very recently (2002-2006), although there are now some signs that this may be changing.

If U.S. sanctions alone are not likely to arrest Iran's nuclear program, what other means of *prevention, containment,* or better still *reversal* are there? Short of regime change there is the possibility that the regime could be prevailed upon to reconsider its policies as a result of domestic and international pressure. Convincing demonstration that there will be no benefits coming from a nuclear capability (which will be offset militarily) and that the costs (sanctions, regional exclusion, condemnation) will remain high is one way. Imposing economic costs could stimulate a domestic debate in Iran about the wisdom of continuing on a collision course with the West. The United States and Europe have done a poor job of stimulating such a debate and making clear that the issue is not denial of technology in general but objection to the regime as such and opposition to specific policies.[20]

Offering inducements as well as ending sanctions would help. Strengthening the incentives for states not to rely on nuclear weapons seems self-evident.[21] Far from rewarding proliferation, inducements are a means of making renunciation of technology more palatable. The United States has resisted this approach, however, as evidenced by John Bolton's comment: "I don't do carrots."[22]

Engagement, never the preferred choice, has also failed. Iran's rebuff of the Clinton administration's overtures was followed by 9/11. In this new context, especially after Afghanistan, Iran was confronted by U.S. power next door. Cooperation in that war might have led to more formal discussions, but it was aborted by the discovery of a shipment of Iranian arms destined for Palestinians fighting Israel. After the *Karine A* affair in December 2001, the United States promoted Iran into the axis of evil. Tehran's fear that the United States might target Iran next led it to a more accommodating posture, including discussion of a possible grand bargain. But direct discussions in Geneva in May 2003 were again torpedoed, this time because of revelations that Iran was hosting Al Qaeda elements.[23] Ironically, this was a lost opportunity when everything would have been on the table because Iranian leaders sensed a real threat to the regime and were willing to negotiate when the United States enjoyed maximum leverage.[24] By the autumn of 2003, however, Tehran sensed that the U.S. military threat had subsided because the United States was bogged down in Iraq, thus lessening the incentive for Iran to make far-reaching concessions.

From 2003 to 2005, U.S. policy toward Iran was incoherent, characterized by attitude and posturing, giving voice to its ideology, and intended to appease its conservative supporters. From mid-2003 the United States resorted to reliance on regime change, encouraging student demonstrations and giving declaratory support to opponents of the regime and reformers. This theme—that the United States could not deal with an unrepresentative and repressive government—continues. Focus on the regime's tyranny, its loathsome human rights record, and its controlled elections is a constant refrain.[25] More concrete assistance through radio broadcasts and support of activists, NGOs, and unions under consideration in 2005 is now policy.[26] The election of hard-liner Mahmoud Ahmadinejad as president in June 2005 served to confirm Washington's skepticism about any form of engagement strategy.[27]

U.S. policy toward Iran is characterized by a special antipathy going beyond distrust or the legacy of past events such as the hostage crisis and Beirut bombings. For a certain category of Americans, Iran is the very embodiment of evil, more so than North Korea or even Iraq, which may be explained by Iran's opposition to Israel, the regime's shifty behavior, or the lack of a domestic constituency or congressional support in the United States.[28] Ultimately, the United States has had less difficulty in supporting diplomacy with Pyongyang than with Tehran, and the gap between rhetoric and worked out policy is noticeable with regard to Iran.[29]

U.S. policy weakness, in part, can be attributed to rivalries within the U.S. administration, which saw expression in simultaneous calls for regime change and negotiations. Senator Richard Lugar (R-IN) alluded to these divisions evident in policy toward North Korea and Iran in criticizing the "ambiguity that was neither constructive nor intended."[30] Behind his concerns were serious issues: Could Iran be brought around to renounce nuclear capabilities through a combination of diplomacy and threats? How durable or reliable would such an agreement be? Would not the act of direct negotiations (and possible agreement) confer legitimacy on the "repressive theocracy," which would be a repudiation of the kind of

Middle East that the United States was now seeking? Would it be a betrayal of Iran's democratic opposition?[31] Some politicians such as Senator John McCain (R-AZ) preferred "rogue state rollback," while neoconservatives still argued that "only democracy in Iran will finally solve the nuclear and terrorist problems."[32]

By the end of 2004, U.S. policy had hit a brick wall. Unable to count on regime change in time to affect the nuclear program, with little prospect that unilateral sanctions could be tightened much further, and unwilling to engage Iran directly, the United States had to reconsider its policy.[33] Instead of being "an excited bystander," the United States needed to get involved more directly.[34] By default, this meant supporting the EU-3 initiative, which Washington embraced skeptically and conditionally in March 2005.

The U.S. approach during the 2003–2005 period consisted of attempts to get the IAEA to refer Iran to the UNSC for its various failings and deceptions. But there is little indication that the United States had prepared the diplomatic groundwork for a successful application of sanctions if the matter were taken to that body. Even more problematic was the U.S. insistence on its certain knowledge that Iran had a nuclear *weapons* program, something the IAEA was unable to confirm. Given doubts about U.S. intelligence, even friendly states gave priority to seeing whether a diplomatic solution was possible before referring the issue to the UNSC.[35]

Another consideration for the United States was the unhappy experience with the 1994 Korean Agreed Framework. The United States now insisted that any agreement be "complete, verifiable, and irreversible," a formula it adapted to the case of Iran. Therefore, the United States equated permanent cessation and objective guarantees and refused to countenance any, even token, amounts of enrichment. Moreover, the U.S. decision to embrace diplomacy was hedged. While there was a need for a common front, especially after Iraq, the United States still saw the Europeans as "wobbly," and the EU, in turn, saw Washington as too unilateralist. So the U.S. aim in agreeing to support the initiative was to stiffen the EU-3 resolve and ensure that the terms of any agreement were clear and rigorous. The United States was particularly concerned to ensure that having committed to diplomacy, the EU-3 also committed to follow through with sanctions and referral to the UNSC in the event of diplomatic failure.[36]

The United States and the EU-3 easily came to an agreement on what to ask of Iran: complete and permanent cessation of its fuel cycle activities as the only basis for confidence that technology would not be diverted to weapons uses.[37] However, how this would be implemented and inspected and, if Iran refused, what would constitute the trigger for referral to the Security Council remained to be defined. More important from the EU-3 perspective was the need for the United States to be involved in the *incentive* as well as the punishment side of the package.

Although the United States showed a willingness to make symbolic gestures by lifting objections to World Trade Organization (WTO) membership and to the supply of civilian aircraft parts, Washington was unwilling to consider the kind of comprehensive package that the Europeans considered necessary if Iran were to be convinced to forgo nuclear technology.[38] Such an agreement would have to include security assurances, inclusion of Iran in a regional security structure, as well as economic and technology assistance. Europeans emphasized the need to acknowledge Iran's "legitimate security concerns," whereas the United States was keen to be convinced that the Europeans and others were prepared to take the proliferation threat seriously enough to take "risks and make any sacrifices to avert it."[39]

The United States and Europe both see diplomacy as a necessary first step if the matter is to be settled by coercion, but there is a difference of nuance between the two: The Europeans are less focused on the nature of Iran's regime and would prefer the diplomacy to "succeed," and the United States is not.[40] Thus, while the allies agree on what to demand of Iran, there is still much room for division and disunity in their positions. Although these divisions were largely narrowed after Iran hardened its approach in mid-2005, the issue of sanctions (and military strikes) and the refusal of the United States to contribute to an incentives package could see divisions resurface and widen again.

The United States no longer insists that Iran has no need for *any* nuclear energy (that is, that the reactor in Bushire, due to come on-stream in 2006-2007, should be dismantled). The official position announced by President Bush in 2003 is that the United States "will not tolerate the construction of a nuclear weapon." More recently, the reference has been broadened to the intolerability of a "weapons capability," suggesting opposition to any activity that involves sensitive technologies that could be diverted to weapons uses.[41] The latest formulation is that "a process which permits Iran to develop nuclear weapons is unacceptable."[42]

After Iran's rejection of the EU-3 package in mid-2005, the United States did in fact become more involved. President Bush emphasized U.S. support for the EU-3's "lead" in a diplomatic solution. The U.S. switch to support for diplomacy and support for the March 2005 EU-3 initiative implied a recognition of the trade-off between obtaining a broad international consensus and the need for haste. A graduated, deliberate approach that took along all the major powers was preferable to a rush to judgment that left many unconvinced.[43] The U.S. shift was aided by two factors in mid-2005. First, the administration still had not clarified its Iran policy in a convincing way, split as it was between those who emphatically rejected dealing with the "*mullahs*' regime" and those who saw the risks of proliferation as requiring a workable policy. For those advocating regime change, it was important to demonstrate that there remained time for this (and a sanctions) policy to be viable, which may have accounted for the "new intelligence estimate" in August 2005 that assessed Iran to be technologically further away from a nuclear weapon than many had assumed.[44] Second, the arrival of Ahmadinejad and his behavior made the argument that Iran was an "irresponsible" state easier, facilitating a broader coalition.

Making up for lost time, the United States invested more effort in diplomacy from September 2005 on by intensively lobbying key states including India, Russia, and China. None of these states initially supported Iran's referral to the UN, absent a major new transgression, preferring a settlement within the IAEA (Iran's resumption of enrichment under the label of "research" in January 2006 changed this).[45] Washington sought to counter the idea that the nuclear issue is a continuation of a feud with Tehran, labeling Iran's nuclear ambitions a "global menace" and a "universal" interest to prevent it.[46]

U.S. diplomacy has also benefited from the sense abroad that the military option, however unattractive, was by no means unthinkable even if the image of a trigger-happy United States gave allies pause. The official formulation that all options are on the table has been consciously repeated.[47] The military option has been made more credible by domestic polls in the United States that indicate considerable public support for both sanctions and military strikes against Iran.[48] The veiled threat of recourse to a military option if diplomacy is not seriously attempted has spurred Russia and China to action. Though averse to the change in forum from the IAEA to the Security Council (and to sanctions), these two states have reluctantly agreed to referral in order to brake any momentum and prevent giving the United States the pretext for unilateral action.

While seeking to maintain pressure on Tehran, first with IAEA resolutions threatening action in the Security Council and now with the threat of sanctions in that body, the United States still shows reluctance about getting *directly* involved. This reluctance may be due to the press of other events, or it may be the inability to hammer out a clear policy acceptable to all elements within the administration.[49] Therefore, there is a decided policy preference for the more general approaches of regime change and Security Council referral and sanctions.

Washington still lacks a convincing answer to the question of what happens after referral. Certainly, a Security Council condemnation of Iran as an internationally certified pariah would in itself be a serious sanction that would hurt the regime domestically. Multilateral sanctions, even if not mandatory or universally applied, would impose more costs on Tehran, which may buy time for reconsideration since the nuclear program may not be as far advanced as Iranians claim.

To summarize, then, the Bush administration has had no agreed, clear, or consistent Iran policy. The U.S. stance has evolved unacknowledged from a policy of regime change along the Iraqi model to policy change along the Libyan model. Its position on nuclear technology has a similar evolution from no nuclear technology to some as long as it is not sensitive. Similarly, from initially disparaging diplomacy, Washington now relies on it for international support. The Bush administration has insisted that a nuclear-capable Iran is unacceptable and has kept the military option in play, resisting any direct diplomatic discussions on this issue. Constrained by its ideologues from diplomacy, the administration has been unable to test Iranian intentions. The result is a stance that reflects a set of attitudes rather than a considered policy that holds diplomacy hostage to ideology, and that reduces U.S. options accordingly.

It is clear that after a series of missteps the United States is determined to prevent Iran's acquisition of nuclear weapons. It has now settled on a method that takes its allies and P-5 with it and stands a better chance of increasing the pressure on Iran. Multilateral diplomacy may result either in Iran's acquiescence in the terms offered or eventually in the imposition of sanctions by a coalition of the willing or through the Security Council.

IAEA Approach

The IAEA labors under several inherent constraints in its mission. First, the agency has a twin mandate—to verify the *peaceful* uses of nuclear technology and to *promote* the use of that technology with an extensive technical assistance program, which creates budgetary and other tensions.[50] Second, the IAEA is not the secretariat of the NPT, nor is it empowered to enforce NPT compliance. To do so, it would need the backing of the UNSC, which may or may not be forthcoming. And, third, if special inspections are refused, the agency's only recourse is to go to the UNSC.[51]

In addition, there are also problems with IAEA's corporate culture, ranging from a penchant for compromise and the assumption of cooperation to a general reluctance to adopt an aggressive approach to verification. It assumes all is well until proven otherwise. Furthermore, in all recent cases of proliferation, the agency has only acted after strong U.S. political pressure.[52]

There are still other more specific problems with verification. One is the problem of the technology: States can legally acquire all the technology and techniques necessary for the production of fissile materials without actually producing them, thereby shortening the gap between being a member of the NPT and being a nuclear weapons state, should it withdraw.[53] Verification itself has inherent limits because it can never clear a state or prove a negative; at most it can only report that nothing has been found to indicate a weapons program. Undeclared facilities cannot be inspected or located without specific intelligence, which the agency itself lacks. By their nature, violations are rarely clear-cut, which necessarily complicates responses. The quest for a smoking gun is thus a chimera, and the system can be manipulated through deception, delay, and denial.[54]

All of these issues dictate caution. A strong criticism of the IAEA is that having ascertained that Iran failed to declare *inter alia* the construction of its enrichment facilities, the agency found Iran in material breach of its *safeguards* agreement but made a distinction between a technical infraction (failure to report) and a substantive one, that is, noncompliance with *NPT obligations*.[55]

Despite these limitations, however, the agency should be judged by its achievements, though modest, and against the feasible alternatives. The IAEA policy has been shaped by Director-General Mohammad Al Baradei, who defines noncompliance narrowly as the diversion of materials to nuclear weapons uses.[56] He sees Iran as one of a class of problems that needs to be tackled by political as well as technical means. His approach has been informed by recent experience: "The most important lesson is the confirmation that verification and diplomacy, used in conjunction, can be effective." At the same time, the challenge posed by Iran is not unique, given the gaps in the treaty that allow for acquisition of sensitive technologies that bring states close to a weapons capability. The way to minimize security risk, Al Baradei argues, is not through technology denial, which cannot work over time, or by creating new distinctions among states inside the NPT. Rather, it must be handled first by a moratorium on all enrichment activities and then by the internationalization of the fuel cycle under multilateral control.[57] This approach to a category of problems posed by holes in the treaty appears to be gaining ground as the alternatives (coercion and sanctions) prove elusive and uncertain in their results.

The director-general sees the issue of proliferation broadly, not in narrow terms of technology, arguing that a nuclear program is the tip of an iceberg masking other security, political, and economic issues.[58] At the same time Al Baradei sought to assure Iran of his *bona fides* in posing the issue in terms of a "need to strike a balance between the right of Iran to use nuclear technology and the concern of the international community that any nuclear program is a peaceful one" and going to some lengths to assure Iran that he would not act as "an instrument of harassment."[59] By positioning the agency as an independent and objective interlocutor, Al Baradei has given the agency credibility, especially with the nonaligned states on which Iran has counted and has made it harder for Iran to escape from its assessments and requests.

IAEA's response dates from August 2002 when an Iranian opposition group, the MOK, revealed the existence of nuclear facilities that Tehran had failed to declare to the agency as it was bound to under its safeguards agreement. This revelation raised the issue of what other undeclared, sensitive facilities might exist and how to respond to what was clearly (at the least) a breach of the safeguards agreement, if not of the NPT itself. The IAEA responded by using the revelations, resultant publicity, and political pressure to widen the scope of its operations to dig deeper into the program.[60] This approach was complemented and reinforced by the subsequent agreement reached between Iran and the EU-3 in October 2003 (Tehran agreement). This in turn built on the pressure exerted first by the U.S. government's attempt to have the matter referred to the UNSC, and by the firm demand of the agency's Board of Governors in September 2003 that Iran demonstrate cooperation or face the consequences. The same pattern emerged once Iran sought to escape from its Tehran agreement by reinterpreting it in the spring and summer of 2004. First, the EU-3 and then the IAEA threatened to side with the U.S. position and take the issue to the UN. The result of this new pressure was a tighter agreement in Paris in November 2004 between Iran and the EU-3, with the IAEA making clear its support for the EU-3 demands. Again in the spring of 2005 when Iran threatened to restart some of its enrichment activities, the EU-3 and the IAEA made clear their common approach and the consequences of a breakdown, forcing Iran to back down from the threat. This is where matters stood before Iran unilaterally restarted conversion activities in August 2005.

Diplomacy moved into higher gear in January 2006, reflecting the sense of urgency and new determination of the EU-3 and the United States to report Iran to the Security Council, after Iran's resumption of "research related to enrichment." The Board of Governors' meeting in February produced a tough resolution recalling that Iran was a "special verification case" with "its many failures and breaches of obligations" and noting that "full transparency is ... overdue." The resolution asked Iran to suspend "all enrichment and reprocessing activities including research and development" and be subject to IAEA verification, and it "deeply regretted," "despite repeated calls," Iran's resumption of conversion and enrichment activities. The resolution also asked that Iran "reconsider the construction of a research reactor moderated by heavy water." It noted that "there is a lack of confidence in Iran's intentions in seeking to develop a fissile material production capability against the background of Iran's record on safeguards." Finally, the resolution asked for the director-general to report on the implementation of this resolution at the next board session. This report, together with the accompanying Board of Governors' resolution in March, would then be conveyed to the Security Council.[61]

For the first time, the threat of reporting the case to the Security Council and taking the issue from the technical-legal agency to the political-security Security Council forum had been made. The IAEA, reflecting this, found itself moving away from the center. Al Baradei's February 2006 report examined developments since November 2005 and then made a critical overall assessment.[62] Among his findings, Al Baradei suggested pragmatically that Iran should be allowed *some* enrichment capability, which underestimates the distrust fostered by Iran's tactics. Not surprisingly, this suggestion has been received coldly by the United States, France, and Great Britain, who consider the issue to be both political and technical.[63] First, an Iranian freeze on large-scale (industrial) enrichment would not be a meaningful concession because Iran currently lacks such a capability. Second, any enrichment capability could serve as a cover for a clandestine program, making monitoring more difficult. Also "some enrichment" could serve as a means for perfecting the technology for a broader program in the future. Finally, allowing a compromise now would send the wrong message: rewarding Iran's deceit and cheating, with no guarantee that it would not be repeated in the future.

Assessment of IAEA Response

The IAEA's role has been notable in its ability to ratchet up the pressure on Iran, while resisting U.S. calls for moving the issue (prematurely) to the Security Council. The director-general put the agency's weight behind the EU-3 in resisting attempts by Iran to define the activities covered by the voluntary suspension narrowly enough to exclude preenrichment or the assembly and production of centrifuges. This meant that Iran was in dispute not with three states but the wider international community. The IAEA used Iran's

breach of its safeguards obligations to improve operating procedures. Instead of putting the burden of proof on the agency (to find
any illegal activities), the situation was reversed: Now Iran was told
to make up for its past transgressions and demonstrate its good will
by confidence-building measures that went beyond any legal
requirement. The IAEA was able to do this by adopting a neutral
stance while cajoling and dispensing a mixture of friendly advice
and implied threat. For example, Al Baradei argued that "the ball
is in Iran's court" and that the deficit in confidence could only be
restored by transparency. He asked that Iran restore full suspension
of "all enrichment-related activities" with no time limit.[64] His
approach was based on the proposition that Iran had "tried to cheat
the system" and that it now had to take the consequences. Because
Iran had had a "clandestine program for almost two decades," it was
a "special case." The agency therefore asked for widespread inspections to make up for the confidence deficit.[65] Requests for special
inspections that Al Baradei termed "transparency visits" were
expanded to examine military sites not covered by the Additional
Protocol (such as Parchin and Lavizan) that might have been used
for the weaponization of nuclear materials. The director-general
was "pushing the envelope under transparency," pressing the Iranians on the need to rebuild confidence.[66]

The success of the agency to date can be measured in part by reference to Iran's goals and achievements. Iran values the agency for
its technical assistance and independence. Its officials differentiate
the IAEA's stance from that of the United States as follows: "The
American statement is not very important for us. What is important
to us is the fact that our activities are based on laws and treaties that
are approved by the IAEA, and that we are fully cooperating with
the IAEA and will continue to do so."[67] That said, there is no illu-
sion about the IAEA's role, as Hasan Rowhani observed:

> The agency and Al Barade'i are international legal entities,
> and given that within these institutions an eye is always fixed
> on the great powers, they are forced to adopt multifaceted

positions ... Al Barade'i makes one positive remark followed by a negative one; two negative ones followed by a positive. He does so because he does not want our cooperation with the agency to be severed, while at the same time he wants to please the world powers.[68]

The IAEA remains an important buffer against U.S. pressure and a sign that Iran takes its international commitments seriously. Consequently, Tehran cannot accuse the agency of bias or afford to antagonize it. Demonstrating cooperation with it becomes an earnest of its intentions, and ignoring its recommendations can alienate the nonaligned states on which Iran relies for diplomatic support. This cooperation has been costly in terms of Iran's stated aims. Iran has not been able to achieve its aim of having its relationship with the IAEA normalized and its nuclear file closed.[69] Prior to 2003, Iran had resisted accepting the Additional Protocol, linking signature with the ending of the embargo of technical materials on its nuclear program. At the insistence of the IAEA, its Board of Governors, and the nonaligned states, Iran has signed the AP and is under pressure to ratify it. Furthermore, it has been under pressure to give access to military sites not covered by the AP, as a confidence-building measure to rebuild trust and has done so as a "voluntary measure," and has been commended for it.[70] Iran has also found itself opposed by the agency in its efforts to stretch the meanings of what is and is not excluded from its suspension of enrichment activities. The only victory that Iran could claim (domestically) was that it avoided being referred or reported to the UNSC between 2002 and 2005.[71]

The IAEA has dealt with the Iran case with considerable success. It has conducted by one estimate over 1,600 man/days of inspections, averaging three inspections per day.[72] Iran's dossier remains very much open, with the international spotlight focused on its nuclear program and the agency's reports on the quality of its cooperation. Through the agency's inspections much more is known about Iran, and the international community has "made good strides in understanding the nature and scope of its program."[73] Iran's signature and application of the AP provisions complicates and makes more risky (though not impossible) any clandestine activity it might engage in, especially running an elaborate parallel nuclear program. The pressure on Iran to suspend its enrichment program (broadly defined) amounted to a freeze on Iran's development of sensitive technologies for the past two years. The agency's role as an international institution has made it easier for Iran to retreat from established positions and also for others like the nonaligned states or Russia to appeal to Iran to meet the agency's demands.[74]

The IAEA's support has also strengthened the EU-3 diplomatic initiative. They in turn have used the agency to validate their concerns and implement their queries. Al Baradei's big picture approach to the question of proliferation (not strictly a part of his professional mandate) parallels the EU-3 initiative, taking it out of the narrow technical realm toward the broader motivations underlying the program.[75] The major criticism of the agency that can be made is to question whether a "diplomacy at any price" approach is always the right answer. However, the case of Iraq makes it harder to fault an approach that seeks to build the case slowly through inspections without closing down a source of information that would leave the agency and governments in the dark.

EU-3 Approach

The 9/11 terrorist attack on the United States and the Iraq war have galvanized the EU to define its position on WMD proliferation. The EU-3, determined to avoid a repetition of the transatlantic rift opened up by Iraq, decided to define Europe's policy proactively and robustly. European interests in this issue were clear enough on several fronts. Proximity makes Europe and the Middle East virtually part of the same neighborhood. It is within missile range of any proliferators. It has large Muslim populations who could be upset by further crises or radicalization of the region. It depends on the region for energy security. And, finally, it has a more general interest to tackle an important security issue to demonstrate the EU's international role and effectiveness.

To meet new threats preventively and if necessary through forward defense, the EU defined its strategy on security and WMD as envisioning a transatlantic partnership (which came to embrace the PSI and cooperation in the G-8) with the use of force, if necessary.[76] A non-proliferation clause was added to agreements with countries seeking relations with the EU. A major difference with the U.S. approach is the EU focus on the regional sources of motivations for nuclear weapons acquisition and thus on addressing the legitimate security concerns of proliferators.[77]

The EU-3 negotiations with Iran, first in the Tehran agreement (September 2003) and then with the more detailed Paris agreement (November 2004), were more than negotiations between Europe and Iran.[78] In reality they constituted three-way negotiations, between the EU-3 and Iran, between the EU-3 and the United States, and, albeit indirectly, between Iran and the United States. This triangular set of interactions raised a number of problems and questions in the negotiations. For the EU-3, it was necessary to coordinate positions with the United States, despite different approaches and the skeptical and lukewarm attitude of the United States toward the diplomacy. The EU-3 was negotiating with its ally, the United States, as much as with Iran. For Iran, there was and still is a need for an interlocutor, and the EU-3 was the best it could "afford."[79] Iran sought to play on possible differences between Europe and the United States but failed to use the EU-3 to build bridges with the United States.

The EU-3 and the United States started from similar points: the imperative to block Iran's nuclear aspirations, by the use of force, if necessary. They shared a broader perspective as well. Both agreed that the underpinnings of security are most assured where there has been a spread of freedom and democracy. Differences arose, however, after this point. For example, the United States believes the

Iranian *regime* to be the primary problem, whereas the EU-3 sees Tehran's *nuclear program* as the key issue. These different assumptions lead to different approaches. Whereas key elements in the United States see engagement and diplomacy as endorsement of the regime and a sellout of its opponents, the EU-3 sees it as the best means to effect regime change.[80] The United States prefers sanctions and isolation of a regime that equates regime maintenance with the national interest.[81] On the one hand, if one accepts that the regime is illegitimate, how can one argue for its legitimate security interests, as European leaders have done?[82] On the other hand, however, the United States taking a morally inspired passive position of disengagement amounted to a "nonpolicy" that threatened to exacerbate differences between the two. Therefore, if the EU-3 were to devise a package of incentives for Iran to forgo its nuclear ambitions, it had to not only coordinate with Washington but also gain its active support.[83]

Before the United States decided to support the EU-3 indirectly in 2005, it sought to get a commitment from its allies that, in the event of failure, they would refer Iran to the Security Council.[84] Even with the EU-3 accepting agreement on referral to the UNSC and the indirect involvement of the United States, there remained the question of the point of the negotiations. Both agreed on what Iran should *not* be permitted to retain, yet differences remained on the best means to that end. For the EU-3, limiting the nuclear program was the aim and diplomacy the preferred means. For the United States, diplomacy appeared to be the means to demonstrate that no agreement was possible, which implied the need for more forceful measures to see the Iranian regime exit the scene.

In its negotiations, the EU-3 has given Iran a structured choice: continuation of the development of the fuel cycle and referral to the Security Council—with all that sanctions, condemnation, and isolation would entail—or acceptance of a package of inducements to forgo the fuel cycle.[85] After the Paris agreement the EU-3 tightened the terms of its negotiations. While Iranian suspension of enrichment is voluntary (rather than legally binding) pending agreement or collapse of the negotiations, this suspension (including preenrichment, assembly, or production of centrifuges) would continue. The aim of the agreement was to ensure Iran's peaceful uses of nuclear technology. For this, the EU-3 insisted on objective guarantees regarding Iran's program, which it defines in practice as *cessation* of fissile material production. Iran in turn defines its suspension as voluntary, limited in time, and a confidence-building gesture. Iran sees objective guarantees as equivalent to the provisions of the Additional Protocol (that is, guarantees through enhanced inspections). Iran insists that its redline is enrichment, which it is not prepared to forgo.[86] The EU-3 and the United States, however, agree that Iran's acquisition of enrichment was *their* redline.

The EU-3 prepared a package to propose to Iran, stipulating that in exchange for Iran giving up its fuel cycle ambitions, the EU-3 would guarantee its fuel supply from more than one source (EU and Russia), offer Iran proliferation-resistant nuclear technology (light water reactors), bolster investment and trade ties, and increase Iran's involvement in regional security discussions and possibly institutions. In addition the question of security guarantees was also broached.[87]

The United States saw its role as stiffening the spine of the EU-3. For example in response to Iranian attempts to get acceptance of its retention of a pilot project of centrifuges that it argued was symbolic (numbers vary between 500 and 3,000 centrifuges), the United States made clear that cessation meant *none, not even a few*.[88] The EU-3 agreed with the U.S. position because it would be technically difficult to monitor and assure peaceful uses. The EU-3 approach was diplomatic—not to reject but to study, evaluate, and suggest alternatives.[89] Keeping the talks going assumed importance not because a breakthrough was in sight but because of the risks of a crisis that would accompany a breakdown in the talks. This did not imply weak diplomacy however. It was clear to the EU-3 that there was little room for maneuver: "The problem is political but the solution is technical, and the only technical solution we have found is cessation."[90] While there was no difference between the

EU-3 and the United States on the need for cessation as such, there was more give in the EU position. The Iranians rejected the suggestion of suspending activities for a period of years, and the United States rejected the suggestion of allowing Iran to retain *some* enrichment capabilities. Both rejections effectively narrowed the scope for compromise. At the same time the EU-3 did not hesitate to threaten Iran with immediate referral to the UNSC when Tehran made moves toward resuming conversion activities in June 2005.[91]

Relations between the EU-3 and Iran steadily deteriorated after Tehran's brusque rejection of the EU-3 offer of a package deal in July 2005. The November meeting of the IAEA delayed a decision on whether to send the issue to the Security Council to give the Russian proposal a chance.[92] Nonetheless, that meeting showed that the votes existed in the Board of Governors for such a transfer. The following month the EU "unreservedly condemned" the comments made by Iran's president on the Holocaust and Israel's right to exist, hinting at diplomatic sanctions.[93] In response to Iran's resumption of enrichment research in January, which the United States dubbed a serious escalation, the EU-3 convened a special meeting in Berlin.[94] In a statement after the meeting, the member states noted that the dispute was not "between Iran and Europe, but between Iran and the whole international community." While still committed to a diplomatic solution, "We believe the time has now come for the Security Council to become involved to reinforce the authority of IAEA resolutions."[95] This meeting was followed at the end of the month by another meeting in London of the EU-3, the United States, China, and Russia. At this milestone gathering, the states agreed to report Iran to the Security Council. Within a week, an extraordinary meeting of the IAEA's Board of Governors was convened, and on February 4, 2006, in a vote of 27 to 3 (with five abstentions), the board agreed to report the Iranian dossier to the Security Council. At the urging of Al Baradei and Russia, it was agreed to give diplomacy another month, after which the director-general would present an agency report prior to definitive action.

The result, as has been seen, is a report that provides an overview of the issue. The Russian proposal has floundered as it is not consistent with Iran's quest for an indigenous enrichment capability. The March 2006 agency meeting thus agreed to report Iran to the Security Council.

Assessment of EU-3 Response

The EU-3 has taken an unhurried approach to negotiations, refusing to be harassed by Iran's self-imposed deadlines, ultimatums, and brinkmanship, while seeking a solution that could meet Tehran's security interests and demonstrate the success of Europe's diplomatic strategy. [96] Playing for time, trying to build confidence, but taking a firm line on essential points are tactics in the service of a diplomacy that is practical and nonideological—classic *realpolitik*. As the Iranians have observed, the Europeans have a stake in a successful outcome and in demonstrating that they can fly solo. But Iranian actions and attitude after mid-2005 hardened the European position, bringing it closer to the U.S. view that a nuclear Iran is intolerable and must be prevented. Iran's belligerent statements about Israel in October, in particular, made it easier for the Europeans and Americans to agree on the need to take a harder line with Tehran. But while the United States has shown some willingness to associate itself with this diplomacy, it continues to sharpen the sanctions at its disposal by extending its secondary sanctions. It remains unclear whether the EU-3 even with the direct and active input of the United States, can offer Iran enough carrots to give up its insistence on the full fuel cycle, or whether Russia or China can do more than delay a crisis. As things currently stand with the breakdown of negotiations due to Iran's resumption of conversion activities and enrichment research, the threat of mandatory sanctions under Chapter 7 in the UNSC appear to be the greatest leverage for the resumption of diplomacy. For although sanctions may be difficult to realize or implement, even partial sanctions and a drawn-out crisis are bound to impose costs on Iran.

What then has the EU-3 accomplished? It has demonstrated that there is little dividing the United States and Europe on this issue. The EU-3 threw Iran a lifeline that Tehran rejected. It has given Iran a choice between a crisis and a negotiated settlement. It has bought time. Its negotiations have at least retarded Iran's nuclear program. It has brought the United States on board, at least indirectly, giving the negotiations more chance of success, since diplomacy has not necessarily run its course.[97] Diplomacy—and the need to reinstate suspension prior to negotiations—may resume, precisely because the alternatives are unpalatable to all parties, but it may need a broader bargain to stand a chance of success.

Russian Approach

Since the breakup of the Soviet Union, Russia has had good relations with Iran. In addition to being Tehran's major arms supplier since 1989, Russia has cooperated with Iran in Tajikistan, Afghanistan (anti-Taliban), and Armenia (against Azerbaijan). Moscow considers Iran an important stabilizing element in the region, not least because Tehran has not encouraged radical forms of Islam or fomented troubles in Russia's south (for example, in Chechnya). Iran's arms purchases in hard currency have been welcome in post-Soviet Russia, where plants lie idle. The agreement in 1989 to build a nuclear reactor at Bushire had a similar commercial rationale. This quasistrategic relationship has been cemented by the two states' opposition to NATO enlargement eastward and since 9/11 by similar concern about U.S. unilateralism and acquisition of bases in the region.

In the Yeltsin era, despite U.S. pressure, the arms and nuclear technology relationship grew, whether through official or semi-official channels. This was in part a reflection of the continued zero-sum thinking vis-à-vis the United States typified by the Soviet-era Middle East expert Yevgeni Primakov.[98] In 1995 through the Gore–Chernomyrdin Commission, the United States and Russia agreed to limit further arms sales to Iran, but the reactor deal on Bushire (initially valued at $800 million) continued and Iranian technicians were trained in Russia.[99]

Russia's relationship with Iran, however, changed somewhat with the arrival of President Putin. Iran's strategic importance was initially given new importance. In 2000 Russia repudiated the Gore–Chernomyrdin agreement and revived the arms relationship with Iran. Russia appreciated Iran's potential as a regional ally and its stubborn, defiant independence regarding the United States. As Putin put it, "Economically, Russia is interested in cooperation ... and politically Iran should be a self-sufficient state that is ready to protect its national interests."[100]

This view shifted with the revelations of Iran's nuclear activities in mid-2002, and since then Russian policy has attempted to balance the need for good relations with its "old and stable partner" and the imperative of preventing Tehran's acquisition of nuclear weapons.[101] Balancing strategic and non-proliferation interests, as well as commercial and political interests, Russia has found itself using the IAEA as the reference point for policies that Tehran might find unpalatable and in the process moving closer and closer to the position of the EU-3.[102] As non-proliferation concerns have grown during the 2003–2005 period, Russian policy has become clearer, and there is less apparent concern about losing Iran as a commercial or strategic partner. In reality Iran has few strategic alternatives for arms, technology, or diplomatic support. Nevertheless, Russia continues to see Iran as an important state that it would prefer to accommodate if possible; as Putin put it, "to infringe upon a country like Iran is counterproductive and could lead to quite complicated and serious consequences."[103]

From 2003 forward, Russia aligned its position with that of the EU-3, supporting its initiatives, closely consulting with the EU-3 in their negotiations with Iran, and conducting its own contacts with Tehran in parallel.[104] At the same time Russia made clear its opposition to Iran's acquisition of nuclear weapons. As Putin put it forcefully, "With the possession of nuclear weapons, none of the problems confronting Iran, including the security issues in the region can be solved ... We are categorically opposed to the enlargement of the club of nuclear states."[105] Putin and his experts (like those in the EU-3) have extended this opposition to Iran's development of the full fuel cycle: "Our Iranian partners must give up development of nuclear (fuel) cycle technology."[106]

While insisting on the continuing validity of the partnership between the two countries, Russia has given priority to preventing the emergence of a nuclear Iran and exerting diplomatic muscle to that end. For example, at U.S. insistence Russia concluded an agreement with Iran to ensure the return of spent fuel from Bushire.[107] In support of the EU-3 in 2004, Russia warned Iran that failure to arrive at an agreement would lead to the end of nuclear cooperation between the two countries.[108] And Russia tied the completion of the Bushire project to a satisfactory outcome of the discussions with the EU-3. Both the date of completion and the dispatch of fuel for the reactor were geared to the outcome of this diplomacy.[109]

Russian diplomacy took a slightly different turn after the failure of the EU-3 package proposal in June 2005. Russia appeared to relish the defeat and the opportunity it presented for Moscow to play a more prominent role. Balancing between the desire to keep Iran friendly and to play a leading role in the international coalition (and G-8), Moscow's traditional ambivalence became more pronounced.[110] On the one hand, Russia agreed to sell Iran $1 billion in air defense missiles and argued against any precipitate act, such as sanctions, that might "aggravate things."[111] On the other hand, Russia insisted that its proposal to carry out enrichment on Russian soil constituted a logical way out of the diplomatic impasse and some form of Security Council sanctions. In general Russia sought to hew closely to the international consensus, hiding behind the IAEA and the consensus therein, doing little to strengthen or weaken it, and avoiding a conspicuous or forward role.

The principal explanation for the evolution from a lukewarm response to Iran's resumption of conversion activities in August to Russia's greater support for the coalition after November 2005 seems to have been twofold: first, the existence (to some extent) of a Russian formula and a leading role in the crisis, and second, the desire to embrace diplomacy to forestall a possible military alternative from an exasperated United States, a point that Russian Defense Minister Sergey Ivanov noted explicitly.[112] In its negotiations with Iran, Russia has been tough in arguing that Iran has violated its obligations to the IAEA and that for diplomacy to work Tehran should resume its suspension of enrichment for an indefinite period and accept inspections.[113]

The Russian proposal—which still provides a last chance for Iran to avoid sanctions and which has U.S. and European support—is a clear attempt to take enrichment out of Iran's hands for a considerable period of time (ten years perhaps) while *possibly* allowing it to retain some parts of the fuel cycle. It remains to be seen whether Iran will consider Russia a more reliable supplier of fuel than the Western countries. In any case, in the nuclear diplomacy that has unfolded, it is the only currently active proposal, which Iran can reject at its own risk. The proposal, which is by no means complete (and which might include other states such as China), is seen by the Russians as a step toward the development of international centers for nuclear fuel production. Russian experts stress their global perspective: "If such a network (of international fuel centres) existed, the sort of problem that exists with Iran today would not occur."[114]

Although Russia may be acting constructively for the international community, it is clear that its proposal is not attractive for Iran economically and that control over Iran's fuel supply (as well as its reactor programs, technical training, and arms supplies) gives Moscow considerable future leverage over its unpredictable neighbor.

At the same time Russia's reluctance to impose sanctions on Iran in the Security Council serves to underline Moscow's independence from the United States and its privileged ties with Tehran. At what point Moscow's support for diplomacy without teeth is exhausted remains to be seen.

6

Iran and Regional Security

Iran seeks a leading role in the Muslim world and the Middle East regional order. Its efforts have focused on reshaping this order to make it more conducive to Iran's interests. This objective implies a correspondingly diminished role for the United States and the West, which are seen as rivals having a different vision of the regional order—a vision that is antithetical to Iranian interests and aspirations. Iran's determination to have a dominant role in the region stems from Iranian nationalism in general, but the emphasis on revolutionary Iran as a role model, the exploitation of Islam, and the zero-sum approach to the Western powers are specific to the Islamic Republic of Iran.

Iran is motivated by both offensive and defensive considerations, but its aims correspond more to its ambitions than to its fears. After all, U.S. encirclement is relatively new and was preceded by Iran's export of the revolution and determination to stymie the various efforts at a Middle East peace process. The content of the order Iran envisions—beyond being Islamic and ratifying Iran's leading role—is fuzzy, but it clearly includes the elimination of the Western presence and a reduction of its influence. A nuclear capability would help to counter and compete with that influence and demonstrate the arrival of Iran as a regional great power.

The defensive aspect of Iran's ambitions stems from structural conditions in the region rather than hostility toward the West. As a Persian Shiite state, Iran is in the minority in the largely Sunni Middle East with no natural ally or constituency upon which to rely.[1] Sunni Arab nationalism is a potential rival and certainly a constraint on Iran's leadership pretensions. The specter of Iran–Arab polarization and Iran's containment is thus dealt with by an activist policy that redefines issues such as Palestine as Muslim rather than simply an Arab or national/territorial question. By outbidding the Arab states in its extremism (or support for the resistance in its terminology) on Palestine, Iran appeals to the Arab street and embarrasses and puts the Arab states on the defensive. So, preventing a united Arab front against it is an additional incentive for Iran to assume a leading role. At the same time Iran hopes to exploit the political instability in the region taking shape in the form of Islamist movements and parties (for example, Hamas). These groups are less disposed toward compromise or moderation in the achievement of their political objectives.

Similarly, to weaken the United States in the region, Iran tries to exploit existing crises, discontent, and anti-Americanism, which can be done most effectively on the Palestine issue—the "Achilles' heel" of the United States in the region.[2] Turmoil in Iraq is clearly another source that feeds the opposition of many to a U.S. regional presence. The spoiler needs leverage, and Iran cultivates its sources with little regard for ideology: for example, Islamic Jihad, Al Qaeda, Hamas, Muqtada al Sadr, among others.[3] Iran seeks to cultivate states in formal relations as well, with periodic peace offensives.

As a Persian, Shiite state with an important pre-Islamic past, Iran shares few bonds with its Arab Sunni neighbors. Iran cannot rely on any other state for automatic sympathy or support, which makes its ambitions for greater status and power more problematic regionally. In the north, Iran has relied on Russia as a strategic partner, based on a common interest in excluding or reducing U.S. power in the region. This has led to cooperation on Azerbaijan, Tajikistan, and Taliban Afghanistan. Moscow values Iran's silence on the Chechen issue and its willingness to forgo any attempt to exploit Islamic extremism in the Caucasus. The convergence in interests is not perfect, however; for example, the two have differed on the division of the Caspian's resources. Similarly on the issue of nuclear technology, Russia has been unwilling to see Iran acquire an enrichment capability and has broadly supported the EU-3 attempts to constrain it. As discussed in chapter 5, Moscow has argued for more patience and diplomacy, hidden behind the IAEA, and has been reluctant to lead any sanctions or condemnation, preferring to follow rather than lead any international sanctions that might result.[4]

Iran's reliance (actually dependence) on Russia for arms, technology, and diplomatic support reflects a strong current in Iranian thinking that seeks to align itself with a "rising Asia" behind China, Russia, and India to challenge the U.S.-dominated world order.[5]

Islamic Iran's preoccupation with the United States is not simply a result of the United States' dominant role in international affairs. It also stems from the Iranian leadership's perception that a U.S.-dominated region and the regime's own survival are not compatible. Therefore, opposition to the United States, a "founding myth" of the revolution, has become a permanent goal of the Islamic Republic.[6] This suggests an Iranian view that is zero-sum, in which even common interests cannot be built upon because an increase in U.S. influence can only translate into Iran's disadvantage.

In the context of a substantial U.S. regional presence, Iran's objectives are largely defensive, characterized by a combination of hedging strategies and a spoiler role. They entail using whatever issues and conflicts exist to dilute and weaken U.S. influence and increase Iran's. In the process Iran has aggravated the suspicions of its neighbors, who rely on U.S. power.

United States as Threat and Strategic Rival

Since 1945, U.S. and Western policy in the Persian Gulf can be encapsulated by the terms *access* and *denial*: access to the region's oil supplies and denial of the region and its resources to a hostile power. After the Cold War the threats to these interests have come from regional states. Since 1990, when U.S. forces were first placed in large numbers on the Arabian peninsula, Iran has sought to reverse the trend toward forward presence. Iran attempted to counter dual containment by offering to cooperate with the Persian Gulf states on security issues. Iran's military, especially naval, procurement, including antiship missiles, mines, and submarines, suggested an intent to develop a sea-denial capability to counter the United States.[7]

The extension of U.S. military presence in the region—after 9/11, with bases in Afghanistan, Central Asia, the Persian Gulf, and after 2003, in Iraq—increased Iran's sense of insecurity. At the same time the stakes in the region increased as the issue of energy supplies became mixed with those of terrorism, Islamic extremism, and weapons of mass destruction. As it became embroiled in Iraq, the United States enlarged its strategic objectives to include a makeover of the Middle East, encouraging democratic reform and change and speaking of its goals as a "task for a generation." This rhetoric implied a continuing determination to play a major role in, and continued access to, the region.

The U.S. role in trying to exclude Iran from regional politics and by way of sanctions to prevent it from cooperating in energy with the Caspian states has imposed significant costs on Iran. But the exclusion transcends the bounds of commerce: Washington and its allies, the Iranian leaders believe, have never accepted or acknowledged "the rule of the Islamic system, our national security and territorial integrity" and have sought to "change the conduct and nature of the Islamic republic."[8] Iran sees the U.S. greater Middle East plan as a "project for a sustained presence in the region."[9]

In countering U.S. influence, Iran has gained some advantages in that its defiant stance and insistence on independence evokes a certain admiration.[10] The decline in U.S. credibility and moral stature as a result of the war in Iraq and revelations at Abu Ghraib has given Iran an opening to exploit the ambivalent relationship between the Arabs and the United States. At the same time, Iran itself suffers from certain disadvantages. One is structural: As a large non-Arab state, Iran is seen as a potential threat and has difficulty in piercing the automatism of Arab solidarity and rank closing in disputes. Thus a dispute with one becomes a dispute with all, as in the case of the islands contested with Abu Dhabi. Similarly, any Iranian influence in Iraq is seen as undesirable by the Arab states, whatever the nature of the regime in Iran or Iraq and whatever the status of Iran–Arab ties.[11] A second set of obstacles for Iran with regard to the Arab states arises from the nature of the regime in Tehran. Active export of the revolution and covert interventions in the Arab states, together with Iran's support of terrorism, have left a durable legacy of distrust, making cooperation with a professedly reformed Tehran problematic.

Iran's Regional Ambitions

Iran wants to make itself the indisputable regional power without which no regional issue of any importance can be addressed.[12] As the United States has become bogged down with Iraq, thus reducing its threat to Iran, Tehran has become emboldened.[13] In reply to Rowhani's comment that "wherever Iran goes, it faces the United States. This includes Iraq," Mousavian, another senior negotiator, observed, "That is right, but there is another side to it. Wherever the US goes, it faces Iran."[14] Outgoing Defense Minister Ali Shamkhani referred to Iran's missiles as giving the country regional deterrence. He said that "Iran is following a path aimed at making others, despite their will, accept Iran as a regional power." Shamkhani earlier noted that Iran was "prepared to sign non-aggression pacts and pacts to prevent the use of bases by a third force with all regional states," and Iran has "always sought such regional pacts against the wishes of outside powers."[15] President Ahmadinejad's chief security advisor, Ali Larijani, ran for president arguing that the United States sought to exclude Iran from regional groupings and that Iran ought to leverage its regional power into geostrategic power. After the election Larijani defined Ahmadinejad's policy as creating strategic relations with neighbors and creating "new regional arrangements and coalitions."[16] Larijani has suggested to his counterpart in Iraq that the two countries could be the nucleus of a new regional security system.[17] When faced with the threat of referral to the Security Council, he pointedly observed that "considering the power it enjoys in the region," Iran need not fear Security Council measures.[18] Iran's reduced sense of vulnerability (and shift in perceived relative balance of power) between 2003 and 2005 was exemplified by nuclear negotiator Sirus Naseri's comment that "Iran is not Iraq and the US is not the self-appointed policeman of the world anymore."[19]

Iran's conception of a regional security arrangement for the Gulf involves building confidence through practical bilateral cooperative measures (extradition agreements on terrorists) and tying an eventual agreement to the allusions to it in paragraph 8 of Security Council resolution 598, which ended the Iran–Iraq war. Some of the smaller states have sought the inclusion of Yemen and Pakistan in any eventual agreement.[20]

The GCC states, however cordial, entertain few illusions about Iran's aims. Iran's size and its past record make them suspicious. Iran's possible exploitation of their often significant Shiite populations (varying from 5 percent in Saudi Arabia to 30 percent in Kuwait to nearly 60 percent in Bahrain and Iraq) is an additional cause for concern. This fear is amplified by the prospect of the first Arab Shiite state emerging in Iraq. This might embolden other restive Shiites in the Gulf, allowing Iran the possibility to use this as a basis for an alliance. Many in the region share Saudi King Abdullah's fears about the emergence of a "Shia crescent" stretching from Lebanon through Iraq to Iran and south toward Bahrain and beyond.[21] Iran's border dispute with Iraq and a territorial dispute with the United Arab Emirates continue to upset relations periodically. For example, there is the ongoing disagreement over the name of the waterway: Persian or Arab? Iran's arms programs come under criticism as well.[22]

There will be no great enthusiasm for exploring new security arrangements until the outcome in Iraq (and U.S. standing) becomes clearer, and as long as Iran's nuclear ambitions remain ambiguous. Given the limited scope for replacing the United States as the region's security guarantor in the Persian Gulf states, Iran has sought to use two current conflicts to improve its position in the region and weaken that of the United States. On the issue of Palestine, Tehran outbids the Arab states in its support for rejectionism, putting them on the defensive and inhibiting any criticism of Iran's other regional policies. At the same time, Tehran seeks to discredit those states close to the West. This stance requires a spoiler strategy, undermining cease-fires and sabotaging peace processes by aggravating tensions and preventing peacemaking. Iran achieves this through providing arms, training, and funding to proxies—directly to Hezbollah (with Syria) and indirectly to Hamas and Islamic Jihad. Its strategic rationale goes as follows: The United States seeks hegemony in the region and its natural resources and wants to achieve it as a first step through the roadmap foisted onto the hapless Palestinians. It is therefore, so the thinking goes, the duty of all Middle East countries, including Iran, to oppose Israel and any compromise peace, which would be tantamount to surrender.[23]

Iran is the only state in the Middle East that denies Israel's right to exist. Its bellicose policies are clearly intended to divert regional attention from Iran's own missile and nuclear programs. The question posed is whether, given its record of indirect conflict with Israel, a nuclear and more confident Iran might not choose to confront Israel more directly, or take greater risks through its proxies, than before? At the very least, the risks of a misjudgment increase considerably.

On Iraq, Iran faces another choice: Should it seek to weaken the United States by bleeding it and taking the risk that a U.S. failure there could translate into regionwide instability (and Sunni–Shiite polarization) or should Tehran set aside competition with the United States and build on the convergence of interest in Iraq? That overlap in interest is substantial: Both states want a unified, stable, moderate, and democratic (and therefore Shiite-dominant) state. Neither Tehran nor Washington wants a weak or disintegrating state, an Arab nationalist state, or an extremist Islamist state. The differences arise from mutual suspicions that each seeks to dominate the future Iraq at the expense of the other's interest. The reality is that neither has the ability to determine outcomes but each can probably harm the other and its own interests in the stubborn competition.

As a neighbor Iran has a considerable stake in the stability of Iraq. With a majority Shiite population in both countries and major Shiite shrines located in southern Iraq, there has long been interaction between the two countries. The eight-year war between the two states in the 1980s left a number of issues unresolved (border agreement, prisoners of war, compensation or reparations). In addition a number of groups—notably the Iraqi Shiite grouping, the Supreme Council for the Islamic Republic of Iraq (SCIRI) with its Badr Brigade militia—were given sanctuary, funded, and trained in Iran. In the current near-civil war in Iraq, Iran retains some influence with this group, and other Shiites (such as Prime Minister Jafaari of the Dawa Party) are naturally suspected of nefarious aims. Iran's Revolutionary Guards also have a presence and retain contacts and influence in Iraq. On a visit to Iraq in mid-2005 the Iranian Foreign Minister Kamal Kharrazi was received by Ayatollah Sistani (which no ranking U.S. official has yet managed). Kharrazi pointedly reminded his hosts that Iran would remain a neighbor long after the United States has departed.[24]

Iranian leaders say that Iraq "is a turning point in [the] region."[25] Unable to predict Iraq's future, Tehran seeks to maximize its options in the fluid circumstances, which means creating multiple contacts and links across the spectrum of opposition and government forces for possible leverage. Iran has sought to reassure the Iraqi government of its goodwill by offering assistance, while maintaining ties with the Dawa Party, SCIRI (and its Badr Brigade militia), Muqtada al Sadr, and Ayatollah Sistani. There are also reports that Iran is funding Sunni insurgent forces, because they target U.S. forces.[26]

Although Iran shares U.S. concerns that Iraq remain intact, become democratic by giving increased power to the majority Shiites, and avoid becoming a radical Arab nationalist or Islamist state, the differences between Tehran and Washington preclude any cooperation to that end. Agreement to discuss Iraq will not change this. Above all, Iran's strategic priority has been to ensure that the United States remains bogged down in the Iraqi quagmire while maintaining its own options (and contacts or proxies) as to how it will play the endgame. [27] This strategy has entailed a complex set of policies, mixing disruptive behavior with offers to the United States to help stabilize the country. Iraqi Sunnis and others, including the United States, are suspicious of Iran's intentions and issue frequent warnings to Tehran.[28]

Iran links the nuclear issue to the U.S. regional presence and to the future of Iraq and Afghanistan. While seeking to deflect military pressure and limit U.S. options, Iran has offered to use its influence to assist the U.S. stabilization of these countries in exchange for greater tolerance of Iran's nuclear program.[29] In effect Iran holds regional stability hostage to U.S. policies on the nuclear issue, which have been inconsistent: "The Bush administration has vacillated between two very different approaches. At times it signaled support for regime change[;] at other times it engaged in direct discussions with Tehran over Iraq and Afghanistan."[30]

Iran may find it difficult to calibrate the correct balance among maintaining links with various groups, its desire for stability, and its intention to deny the United States a success or honorable exit. Reports of Iran providing insurgents with shaped charges for explosives and increased assistance could lead, if sufficiently blatant, to an Iranian–U.S. confrontation.[31] Iran wants stability in Iraq, but not at the price of continued U.S. bases in that country or its own containment by U.S. power.[32]

In sum, Iran is developing a sea-denial capability and missiles while cultivating the GCC states with confidence-building measures and talk about a new security arrangement. Iran seeks to outdo the Arab states in support for the Palestinians while inhibiting their reactions to its own policies. Tehran enjoys special relations with Syria and Hezbollah and exploits anti-Americanism and the sensitivity of regimes being labeled U.S. clients. Iran is cultivating its ties with Shiite populations in the region and hedging its bets on the future of Iraq, which Tehran would like to have as a strategic ally. Although the shape of the regional order that Iran would like to see is unclear, it has certain identifiable features: it is hostile to the United States (West); it is Islamic and independent; and Iran has a leading role in it. A nuclear-capable Iran would be better placed to bring such an order into being.

Iran in the New U.S. Strategic Context: From Regime Change to Democratization

Iran's bid for a nuclear capability is of inherent political importance, but it is magnified by both the kind of regime it is and the regional context within which its proliferation is taking place. This context, sensitive and unstable, has been made the more so by U.S. policy in Afghanistan and Iraq. Furthermore Iran's policies in the region and beyond, opposed to U.S. interests, were one of the criteria that made the United States so implacable and hostile to Iranian proliferation. The unanticipated U.S. entanglement in Iraq gradually saw a shift in U.S. policy goals to rationalize the costs of the deeper engagement. The United States elided from a policy of regime change to the more ambitious and open-ended one of democratization. The new rationale for a generational commitment in the Middle East became the necessity of democratization that alone could guarantee an end to radicalism and proliferation.[33] It is this approach that colors policy toward Iran today.[34]

U.S. involvement in the region reflects and shapes the strategic context of the contemporary Middle East. The United States has become a regional player and revolutionary state with a long-term commitment to promoting change. The implicit trade-off is among short- and long-term stability, supporting allies, and encouraging democratic opposition and reform. Deeper U.S. involvement comes at a time of transition in the region, where the pressures for political reform have grown, oil incomes have risen, and competition for Persian Gulf oil has increased. Together with its long-standing commitment to Israel, which remains unaffected, the United States has assumed a greater role in the Caucasus and Central Asia, where it has access to an arc of military bases. In the south, the United States has diversified its base structure among the smaller Gulf states, notably Bahrain and Qatar. Iraq and Afghanistan will provide access facilities to the United States for the foreseeable future. While militarily present and politically active in the region, the United States is also overextended militarily, which makes it vulnerable to crises and demands on its forces elsewhere and to reverses that could call into question whatever progress has been made in Afghanistan and Iraq so far.

In this context, discussions of a military option to prevent Iran's nuclear ambitions have an air of desperation and bluff. Although this course can never be totally discounted as a last resort or prudently devalued in diplomacy and negotiations before that stage, in practical terms it is an unattractive and probably counterproductive option.[35] An attack would need to destroy all sites and be able to assure that the nuclear program would not resume or accelerate outside of the NPT. It would need the full support of the international community, following prolonged attempts toward a diplomatic effort, and demonstrate incontrovertibly that Iran was seeking or in possession of nuclear weapons. A strike would need to cover enough targets to destroy the infrastructure but not enough to constitute an act of war against the Iranian people or to strengthen the regime. Iranian responses would have to be anticipated, whether they be missile strikes or terrorism against the United States or its regional allies. In this context, the United States' overexposure in Iraq surely constitutes a liability (with U.S. forces a form of hostage to Washington's good behavior).[36]

The intelligence debacle surrounding Iraq has made tackling Iran more difficult. Some have argued that the United States invaded the wrong country; Iran filled more of the criteria than Iraq. What Hans Blix calls "faith-based intelligence" has been, at least temporarily, discredited.[37] Today, the lack of good (that is, actionable) intelligence on Iran means U.S. policy is flying blind on most issues affecting Iran, most especially its secret programs. An official and comprehensive report underscoring this suggested to professionals the need for greater caution where Iran was concerned. But senior U.S. officials argued that this should not lead states to "underreact" and that "there are no guarantees where intelligence is concerned."[38]

U.S. Response to the Regional Implications of a Nuclear-Capable Iran

Iran has sent mixed signals about its nuclear intentions. Sometimes its leaders have argued that a nuclear capability would only complicate relations with neighbors; at other times they claim possession of a regionwide deterrent.[39] From the U.S. perspective, Iran's status as "the most active state sponsor of terrorism in the world" makes its move toward a nuclear capability particularly threatening.[40] Where the United States is concerned, rogue states and WMD are indistinguishable from terrorists and WMD, and it is the nature of the regimes proliferating, not the weapons, that count. Since Iran's policies "directly threaten US interests in the region and beyond,"[41] Iran would constitute a challenge on several levels.

The most abstract threat is to the non-proliferation regime itself. A long-standing member either leaving the NPT or openly flouting it would create doubts about the regime and set a precedent for others. Iran's withdrawal might serve as a catalyst and even a model for others—the "tipping point" analogy.[42] Weakening the NPT regime by defecting from it and setting the stage for others to do so would unravel the most important and universal arms control treaty in existence and could result in regional arms races, shifts in alliances, and further proliferation.

Iran's refusal to recognize Israel and its opposition to the peace process puts it in a special category of states. Iran might seek to confront Israel, or more likely, use Hezbollah to do so, while sheltering behind its nuclear capability. As John Bolton put it, "Their repeated support for terrorism makes it particularly dangerous if they were to acquire a nuclear weapon ... Whether they would use it directly as the government of Iran or whether they would transfer it to a terrorist group leaves us very concerned." Bolton, however, argued the opposite in the case of Israel, suggesting that Israel's possible use of nuclear weapons was less a source of concern, because it was less likely to do so as a democracy and ally of the United States.[43]

A more direct threat would be the impact of a nuclear Iran on U.S. security commitments. As President Bush suggested before 9/11, proliferators "seek weapons of mass destruction ... to keep the United States and other responsible nations from helping allies and friends in strategic parts of the world." A nuclear Iran would inhibit cost-free interventions, creating uncertainty and acting as a deterrent.[44]

The United States has been clear that an Iranian nuclear capability would throw a shadow over the area not least because Iran's policies "directly threaten US interests in the region and beyond."[45] President Bush observed, "We share the view that Iran's acquisition of nuclear weapons would be destabilizing and threatening to all Iran's neighbors."[46] John Bolton noted, "Iranian nuclear capabilities would change the perceptions of the military balance in the region and could pose serious challenges to the [United States] in terms of deterrence and defense."[47]

U.S. fixed bases in the region as well as access are already put under threat by missile proliferation, and this would be magnified by a nuclear Iran.[48]

U.S. officials also underlined that a nuclear Iran is destabilizing not only to Iran's neighbors but "for peace and security internationally"; that the "pursuit of weapons of mass destruction and delivery systems makes Iran less secure and the region more unstable";

that Iran's quest for nuclear weapons might invite an attack from another regional state; and that money would be better spent on conventional means of offsetting superior US forces in the region.[49]

Another problem caused by a nuclear Iran is the context in which this proliferation would take place—a region of instability, competition, and recent conflict. Given the intersecting rivalries—Arab–Iranian, intra-Arab, Sunni–Shiite, and national—combined with the short distances involved, it would be difficult to identify the source if any weapons are used. The risks of catalytic war and indeed of the end of the taboo against nuclear weapons use are most likely where extremism in the name of religion has become an identifying feature. Given this reality, even a moderate and satisfied state would cause concerns in seeking a nuclear capability. A nuclear Iran, if rent by domestic disorder, might seek to burnish its leadership credentials through nuclear brinksmanship.[50] All of these are considerations that arise from the prospect of a nuclear Iran. While their implications are not well understood, the imperative to arrest any further movement in that direction seems evident.

U.S. diplomacy has been slow and largely failed in mobilizing Iran's immediate neighbors, the states most directly affected by an Iranian nuclear capability.[51] The most visible effort, the visit of John Bolton to the Persian Gulf in January 2005, was illustrative. Though concerned (especially about possible environmental consequences), none of the GCC states publicly denounced Iran's nuclear program or actively lobbied against it at the Review Conference. Coming rather late, the Bolton visit underlined the liabilities of being associated with a state that has lost moral authority as a result of Abu Ghraib and credibility as a result of Iraq. The United States' association with Israel (which possesses a large weapons inventory) also made denunciation of the still embryonic Iran program problematic for the Arab states. This was to change, however, by the end of 2005 as the protracted crisis over Iran's nuclear program intensified with the arrival of a more hard-line government in Tehran. The Gulf states, concerned by Iran's activities in Iraq, were more receptive when Secretary Rice undertook a similar (and this time locally well received) visit to the Gulf in February 2006.

The United States has also tried and failed to impress on its new strategic partner, India, the need to avoid major economic agreements with Iran. New Delhi—which is increasingly dependent on the Gulf for energy supplies, is currently negotiating a gas pipeline from Iran, and considers Tehran an important, largely dependable regional state—has demurred.[52]

Regional Responses

The most direct impact of a nuclear Iran will be on its immediate region. Its neighbors will have to adjust to living in the shadow of a nuclear-capable and missile-equipped Iran. These military capabilities will aggravate already existing geopolitical disparities—Iran's demographic and geographical weight and the possible political ascendance of the Shiite in the Gulf region. This comes at a time of change in relations with the United States. In every state in the region, the reputation of the United States has suffered, and although reliance on the United States may continue, it is marked by reluctance or by the absence of choice rather than enthusiasm. Saudi Arabia's and Turkey's relations with the United States are lacking their earlier warmth. Uncertainty about Iraq, about Iran's intentions, and about how to assure Gulf security is mixed with the recognition that regional solutions are needed and that political exposure vis-à-vis the United States is dangerous.

Riven by wars, transnational terrorism, and inherently cautious, the regimes of the region have not taken a very active role in response to Iran's current programs. This is not because they are not concerned. Rather, other more urgent issues like Iraq preoccupy them. Nonetheless, silence cannot be taken for consent. The following gives the broad outlines of likely regional responses rather than detailed country-by-country reactions that are available elsewhere.[53]

A flavor of the reactions to Iran's programs is captured by two responses in the Persian Gulf. A Saudi newspaper in 2003 observed that nobody could believe that Iran sought nuclear weapons against Israel or the United States: "The real target is the neighboring countries."[54] A Gulf Research Center report concluded that the GCC and Arabs generally do not see Iran's nuclear weapons program as constituting "an instrument of deterrence, nor does it represent a counterbalancing lever against Israel's nuclear capabilities."[55]

Since late 2005 the GCC states have become more vocal in their opposition to the Iranian nuclear program. Initially careful to focus on the environmental risks and on Israel's nuclear weapons, they are no longer inhibited from expressing concern about Iran's program. The Secretary-General of the GCC criticized the program, and at the GCC summit in December 2005, the members refused to emphasize the Israeli threat, focusing instead on Iran. Significantly, the GCC now emphasized a Gulf WMD-free zone (WMDFZ) as a first step toward a wider Middle East zone.[56] Equally significant, Saudi Arabia has been less bashful about its concerns, with both the crown prince and the foreign minister clearly promoting a Gulf WMDFZ without making Israel's disarmament a precondition.[57]

This recent vocal opposition to Iran's nuclear program by its neighbors serves notice on Tehran of the *regional* costs to be paid for continuation of the program, apart from that which might come from the Security Council.

A nuclear Iran will tilt the balance of the region away from the Arabs; it must necessarily be a card for non-Arabs and Shiites. It will challenge and complicate, if not end, U.S. hegemony, raising questions about the wisdom of relying on the United States exclusively. A nuclear Iran will seek to cash in on its new status to seek hegemony and leadership in the wider Muslim world. A nuclear Iran would seek to inhibit pro-Western-inclined Arab states. Such an Iran may also seek to increase its influence in its immediate neighborhood, in effect separating the Gulf–Arab states from those further afield.

Broadly, the GCC states have several options. First, they could *seek to appease* Iran, mollify it, bandwagon, meet its needs, and procure security by joining it. This might include seeking to entangle Iran in regional arrangements including trade and security. This option accepts the limitations involved and prefers to rely on rather than counter Iran.

Second, the GCC states could *seek to balance* Iran (that is, look to a proximate or distant balancer). The United States is the only contender for such a role. This would entail tightening ties with the United States and seeking security guarantees and military links, including a theater missile defense system. Such a decision would be more attractive if Iran were considered a serious threat *and* if there were confidence in a U.S. guarantee.

Third, the GCC states could *acquire a countervailing capability* (that is, a national nuclear option). This may be an attractive option, but few states in the region have such a capability. Fewer still have a nuclear infrastructure they could set into motion to acquire such a capability within even a decade. Choosing this option would also risk relations with the United States. The alternative might be to seek nuclear weapons or the stationing of nuclear weapons from a friendly power. Saudi Arabia is sometimes cited as following this model with an assist from Pakistan and already follows a policy of opacity in regard to IAEA safeguard inspections. Saudi Arabia might also seek to buy or lease nuclear warheads from Pakistan for its existing missiles or have them stationed on Saudi soil under Pakistani control (technically legal). It is open to question whether Pakistan would be willing to guarantee Saudi security or accept the costs of offending the United States.[58]

Turkey's response in this scenario is also uncertain given its weak nuclear infrastructure. Moreover, Turkey's political evolution is uncertain, domestically, regionally, and internationally (with the EU and the United States). Egypt, which considers itself the natural leader of the Arab world and puts considerable weight on its status, has not had diplomatic relations with Iran for over a decade.

Any suggestion of the achievement of nuclear status by another regional state—especially Iran—is bound to give rise to pressures on Egypt to follow suit. This may be difficult given Egypt's lack of significant nuclear infrastructure. Also Cairo's ties with the United States (and Israel) would complicate any overt attempt to seek nuclear weapons.

In general, the most likely short-term response of regional states will be a tendency to hedge, while examining all these options.

A fourth possible approach for the GCC might be one of arms control and attempts to realize the long-discussed WMDFZ. The success of either of these, however, depends on political solutions that are not apparent (for example, Egypt prefers to emphasize Israeli nuclear weapons, whereas the GCC states focus on Iran's program). A grand bargain between the United States and Iran in parallel with serious movement on the peace process front, however, *could* make at least progress on a regionwide approach to tackling WMD more likely. But while Iran's Arab neighbors are less reticent in voicing their concerns about Iran's program, a joint or regional response, whether diplomatic or military, appears unlikely, leaving the United States and Europe to do the heavy lifting.

The implications of a nuclear-capable Iran are serious but are not seen as an *imminent* threat in a region beset by immediate crises. None of these options look attractive to the states of the region. Increased reliance on the United States (though not welcome) may be the most practical. Some states may position themselves to develop nuclear options, but none are well placed to do so in the short term.

Israeli Response

Iran refuses to recognize Israel's right to exist. For the past decade and a half Israel has been aware that the proximate existential threats it faced have been displaced to the East. Israeli strategists and the Israeli Air Force first talked of military strikes against Iranian nuclear installations in 1992.[59] In the 1990s Israel saw Iran rather than Iraq as the more serious threat, and believed that with Baghdad contained, Iran would be free to pursue its programs unobserved. Even the war with Iraq in 2003 took the spotlight off the greater threat that Iran was beginning to represent. Israel sees Iran as an implacable foe, unpredictable and shrewd, posing an international rather than bilateral threat. Throughout the 1990s, Israel was in the forefront of those seeking to sensitize President Yeltsin's Russia to the dangers from transfer of nuclear technology to Iran. Its alarmism was deliberate, aiming to act *preventively* before Iran became self-sufficient instead of waiting for Iran's program to reach the point of no return and become less subject to influence from outside. The 2002 revelations of Iran's nuclear program therefore served as confirmation of Israel's own estimates and warnings over the previous decade.

An obvious feature of the Iranian program that causes particular concern for the Israelis has been its development of long-range missiles configured apparently for specialized warheads. Iranian slogans against Israel on missiles do nothing to reassure Israel about Iran behaving responsibly. Of equal concern has been Iran's attempt to deploy its Russian-built submarines outside the Gulf and to project power throughout in the region.[60] Also of concern is Iran supplying missiles to Hezbollah together with funding and the overall strategic relationship, which might become more pronounced if Iran were to acquire a nuclear capability.

A nuclear Iran raises a host of questions for Israel ranging from Iran's propensity for risk-taking to its attempts at extending deterrence to Hezbollah to its behavior and posturing in crises to its possible attempts to sanctuarize itself with nuclear weapons while continuing to support or upgrade support for rejectionist elements and terrorists. Although reformists in Iran have questioned Iran's policy of being "more Palestinian than the Palestinians," the regime, and the new government in particular, shows no sign of reducing support for hard-line Palestinians. Yet few Iranians consider the Palestine issue one of national interest; at most it is an issue of

Muslim solidarity. Still, Tehran finds it expedient to magnify the issue and demonize Israel. Israel therefore must anticipate the worst.

Israel has responded to this threat in several ways. It insists that Iran is an international issue first and foremost, and to that end it coordinates its diplomacy closely with the EU-3, sharing intelligence and estimates. It takes seriously Iranian threats of retaliation *inter alia* against Dimona, in the event of a military attack on Iranian facilities. Israel must necessarily consider and plan for the possible need for preemption against facilities if all other alternatives (diplomacy, sabotage, assassination) fail, which lends credence to allegations of an Israeli presence in Northern Iraq and Israeli use of Turkish airspace, given regular exercises.

Israel has also responded by moving its deterrent to sea. *Dolphin* class submarines that can reach and navigate the Persian Gulf are now part of a second-strike capability that makes Israel's deterrent more robust and survivable. The ARROW antimissile system constitutes the other part of this upgrade.

Israel may consider moving from its opaque doctrine on nuclear weapons to a more overt stance. A move from ambiguity to quasi-public acknowledgment, intended to act as a deterrent to Iran, could have the effect of putting greater (domestic political) pressure on states like Egypt to follow suit.

Israel will have to initiate a strategic dialogue with Iran to clarify redlines and avoid misunderstandings. For example, Iran will need to know that Israel cannot accept the concept of limited strikes. Given the experience of the Holocaust, any attack on Israel will be met by a full-scale, devastating response about which there should be no doubts (that is, there will not be proportional responses). Iran needs to be disabused of any notion of using numerical superiority or the geographical asymmetries of the region to advantage.[61]

Unable to deal with it unilaterally, Israel has insisted that Iran's nuclear ambitions are, first and foremost, an international problem. Israel's main concern has been to keep the international spotlight and pressure on Iran. This means close and frank coordination with Washington. Israel's primary concern is that focusing on estimates of the dates at which Iran will be able to produce fissile material (3 to 5 years) will obscure the point at which Iran will have effectively achieved self-sufficiency regarding the fuel cycle. This "point of no return" will make Iran less vulnerable to sanctions and embargoes and will come *before* the date of actual production. It is this earlier date that is salient for diplomacy. Israel, which will be in the front line in the event of an Iranian nuclear capability, is bound to influence policy and calculations.

As the country most affected and most able to respond quickly, Israel's response to Iran's nuclear program is the most important in the region. Israel must consider Iran's refusal to recognize its right to exist together with proxy war waged with it over two decades as an existential threat. A nuclear Iran will complicate the regional strategic landscape by raising the risks of major conflict at a time when most instabilities in the region are transnational and domestic.

Conclusion

I have argued that Iran's nuclear ambitions reflect a broader Iranian challenge to the Middle Eastern regional order. A nuclear capability symbolizes Iran's quest for regional leadership. It provides the means to block a U.S.-inspired regional order, which is seen as domineering, hegemonic, and imperial.[1] Such an order is seen as a threat to Iran and its pretensions to manage regional security.[2] In seeking to block it, Iran gives priority to its relations with Russia and China. In joining the Shanghai Cooperation Organization (as an observer), Iran joins an implicitly anti-NATO and anti-Western grouping.[3] Iran seeks a regional order in which outside powers are excluded and in which it plays a leading role in the Caucasus, Persian Gulf and broader Middle East, and parts of South Asia. As a starting point, this strategy entails a reduction of the U.S. presence and influence in the region.

Iranian leaders are in no doubt about the competition for regional influence under way. President Ahmadinejad observed, "They [the United States] want to silence us on the important issues that are going on in the region and the world of Islam. They want us to follow their discipline in our foreign policy."[4] His principal security advisor boastfully noted the linkage between the nuclear issue and regional politics: "They [the United States] are also concerned that if Iran acquires nuclear technology the situation in the region will be altered."[5] He has already hinted how: "With the power it enjoys in the region, there is no way that Iran can be worried about the threat of the Security Council."[6] Meanwhile the Guards Commander warns that Iran cannot be excluded from the region and that Iran is "not merely a regional power" but "a major power in the Middle East and the world."[7]

Turmoil in the region, insurgency in Iraq with attendant uncertainty about the outcome, combined with the prospect of a Shiite-led state (in which Iran has significant influence and which emboldens Shiites in neighboring Arab states) feeds a sense of regional insecurity. In this context Iran's ambiguous policies in Iraq and strident rhetoric about Israel are amplified.[8] Accordingly Iran's looming nuclear ambitions appear menacing. Relations with Saudi Arabia are strained over Iraq, while Turkish analysts noting Iran's "activism" and grab for regional influence see a "new danger."[9] The smaller Gulf states are preoccupied with terrorism and are not reassured by Iran's careless diplomacy. An Israeli analyst succinctly (and accurately) notes that "Iran is striving to become an Islamic superpower with hegemony over the greater Middle East," which drives the development of ballistic missiles and a nuclear capability.[10]

Since the arrival of the Ahmadinejad presidency, Iran's policy on the nuclear issue has hardened. The new team is more confrontational by nature and more prone to brinksmanship. They are bolstered by a belief that Iran should align itself with Asia and are not interested in the West or Western inducements. The strategic picture seen from their perspective has changed for the better over the past two years. The United States is bogged down in Iraq, which they believe takes the military option off the table. The EU is, or will be, preoccupied with internal matters: elections, terrorism, economies, immigration, and the future shape of the EU. The tight energy market has given Iran a buffer of approximately $15 billion in extra oil revenues for 2005. Moreover, the high price of oil reduces the likelihood that any sanctions on Iran will include the oil sector.

An alternative analysis would be less sanguine about Iran's position, focusing instead on the weakening of Syria, its principal ally, the growing alienation of regional states, the knife edge on which Tehran is poised in Iraq, where hurting the United States risks a destabilization of the country and a prolonged civil war, the tenuousness of any Russian–Chinese tilt toward Iran, and the necessity for good relations with the EU, if not the United States.

Territorially, Iran is a status quo power, not an adventurist state. Yet its opportunism, regime insecurity, and tolerance of ideological militants, together with the shift in power to the Revolutionary Guards, could see the emergence of less restrained policies. Iran's ambiguity on terrorism only increases suspicions about its reliability. Tehran has yet to make the choice between radicalism and being accepted (and treated) as a normal state. Iran continues to exploit hostility toward Israel for leverage in the Muslim world and for bargaining with the United States, yet it is of marginal importance in terms of national, as opposed to regime–factional, interest.

At the same time, while fragile, the regime will not be threatened by opposition, unless it comes from within the system. With strong repressive institutions it can counter threats but cannot generate enthusiasm and popularity except in the constituencies it favors with patronage. Regime evolution, inevitable with generational change, may take too long to be relevant as an answer to Iran's nuclear ambitions.

The wild cards in Iran today are the ultranationalists/Islamists who would welcome a return to a state of siege and embattlement and believe a nuclear capability is an answer for the lack of respect afforded Iran. They are a minority of the elite, but they have intimidated the more internationalist leaders, who see interaction or engagement with the world and the West as inevitable and necessary for development, but who now have to debate the issues on the conservatives' terms.

Iran's challenge to the international order is not a conventional one that can be contained militarily or susceptible to easy co-option. The challenge it poses is civilizational and ideological.

Whether it can be accommodated and whether its behavior and goals can be tempered and changed remains unclear. I have argued that Iran seeks to be recognized as a regional and even global power. It wants to be taken seriously and its quest for nuclear status reflects this impulse. However, there are elements currently in office in Iran that appear to expect to achieve this on their own terms without significantly changing their policies.

These policies are disruptive of regional order and could become more so with a nuclear capability. Iran's sense of grievance, its lack of a natural regional constituency, which leaves it blocked diplomatically, and its self-absorption do not give rise to regionally responsible behavior. Iran exploits strategic ambiguity, does little to reassure its smaller neighbors, and nurtures and cultivates a populist nationalism, rarely consulting or acting through institutions. Iran's regional policies in the Arab world are that of a spoiler or disrupter, maximizing options and leverage for bargaining. Iran's anti-Americanism and hostility toward Israel are heartfelt *and* tactical, to be exploited to promote Iran's version of a regional order.

Some scholars have suggested that the starting point for a nuclear agreement with Iran is "according Iran a guaranteed leading place in a Middle Eastern security order."[11] But this begs the question whether Iran can be accommodated within the existing system or whether it seeks to overthrow the system. Does it seek greater recognition within or against the system? That depends on which Iran you are speaking about.

Iran is seeking a nuclear capability, at least a weapons option, the benefits of which it sees as prestige and domestic legitimation, regional status, and a greater voice in international relations. The strategic aspects are not principal, but with weak conventional forces and missiles, a nuclear capability necessarily assumes more importance. As a deterrent against U.S. regime change, a nuclear capability has certainly increased in value since 2002, similarly as a bargaining chip in any grand bargain.

Iran has no grand strategy to achieve this and has been improvising tactically and defensively since its nuclear program was uncovered. Iran does not want nuclear weapons capability at the cost of international isolation and setbacks for development, but some may have convinced themselves that a *fait accompli* would force others to accept it or that it has an "Eastern" option.

On the one hand, *if* Iran does *not* have a parallel clandestine program *of any significance* (which is not the same as undeclared facilities), then its current capabilities are still limited and rudimentary and vulnerable to sanctions. On the other hand, isolation and sanctions will only reinforce its interest in a nuclear capability. The nuclear issue is an attempt by Iran to force the world to deal with it on *its* own terms, rather than accommodate the terms demanded by others. Iran wants technology *and* independence, hostility to the United States *and* recognition/status.

The United States has handled the nuclear issue badly for over a decade, acting as if sanctions could work in an era of globalization. Its policies have left Tehran free to depict the issue as one of technology denial. Most Iranians are concerned about bread and butter issues but do not like being dictated to or discriminated against.[12] Influencing the debate in Iran a decade ago might have been more useful, but there is still time to point to the difference between sensitive and other technologies and to underscore that it is the government's behavior that raises concern, not the rights of the Iranian people.

The current U.S. administration has insisted, stubbornly but with some reason, that it is not weapons *per se* that are the problem but, rather, certain regimes. Iran after all is not Japan or Sweden. U.S. policy has fluctuated unclearly between regime change and policy change. In essence, the aim of some in Washington seems to be to get Tehran to choose between radical policies and sensitive technology. So far Iran has held out for both. Neither containment nor sanctions have worked very effectively. Seeking to moderate Iran's behavior through engagement (and inducement) has been the approach of the European states. U.S. policy has been largely incoherent, consisting of bluster and bile mixed with optimism about a spontaneous, imminent regime change. Since February 2005, when the United States joined its European allies in supporting diplomacy, the chances of settlement have increased. Iran's summary rejection of the EU package offer in July *may* have had more to do with the contents of the package than with distaste for an overall settlement. A larger package deal or an across-the-board agreement is unlikely, however, given Iranian fears about U.S. aims (and a temporary sense of leverage) and U.S. political constraints.

In the absence of such an agreement, which would deal with all the issues of concern on either side, a limited or technical agreement on the nuclear issue appears more likely. This limited agreement could take the form of giving Iran access to some parts of the fuel cycle (such as conversion but not enrichment on any scale), with the bulk of enrichment and return of spent fuel outside of the country (possibly Russia, which is to provide the fuel for Iran's first reactor at Bushire on these lines). Such an agreement would certainly defuse the current crisis and give the international community some breathing space. One defect of such an agreement, however, is that if Iran has clandestine enrichment facilities, its permitted conversion activities would unwittingly fuel its program. Would Iran accept such an agreement? This depends on both its immediate nuclear ambitions and its perception of the threat involved in Security Council sanctions. Such an agreement supported by the IAEA, Russia, the EU, and the United States might be difficult to reject because China and India would find it much easier to associate themselves with it.

Iran will continue to push for advantage, to slice away at existing constraints, and to make moves that restart its program without providing enough justification for a strong or united international response. Iran will insist on its willingness to continue negotiations, perhaps in a different mode or forum, and on its cooperation with the IAEA. At the same time, Iran has already reduced cooperation with the inspectors, with possible withdrawal from the NPT hinted at as a last resort. Iran's calculation is that its continued cooperation with the IAEA (however imperfect) is preferable to the international community than the continuation of its program without any inspections or monitoring. It may believe a tight oil market increases its leverage, but in this it may prove mistaken. Playing to a domestic audience, while pushing for advantage, has brought Iran into direct conflict with the international community. Iran is now in a trap of its own making, finding it difficult to give up what it has convinced its domestic audience is essential to science and development, while failure to do so could jeopardize its economic prospects and development. Iran may have underestimated the degree to which its behavior has antagonized its interlocutors and overestimated its own ingenuity to devise ways of having its cake and eating it too. In turning down the EU-3 offer of technology and a long-term relationship and insisting on an accelerated drive for enrichment, it scored an "own goal."

I have suggested that a fix for the nuclear issue, however welcome, is not the end of the story. Iran's behavior and its regional ambitions are concerns that will not necessarily change. The primary aim of the regime is to stay in power. It is sensitive to power, and when vulnerable, it will deal. Absent an external threat, it will continue as in the past, opportunistic and reflexively hostile to the United States and Israel. It will use the nuclear issue and foreign policy to shore up its legitimacy. It will be regionally and globally ambitious without the means to achieve such status. A nuclear capability would certainly see Iran's penchant for brinksmanship elevated to new levels.

Tehran's mantra about being discriminated against obscures the degree to which Iran is the victim of its own behavior. Iran's irresponsibility, including unwillingness to assume responsibility for its own acts, lies at the heart of international reluctance to allow the emergence of a nuclear Iran. Iran still acts more like a revolutionary clique than a responsible government that recognizes responsibilities as well as rights. A state deficient in a sense of responsibility cannot be allowed control over dual-use technology. A state that has elevated deniability to a new art form cannot be trusted with nuclear weapons. A state that harbors and promotes terrorists cannot reasonably be allowed WMD. A state that refuses other states' right to exist should not be permitted to acquire weapons that may allow it to act on its rhetoric or encourage (or enable) others to do so. A state with a rather vague and fluid sense of international responsibilities in relation to international treaties cannot reasonably be trusted with technology that needs to be limited by legislation to state parties.

The Iranian government is still so insecure in its legitimacy that it is unsettled by the prospect of normalization with the United States. It wants to claim democratic attributes without trusting democracy; the contrast between its tight control of elections and its rhetoric of the people's participation (and choice) is stark. In its refusal to dispense with the cult of victimhood, revolutionary rhetoric, and subversive acts and in its unwillingness to assume normal relations with others lies the origin of the reluctance of others to see Iran acquire a nuclear capability.

Policy Options

Iran's nuclear program presents difficult policy choices for all the players involved. Nuclear ambition is only part of a broader strategic challenge posed by Iran. Therefore, any solution to the nuclear issue is necessarily a partial one that needs, in time, to encompass the broader threats posed by Iran's ambition for regional hegemony. Policy choices to deal with the nuclear issue are further constrained by the debacle in Iraq and the consequent imperative to maintain an international consensus.

By early 2006, the United States had recaptured the diplomatic initiative. To do so, it had accepted Iran's right to peaceful nuclear technology (including the Bushire reactor) and perhaps even some parts of the fuel cycle on Iranian territory. The United States had also embraced the need for diplomacy, while outsourcing this to its European allies. Washington had accepted Moscow's proposal to take enrichment from Iran to Russia as a potential means of keeping Iran from the full fuel cycle. Above all the United States had accepted the need to maintain an international consensus among the Security Council members (and the IAEA Board of Governors) on the issue. This approach implies a deliberate, slow pace, in which the responses are graduated and pressure is ratcheted up and taken sequentially, giving Iran time to reverse its course (ceasing conversion and research activities and reinstating Additional Protocol inspections) pending a strategic decision to forgo the full fuel cycle.

The U.S. decision in March 2005 to back diplomacy has been mixed. Support for the EU-3 has been a little grudging and skeptical but inevitable given Washington's refusal to engage directly. Supporting a broader multilateral consensus since September 2005, the United States has accepted a more leisurely pace. However, leaving the military option conspicuously on the table has been useful in concentrating the minds of the UNSC members on the need for diplomacy. The question remains whether multilateral diplomacy and the authority of the Security Council will be enough to get Iran to renounce its nuclear ambitions, and if not, what the policy options would be thereafter. The United States needs to do two things to strengthen the coalition to prevent Iran's momentum toward a nuclear option. First, it has to choose between nonengagement and non-proliferation, that is, between its desire to achieve the second without the first. Second, the United States needs to couch any offer to Iran in general terms, to deal with the lacuna of the NPT, rather than by ad hoc arrangements conceived individually (for example, in fuel assurance provisions).[13]

Broadly there are two policy options—engagement and regime change—each with limitations:

Engagement

Policy along these lines is designed to stop, delay, and reverse policies. Some believe that by freezing the program and buying time, the Iranians may reconsider their policies or another government might do so. This policy, which relies on diplomacy first adopted by the EU-3 and then continued by a broader coalition, seeks to convince Iran that the price for continuation of the quest for a nuclear option is too high. Sanctions are part of this dialogue. So are the incentives offered by the EU-3 in August 2005 in the package summarily rejected by Iran, a package now being renewed. In exchange for renouncing sensitive technology and increasing its transparency, Iran would be eligible for nonsensitive nuclear and other dual-use technology and be given trade and other opportunities.

For success this approach requires U.S. engagement and an Iranian government sensitive to costs and isolation and willing to make compromises and build trust. It implies a strategic decision in Tehran to forgo a nuclear weapons option. It also requires a combination of pressures and incentives that make such a decision more compelling.

The Russian proposal currently exemplifies the strengths and limitations of this approach. But an ad hoc technical fix, however attractive for the immediate problem, does nothing for the broader issue posed to the NPT regime by the potential proliferation of enrichment capabilities. More important, it does not address the key strategic issues of which the nuclear question is a part: Iran's broader role as a destabilizing force in the region opposed to the United States.

A technical fix, however, could be part of a sequence of steps that leads to a broader agreement that encompasses all aspects of Iran–U.S. relations. Like others suggested, such as building on the overlapping interests of Iran and the United States in Iraq, this approach depends for success on a willingness of *both* parties to engage with a view to an eventual *grand bargain*. In principle this appears the most logical solution, but it comes up against several obstacles. First, it is not self-evident that the driving force behind the nuclear program is national security in the narrow sense and therefore susceptible to security assurances. The current Iranian government does not wish to bargain but seeks to attain its capability to deter while accentuating its leverage vis-à-vis the United

States. Moreover, like the government that preceded it, it is convinced that any negotiation with the United States entails a slippery slope, in which one U.S. demand follows another, ending only with regime change. In May 2003 Iran was willing to negotiate such a grand bargain, but a perceived change in the balance of power and leverage, together with a new ideological government, makes a repetition of this in the near term improbable.

If, as I have argued, Iran feels threatened by the United States and seeks global recognition and domestic legitimation—and its quest for a nuclear capability reflects all three of these considerations—then the answer to its program is not technical or partial but comprehensive. It is worth sketching out what such a bargain might comprise.

Discussions dealing with specific issues of mutual concern such as Iraq could be used as icebreakers, but they will soon run up against the fact that everything in U.S.–Iran relations is related to everything else. Thus, progress on Iraq (where interests objectively converge) would be contingent on Iran being reassured about U.S. intentions toward Iran after Iraq is stabilized. Similarly, the United States would need to be reassured that Iran would change its policy against Israel and its support for terrorism, as well as forgo nuclear weapons. The United States might offer Iran the following incentives through an engagement policy:

- Full normalization of relations, including the lifting of sanctions and unfreezing of assets; this implies recognition of the Islamic Republic as a legitimately constituted state;

- Provision of access to technology (including dual use, with appropriate controls), conventional arms, and investment;

- Security guarantees, both against regime change and negative security assurances regarding nuclear weapons use; and

- Recognition of Iran's legitimate security and political interests and an end to efforts to contain Iran or otherwise block its regional relationships.

In exchange for offering these measures, the United States would insist that Iran:

- Renounce the closed fuel cycle and ratify the Additional Protocol;
- Cooperate on the stabilization of Iraq;
- End support for terrorists of whatever stripe, for whatever cause;
- End hostility toward the peace process and Israel, which implies any actions or rhetoric stimulating violence or hatred going beyond the accepted practice of diplomacy;
- Initiate discussions with neighbors about mutual security, including arms control with emphasis on missiles; and
- Perform better on human rights.

A grand bargain is unlikely as much due to U.S. reluctance as to Iran's. Washington today is unwilling to engage an "evil regime," giving it an undeserved legitimacy. Current U.S. policy, formulated as policy change on the Libyan model, is in fact to support regime opponents by extending radio broadcasts and assistance to NGOs and students. This may reflect a decision to increase pressure on Tehran rather than any realistic assessment of the regime's vulnerability to externally assisted destabilization. If so, it is a renunciation of a policy that has some chance of working for one that has virtually none.

Regime Change

If a technical fix only covers a narrow band of issues, indirect engagement is an uncertain recipe, and direct engagement is unacceptable, what remains? Regime change. Broadly, this approach is ideologically convenient and conceptually attractive; in one fell swoop repressive extremists are removed and with them the whole range of problems between Iran and the United States. The military option can be seen as a policy midway between engagement and regime change in that it could result in either delaying the program or acting as a precursor to regime change. However, although military strikes might delay the program, they may also act to solidify nationalist support and international sympathy for the regime, which could in turn drive an accelerated program further underground, blinding the international community as to its dimensions. Furthermore, even if the regime were destabilized or changed, there is no guarantee its successor would be less inclined to seek a weapons option.

However, if the problem is as much one of regime as technology, then a different regime, if more accountable, pluralistic, and transparent, would certainly be an improvement. First, such a regime would be more sensitive to its international standing and less insistent on acting as an Islamic revolutionary role model. Second, its moderation in foreign policy would give it less reason to seek a weapons option or for others to fear it. Such a regime may emerge in Iran spontaneously, but it also needs international encouragement.

In the event that current diplomacy fails, other issues arise, or Iran persists in its program, the United States will have to take the lead in containing Iran diplomatically and deterring it from gaining any benefit from an embryonic nuclear capability. This role might entail a range of measures from security assurances to the GCC states to theater missile defenses (TMD). Accentuating Iran's regional isolation through the weakening of Syria and the marginalization of extremist groups depends on the United States' broader diplomacy.

U.S. policy choices for the immediate future revolve around the diplomacy of persuasion. If the U.S. position in Iraq improves and with it its leverage, Washington should seriously consider a grand bargain. Even if this were proposed unilaterally and rejected by Tehran, it would serve to educate American and other citizens to the fact that the United States had gone as far as it could to settle the broad range of contentious issues peacefully.

Notes

Introduction

1. See Leonard Weiss, "Turning a Blind Eye Again?" *Arms Control Today*, March 2005, pp. 12–8; also David Albright and Corey Hinderstein, "Unravelling the AQ Khan and Future Proliferation Networks," *Washington Quarterly*, vol. 28, no. 2, May 2005, pp. 111–28.

2. This appears to confirm Brad Roberts' comment a decade earlier: "The inherently discriminatory character of non-proliferation mechanisms is incompatible with an era in which technology, industrial capability, and expertise are slowly spreading throughout the world. Permanent firebreaks between the haves and the have-nots will only fuel the ambitions of the have-nots to acquire what they have been denied." See Brad Roberts, "Arms Control and the End of the Cold War," *Washington Quarterly*, vol. 15, Autumn 1992, p. 45.

3. See William Walker, "Weapons of Mass Destruction and International Order," Adelphi Paper no. 370 (London: Oxford University Press for IISS, 2004).

4. Philip Stephens, "Breakdown in the Nuclear Family," *Financial Times*, May 13, 2005, p. 15.

5. The phrase is used by the UN Secretary-General's High-Level Panel on Threats, Challenges, and Change that reported in 2004. It is repeated by Secretary-General Kofi Annan, "In Larger Freedom: Decision Time at the UN," *Foreign Affairs*, vol. 84, no. 3, May/June 2005, p. 67.

6. Albert Wohlstetter, "Spreading the Bomb without Quite Breaking the Rules," *Foreign Policy*, no. 25, Winter 1976/1977, pp. 88–96, 145–79.

7. David Sanger, "Bush Seeks to Ban Some Nations from All Nuclear Technology," *New York Times*, March 15, 2005, http://www.nytimes.com.

8. Stephen Rademaker, Assistant Secretary of State for Arms Control, Statement to 2005 Nuclear Non-Proliferation Treaty Review Conference, New York, May 2, 2005, http://www.state.gov/t/ac/rls/rm/45518.htm.

9. For an excellent recent discussion, see Lawrence Scheinman, "Article IV of the NPT: Background, Problems, Some Prospects," in *The Weapons of Mass Destruction Commission Report*, no. 5, June 2005, http://www.wmdcommission.org/files/No5.pdf.

10. This was admitted by Hasan Rowhani recently in a speech at the Strategic Studies Center of the Expediency Council in his reflections on his experience as well as in the background of the crisis subsequently published as an article in the Iranian quarterly journal *Rahbod* and the newspaper *Etem'ad* (Tehran), February 23, 2006, in BBC Monitoring, February 26, 2006.

11. For a striking comment to this effect, see Ephraim Sneh and Graham Allison, "Nuclear Dangers in the Middle East: Threats and Responses," Policy Watch no. 995 (Washington, DC: Washington Institute for Near East Policy, May 18, 2005). See also Daniel Vernet, "Faut-il avoir peur de la bombe iranienne?" *Le Monde*, September 7, 2005, p. 15.

12. Kurt M. Campbell, Robert Einhorn, and Mitchell Reiss, eds., *The Nuclear Tipping Point: Why States Reconsider Their Nuclear Choices* (Washington, DC: Brookings Institution, 2004), p. 345. Einhorn and Campbell emphasize that the threshold to a decision to acquire technology for the nuclear weapons option is high, requiring determination and real effort.

Chapter One

1. Shahram Chubin, "Iran's Strategic Predicament," *Middle East Journal*, vol. 54, no. 1 (2000).

2. See, for example, the senior Ayatollah Fazel Lankarani, who observed that the basis for U.S. opposition to Iran's nuclear program lay in its hostility to "the essence of the Islamic revolution," and that for this reason its pressures must be resisted resolutely to safeguard the revolution and the country. Quoted in "Qom Ayatollahs Advise Minister on Domestic, Foreign Issues," *Iran* (Tehran), September 25, 2005, in BBC Monitoring, September 27, 2005.

3. Indian Foreign Minister Manmohan Singh commented at the UN that another nuclear power in the neighborhood was not desirable. See *Hindu*, "Iran Downplays Manmohan Singh's Remarks," September 18, 2005, http://www.hindu.com/the-hindu/holnus/001200509181428.htm.

4. Antoine Dudalu, "Asia's Alliance with the Middle East Threatens America," *Financial Times*, October 6, 2005, p. 15.

5. For background, see Shahram Chubin and Charles Tripp, "Iran-Saudi Arabia Relations and Regional Order," Adelphi Paper no. 304 (London: Oxford University Press for IISS, 1996).

6. Thus, see Iran's Supreme Leader Ali Khamenei's statement that "no policy can be implemented in the region without taking account of Iran's views." "Khamene'i Tells Commanders No Policy Made in Region without Iran," *Vision of the Islamic Republic of Iran (IRI) Network* (Tehran), vol. 1, October 13, 2004, in BBC Monitoring, October 14, 2004.

7. The new chief nuclear negotiator Ali Larijani is a believer in raw power politics, arguing that threats to Iran can only be removed "when Iran is powerful. The rest is small talk." Quoted in "Iranian Negotiator Gives Press Conference on Nuclear Issue," *Voice of Islamic Republic of Iran News Network* (Tehran), September 20, 2005, in BBC Monitoring, September 22, 2005.

8. Defense Minister Ali Shamkhani (until August 2005) quoted in Amir Taheri, "Eye of the Storm: The Buzz in Tehran," *Jerusalem Post Online*, May 19, 2005, http://www.jpost.com/servlet/Satellite?pagename=JPost/JPArticle/Printer&cid=1116 383.Hossein Mousavian also notes that far from feeling encircled Iran was given leverage. See Najmeh Bozorgmehr, "Interview with Hossein Mousavian," *Financial Times*, February 3, 2005, p. 6.

9. George Perkovich, Joseph Cirincione, Rose Gottemoeller, Jon B. Wolfsthal, and Jessica T. Mathews, *Universal Compliance: A Strategy for Nuclear Security* (Washington, DC: Carnegie Endowment, March 2005), p. 169.

10. See Hasan Rowhani, quoted in "Most Difficult Case," *Iran* (Tehran), February 21, 2005, in BBC Monitoring, February 24, 2005; Information Committee Director of the SNSC Ali Agha Mohammadi, quoted in "Official Says EU Aims to Delay Nuclear Talks until After Iranian Elections," Mehr News Agency (Tehran), April 27, 2005, in BBC Monitoring, April 28, 2005; and Mohammad Saidi, Deputy Director for Planning of the Atomic Energy Organization (AEO) for the Nationalization Comparison, quoted in "Iran to Resume Nuclear Activities in Esfahan—Atomic Official," May 9, 2005, in BBC Monitoring, May 10, 2005

11. See, respectively, Ali Akbar Salehi, Ambassador to the IAEA, quoted in "Envoy to IAEA Says Iran Enriching Uranium Takes 'Positive View' of NPT," *Iran*, July 27, 2003, in BBC Monitoring, July 28, 2003; and senior negotiator Hossein Mousavian, in Bozorgmehr, "Interview with Hossein Mousavian," p. 6.

12. Hasan Rowhani, Secretary of the Supreme National Security Council (SNSC), stated: "Being a revolutionary does not mean we must discard everything and put ourselves on the road to confrontation with the rest of the world." Quoted in "Iran Wants to Settle Its Nuclear Dossier at IAEA: Security Chief," Mehr News Agency (Tehran), March 10, 2005, in BBC Monitoring, March 12, 2005.

13. See Hasan Rowhani, quoted in "Iran Adopted Best Approach to Nuclear Issue, Rowhani Tells Governors," Iranian Labour News Agency (ILNA) (Tehran),

November 18, 2004, in BBC Monitoring, November 19, 2004; and Hasan Rowhani, quoted in "Iran Wishes to Continue Peaceful Nuclear Activities, Security Chief Says," *Iran* (Tehran), February 21, 2005, in BBC Monitoring, February 24, 2005.

14. Statement made by Rowhani, in "Iran Adopted Best Approach."

15. See Hasan Rowhani, "Iran's Security Chief Presents Report on NPT Protocol," *Iran* (Tehran), March 8, 2004, in BBC Monitoring, March 10, 2004.

16. The quote is from the former envoy to the IAEA, Ali Akbar Salehi, an MIT-educated nuclear physicist. See "Ex-envoy Says Iran to Make Own Decision on Possible Nuclear Deal," *Hemayat* (Tehran), August 31, 2004, in BBC Monitoring, September 3, 2004.

17. I have elaborated on these issues at greater length in the following sources. Shahram Chubin, "Whither Iran? Reform, Domestic Politics and National Security," Adelphi Paper no. 342 (London: Oxford University Press for IISS, 2002); Shahram Chubin, *Iran's National Security: Intentions, Capabilities, and Impact* (Washington, DC: Carnegie Endowment, 1994) and citations therein.

18. For a recent expression of this, see Defense Minister Ali Shamkhani, who alludes to the war with Iraq as a reason for Iran's quest for military self-sufficiency. Quoted in "Maximizing National Strength Is Our Agenda, Says Iranian Defence Minister," Mehr News Agency (Tehran), May 8, 2005, in BBC Monitoring, May 9, 2005. Supreme Leader Khamenei more colorfully argues that the blanket denial of technology has led to Iran becoming self-sufficient and standing on its own two feet. Quoted in "Iran: Khamene'i Tells Scientist Iran Should be Self-Sufficient," *Voice of the IRI Network* (Tehran), February 23, 2005, in BBC Monitoring, February 24, 2005.

19. See Khamenei's Friday lecture for all of these and related points, quoted in "Iranian Leader's Friday Sermon Praises Country's Progress, Denounces Israel," *Voice of the IRI Network*, November 5, 2004, in BBC Monitoring, November 6, 2004.

20. In running for president in May 2005, Hashemi Rafsanjani referred to "the vast and powerful Iran" that can "find a distinguished and lofty standing among the nations of the world, a status and standing which befits the civilized nation of Iran." Quoted in "Iran Press: Rafsanjani's Statement Outlines Reasons behind Candidacy Decision," *Iran*, May 11, 2005, in BBC Monitoring, May 14, 2005.

21. Hashemi Rafsanjani told Hans Blix that "the mere signing of a ban on nuclear weapons is not enough. In light of Iran's experience with Iraq it was evident that wherever the vital interests of a country were threatened, states could not obey international regulations." As summarized in FBIS-NES-90-216, November 7, 1990, pp. 50–1.

22. See Khamenei, "Khamene'i Tells Commanders." Other leaders share this view as well. Former Revolutionary Guards commander Mohsen Rezai says that in the next twenty years Iran would be the "centre of international power politics in the region," while former foreign minister and advisor to the Supreme Leader Ali Akbar Velayati asserts that since returning to its Islamic identity, Iran has become

"the most powerful country in the Middle East." See, respectively, "Iran to Play Key Role in Regional Power Politics—Expediency Council Secretary," *IRNA*, March 5, 2003, in BBC Monitoring, March 6, 2003; and "Velayati: Iran Most Powerful State in Middle East," *IRNA*, August 1, 2004, in BBC Monitoring, August 2, 2004.

23. Among many such statements, Khamenei said: "They are against progress in any backward country.... The arrogance [of the United States] is so impudent that it says that Iran does not need nuclear energy. What has this got to do with you? What right do you have to determine whether or not a nation has the right to use nuclear energy?" Quoted in "Leader Says Iran Will 'Punch' Anyone Who Threatens Its National Interests," *Vision of IRI Network 1* (Tehran), May 1, 2005, in BBC Monitoring, May 3, 2005. Iran has been saying much the same thing for the past ten years. See Shahram Chubin, "Does Iran Want Nuclear Weapons?" *Survival*, vol. 37, no. 1, Spring 1995.

24. See also Shahram Chubin, "Iran: The Lessons of Desert Storm," unpublished paper prepared for Los Alamos National Laboratory, November 1991; Charles Duelfer, report for corroboration of the lessons drawn by Iraq, *Comprehensive Report of the Special Advisor to the DCI on Iraq's WMD*, 30 September 2004, http://www.cia.gov/cia/reports/iraq_wmd_2004; David Johnston, "Saddam the Deceiver: A Phoney Arms Threat," *International Herald Tribune*, October 8, 2004; and Evelyn Leopold, "Inspector Says Saddam Wanted to Bluff Iran on Arms," *Reuters AlertNet*, May 25, 2005. Iran's emphasis on morale and improvisation in the Iraq war also led to the cultivation of asymmetrical strategies, including the use of terrorist proxies against the United States and France in Lebanon.

25. Quoted in Geoffrey Kemp and Selig Harrison, *India and America after the Cold War* (Washington, DC: Carnegie Endowment, 1993), p. 20.

26. Rafsanjani stated: "We thought of building missiles only after we were hit by them. We then started to build them from scratch." Quoted in "Ex-president Says Iran Can Launch Missiles with 2000-km Range," *IRNA* (Tehran), October 5, 2004, in BBC Monitoring, October 6, 2004. See also Chubin, *Iran's National Security*.

27. This was a lesson allegedly drawn by the North Koreans. See Philip Gourevitch, "Letter from Korea: Alone in the Dark," *New Yorker*, September 8, 2003, p. 68. Respected experts such as Lawrence Freedman also suggested that this was the lesson of Iraq for other proliferators: "The only apparently credible way to deter the armed forces of the U.S. is to own your own nuclear arsenal." See Lawrence Freedman, "A Strong Incentive to Acquire Nuclear Weapons," *Financial Times*, April 9, 2003, p. 15.

28. This is a continuing theme of the military. See, for example, Revolutionary Guards Commander Rahim Safavi quoted in "Iran: Guards Commander Says the Corps Is to Receive More Research Funding," *ILNA* (Tehran), December 15, 2004, in BBC Monitoring, December 16, 2004; and "Iran's Guards Commander Stresses

Importance of Persian Gulf Security," *ISNA* (Tehran), January 6, 2005, in BBC Monitoring, January 7, 2005.

29. Mohsen Rezai, quoted in "Iran: Senior Official Sure U.S. Will Attack Iran—Financial Times," *IRNA* (Tehran), June 21, 2002, in BBC Monitoring, June 22, 2002.

30. See, for example, the comments of the Deputy Guard's (IRGC) commander, Brigadier General Mohammed Bager Zolgadr, quoted in "Commander Says Iran Will Not Tolerate U.S. Presence in Region," *Fars* (Tehran), January 10, 2005, in BBC Monitoring, January 11, 2005. Also Admiral Abbas Mohtaj, Commander of the Iranian Navy, quoted in "Foreign Forces in Persian Gulf Present Threats to Iran, Says Navy Chief," *ISNA* (Tehran), January 12, 2005, in BBC Monitoring, January 13, 2005; and Defense Minister Ali Shamkhani, quoted in "Maximizing National Strength Is Our Agenda, Says Iranian Defence Minister," Mehr News Agency (Tehran), May 8, 2005, in BBC Monitoring, May 9, 2005.

31. See the discussion by a hard-line Iranian paper: "Iran Says American Nuclear Policy Threatening World Peace," *Resalat* (Tehran), March 16, 2002, in BBC Monitoring, March 25, 2002; and Hashemi Rafsanjani, quoted in "Iran: Rafsanjani Says U.S.A. Could Use Nuclear Weapons against 7 Countries," *Vision of the IRI Network 1* (Tehran), March 10, 2002, in BBC Monitoring, March 12, 2002; and "Iran: Rafsanjani Says Circumstances Will Change If Israel Accepts Arab Decision," *Voice of the IRI Network* (Tehran), March 29, 2002, in BBC Monitoring, March 30, 2002. In June 2002 Rafsanjani observed that "America is now talking very arrogantly to the world and by creating an 'axis of evil' order, is threatening any adverse country with nuclear bombs." Quoted in "Iran: Former President Rafsanjani Says U.S.A. 'Hegemonic Policies' Would Fail," *IRNA* (Tehran), June 27, 2002, in BBC Monitoring, June 28, 2002. For a report on U.S. appropriations of $27 million for mini-nukes, see "Plans for Nuclear Bomb Proof of U.S. New Outlook to Global Security—Iran TV," *Vision of the IRI Network 1* (Tehran), February 2, 2005, in BBC Monitoring, February 3, 2005.

32. "Iran: Rafsanjani says Tehran Ready to Cooperate if There Is Change in U.S. Policy," *Voice of the IRI Network* (Tehran), June 21, 2002, in BBC Monitoring, June 22, 2002.

33. Hashemi Rafsanjani, quoted in "Iran: Rafsanjani Says Washington Changing Tone after Failure of U.S.-Inspired Riot," *Voice of the IRI Network* (Tehran), August 1, 2003, in BBC Monitoring, August 2, 2003.

34. Hossein Mousavian, quoted in "Iran Senior Official Says U.S., Israel Will Not Attack Nuclear Installations," *ISNA* (Tehran), August 2, 2004, in BBC Monitoring, August 2, 2004.

35. See Ali Akbar Dareini, "Iran: Uranium Enrichment Plant Underground," Associated Press, http://abcnews.go.com/International/wireStory?id=558596.

36. Shamkhani stated that even a limited attack "will be regarded as an attack against the existence of the Islamic republic of Iran." Quoted in "Minister Says U.S. Incapable of Military Attack against Iran," *ILNA* (Tehran), July 22, 2004, in BBC

Monitoring, July 23, 2004. Brigadier General Mohammed Bager Zolgadr is quoted as saying that "Iran will not recognize any limit on defending itself...and will come down on the aggressor anywhere that it wills." See "Commander Says Attack on Iran Will Not Stay within Iranian Borders," *FARS* (Tehran), January 26, 2005, in BBC Monitoring, January 27, 2005; the Commander of the IRGC, Yahya Rahim Safavi, threatened U.S. forces, in *Al-Jazeera.net*, March 3, 2005; a March 29, 2005, *Al Hayat* report noted the threat to target U.S. bases in the region (translated by Middle East Media Research Institute, http://memri.org/). On the United States having no monopoly on preemption, see Ali Shamkhani's comments reported in "Iran Warns of Preemptive Strike to Prevent Attack on Nuclear Sites," *DOHA*, August 18, 2004; and Associated Press, "Iran Hints at Preemption over U.S. Threat," *International Herald Tribune*, August 20, 2004, 5.

37. See Thom Shanker, "Pentagon says Iraq Effort Limits Ability to Fight Other Wars," *New York Times*, May 3, 2005, http://nytimes.com/2005/05/3/politics/03 military.html.

38. See Sarah Chayes, "The Riots in Afghanistan: With a Little Help from Our Friends," *International Herald Tribune*, May 27, 2005, p. 8.

39. It is clear that Iran seeks to use the vulnerability of the United States and the United Kingdom in Iraq as a pressure point on the nuclear issue. See British allegations of Iran's supply of explosives to anti-British forces in southern Iraq through Hezbollah. See Christopher Adams and Roula Khalaf, "UK Accuses Iran over Iraqi Rebels," *Financial Times*, October 6, 2005, p. 5; and Christopher Adams and Edward Alden, "U.S. and UK Warn Iran and Syria on Terror," *Financial Times*, October 7, 2005, p. 5.

Chapter Two

1. Mohsen Rezai, Secretary of the Expediency Council, quoted in "Iran: Senior Official Comments on Ties with U.S., Majlis Polls, Nuclear Program," Website (Tehran), August 18, 2003, in BBC Monitoring, August 18, 2003.

2. See Mohammad Hossein Adeli, Iran's UK Ambassador, quoted in "Iran Has a Right to Develop Nuclear Power," *Financial Times*, February 18, 2005, p. 13. According to one Iranian official, unchecked domestic consumption is caused by price subsidies that entail waste on the order of $5 billion annually. See "Official Says Iran Energy Waste Five Billion Dollars," IRNA News Agency (Tehran), June 19, 2004, in BBC Monitoring, June 19, 2004.

3. The figures vary between 7,000 and 10,000 megawatts of electricity and ten to twenty reactors. See "Iran Experts Say Nuclear Power Necessary for Electricity Generation," *Vision of the Islamic Republic of Iran Network 1*, June 13, 2004, in BBC Monitoring, June 14, 2004; Chairman of the Majles Energy Committee quoted in "Majlis

Deputy Says Iran Needs Nine More Nuclear Power Plants," *Voice of the IRI Network* (Tehran), October 25, 2004, in BBC Monitoring, October 26, 2004; and "Iran Majlis Studying Proposals on Construction of 20 Nuclear Power Plants—MP," Mehr News Agency (Tehran), January 30, 2005, in BBC Monitoring, February 1, 2005.

4. Deputy Head of AEO Mohammad Saidi, quoted in "Nuclear Energy Top Priority in Iran's Nuclear Program—Official," *IRNA* (Tehran), March 22, 2005, in BBC Monitoring, March 23, 2005; and Elaine Sciolino, "Iran and the US Have One Thing in Common," *International Herald Tribune*, March 23, 2005, p. 4.

5. Not all observers are unsympathetic. University of California–Los Angeles Chancellor and nuclear expert Albert Carnesale has asked: "If you were building a nuclear power plant would you want to rely on Russia to provide the fuel for the next thirty years regardless of what your diplomatic relations were?" Leslie Evans, "UCLA Chancellor Carnesale on the Risks of Nuclear Attacks on the United States," UCLA International Institute, Los Angeles, May 18, 2005, http://www.isop.ucla.edu/article.asp?parentid=24561.

6. Ali Akbar Salehi, Iran's former IAEA envoy, quoted in "Envoy Says Iran Needs 10 Years to Produce Good Nuclear Fuel," *ISNA* (Tehran), October 7, 2003, in BBC Monitoring, October 7, 2003.

7. Mohammad Saidi, Deputy Head of the AEO, quoted in "Natanz Complex Achievement of Iranian Experts," *IRNA* (Tehran), March 30, 2005, in BBC Monitoring, March 31, 2005; and "Iran Press: On West's Opposition to Iran's Nuclear Fuel Cycle," *Afarinesh* (Tehran), May 14, 2005, in BBC Monitoring, May 25, 2005.

8. Hashemi Rafsanjani, quoted in "Ex-President Says Iran Not Seeking War, Ready to Negotiate," *IRNA* (Tehran), April 29, 2005, in BBC Monitoring, April 30, 2005.

9. Rowhani has said the world must accept Iran's entry into the global nuclear club, while Rafsanjani has said that Tehran expects to become a member of the club of countries possessing nuclear technology. Quoted, respectively, in "World Must Accept Iran's Entry into the Nuclear Club—Hasan Rowhani," *Vision of the IRI Network 1* (Tehran), March 7, 2004, in BBC Monitoring, March 8, 2004; and "Rafsanjani Says Iran Expected to Join Club of Nuclear States," *IRNA* (Tehran), December 3, 2004, in BBC Monitoring, December 4, 2004.

10. "Iran Press: Linking Nuclear Case and 'Holy Defence Week of Iran-Iraq War,'" *Jomhuri-ye Eslami* (Tehran), September 27, 2005, p. 1, in BBC Monitoring, September 29, 2005.

11. See Hasan Rowhani, quoted in "Iran: National Security Council Secretary Calls for Greater Global Interaction," *Vision of the IRI Network 2*, March 13, 2003, in BBC Monitoring, March 15, 2003; Hashemi Rafsanjani, quoted in "Iran: Rafsanjani Says Iran Does Not Want Nuclear Weapons," IRNA News Agency (Tehran), September 8, 2003, in BBC Monitoring, September 9, 2003; and Ali Khamenei, quoted in "Khamene'i Tells Prayer-Leaders Iran Does Not Possess Nuclear Weapons," *Voice of the IRI Network* (Tehran), October 6, 2003, in BBC Monitoring, October 7, 2003.

12. According to Rowhani, Iran is eighth in a list of thirteen states capable of manufacturing equipment needed in producing nuclear fuel. Quoted in "US Should Not Terrify World over Iran's Nuclear Activities—Security Chief," *IRNA* (Tehran), March 8, 2005, in BBC Monitoring, March 9, 2003. On the same theme of pride in the achievements, one Iranian commentator stated: "Today the same nation that was called barbarian by the West is proud and dignified and is one of the ten to fifteen countries that can run their native nuclear technology." See "Iranian Commentary Says Fundamentalism Part of Anti-Globalization Movement," *Keyhan* (Tehran), January 30, 2005, in BBC Monitoring, February 2, 2005.

13. Ali Khamenei, "Leader Says US, Europe Aim to Hinder Iran's Scientific Development," *Vision of the IRI Network 1* (Tehran), March 3, 2005, in BBC Monitoring, March 4, 2005.

14. The first comment is that of former Foreign Minister Ali Akbar Velayati, and the second is that of current Foreign Minister Kamal Kharrazi. Quoted in "Former Iranian Foreign Minister Says Europe Not to Be Trusted, Blair 'Bankrupt,'" *Jomhuri-ye Eslami Website* (Tehran), November 8, 2003, in BBC Monitoring, November 8, 2003; and "Iran's Kharrazi Says America 'Wise Enough' Not to Attack Iran," *IRNA* (Tehran), March 1, 2005, in BBC Monitoring, March 2, 2005.

15. There was a 20 percent fall in stocks between mid-July and October of 2005. For hard-line *Jomhuri-ye Eslami* (Tehran) reaction, see "Iran: Editorial Urges Government Action over 'Ailing' Stock Exchange," October 10, 2005, p. 1, in BBC Monitoring, October 13, 2005. A Western source put the plunge at 30 percent since late September 2005. See Nazila Fathi, "Iran's Stocks Plunge after Vote for UN Review of Nuclear Program," *New York Times*, October 9, 2005.

16. Bennett Ramburg argues that nuclear tension generates support for a failing regime, which might welcome confrontation as "political salvation." See Bennett Ramburg, "Dealing with Iran 11," *International Herald Tribune*, March 24, 2005.

17. For three such poll references, see "Iran Commentator Says 'Enemies' Will Accept Iranian Demands over Nuclear Issue," *Voice of the IRI Network* (Tehran), October 18, 2004, in BBC Monitoring, October 20, 2004; "Daily Says IAEA Case Aimed at 'Preoccupying' Iran, Deceiving Public," *Siyasat-e Ruz* (Tehran), November 29, 2004, in BBC Monitoring, December 14, 2004; "Iran Made 'Impressive' Progress in Nuclear Technology, Says Spokesman," Mehr News Agency (Tehran), January 14, 2005, in BBC Monitoring, January 15, 2005. Hasan Rowhani referred to access to nuclear technology as a "national demand" to his Japanese counterparts. Quoted in "No Government in Iran can Forgo Nuclear Technology—Senior Negotiator," Mehr News Agency (Tehran), May 11, 2005, in BBC Monitoring, May 12, 2005.

18. For a critique on lack of information, see "Iran Daily Urges Government to Inform Public on Nuclear Dossier Talks," *Aftab-e Yazd Website* (Tehran), March 5, 2005, in BBC Monitoring, March 6, 2005; see also the interview of Ray Takeyh by

Bernard Gwertzman, Council on Foreign Relations, March 2, 2005, http://www.cfr.org/publication/7885/takeyh.html.

19. Interview by Edmund Blair, "Tough Nuclear Choices Face Iran's Next President," June 14, 2005, http://www.swisspolitics.org/en/news/index.php?section=int&page=news_inhalt&news_id=5868315.

20. For a discussion, see Farideh Farhi, "To Have or Not to Have? Iran's Domestic Debate on Nuclear Options," in *Iran's Nuclear Weapons Options: Issues and Analysis*, ed. Geoffrey Kemp (Washington, DC: Nixon Center, 2001), pp. 35–54; Shahram Chubin and Robert Litwak, "Debating Iran's Nuclear Aspirations," *Washington Quarterly*, vol. 26, no. 4, Autumn 2003; on the national pride in the program, see also George Perkovich, "For Tehran, Nuclear Program Is a Matter of National Pride," *Yale Global Online,* March 21, 2005, http://yaleglobal.yale.edu/article.print?id=5448.

21. For intraregime differences, see Safa Haeri, "Iran, US: Fissures within Fissures," *Asia Times*, http://www.atimes.com/atimes/printN.html; Kenneth Pollack and Ray Takeyh, "Taking on Tehran," *Foreign Affairs*, March/April 2005, http://www.foreignaffairs.org/20050301faessay84204/kenneth-pollack-ray-takeyh/taking-on-tehran.html.

22. For striking parallels with Iran between conservatives and realists in North Korea divided at the time of the Agreed Framework, see Joel Wit, Daniel Poneman, and Robert Galluci, *Going Critical: The First North Korean Crisis* (Washington, DC: Brookings Institution, 2004), pp. 75–6.

23. In the view of reformist Mohammad Reza Khazemi, leader of the main reform party and brother of outgoing President Khatami, see "Taboo of US Relations Turned on Its Head," *Iran Mania*, June 8, 2005, http://www.iranmania.com/News/ArticleView/Default.asp?ArchiveNews=Yes&NewsCode=32367&NewsKind=CurrentAffairs.

24. See, respectively, Mostafa Moin's speech to the Ghazvin Medical University, quoted in "Moin: If Elected as President, I Will Stop the Uranium Enrichment," *Keyhan*, April 19, 2005, in BBC Monitoring, April 21, 2005; Mohsen Rezai, quoted in "Iran Presidential Candidate Reza'i Says He Will Resume Nuclear Enrichment," *Vision of the IRI Network 1* (Tehran), June 5, 2005, in BBC Monitoring, June 6, 2005; Ali Larijani, "Presidential Candidate Larijani Calls for Nuclearization of Iran," *Vision of the IRI Network 1* (Tehran), June 2, 2005, in BBC Monitoring, June 4, 2005. Larijani characterized the Tehran agreement between Iran and the EU-3 in October 2003, which postponed referral of Iran's nuclear file to the UNSC in exchange for suspension of fuel cycle activities, as the lamentable exchange of "candy for a pearl."

25. Mohammad Bager Qalibaf, quoted in "Iran Election Program: Qalibaf Hints at Developing Ties with USA," *Vision of the IRI Network 1* (Tehran), June 4, 2005, in BBC Monitoring, June 5, 2005.

26. "Conservatives Will Win Iranian Presidency if Rafsanjani Does Not Run— Rowhani," Mehr News Agency (Tehran), February 2, 2005, in BBC Monitoring, February 3, 2005.

27. For the five postelection pledges to the nation, see "Iran Press: Rafsanjani Outlines Five Post-Election Pledges to Nation," *Iran* (Tehran), May 31, 2005, in BBC Monitoring, June 2, 2005; and "Iran Election Program: Rafsanjani Announces Manifesto," *Vision of IRI Network 2*, May 31, 2005, in BBC Monitoring, June 1, 2005. For the evolution of Hashemi Rafsanjani toward pragmatism and national interest, see Sana Vakil, "Reformed Rafsanjani Could Be Force for Change," *Financial Times*, June 16, 2005, p. 13.

28. "Iran Press: Daily Says Next President Must Promote Nuclear Technology Firmly," *Jomhuri-ye Eslami* (Tehran), May 15, 2005, pp.1–2, in BBC Monitoring, May 18, 2005.

29. Ali Larijani referred to the desire to keep Iran an industrial backwater and a pattern of denial of advanced information as well as biological and nanotechnology. Ari Larijani, interview, *Financial Times*, January 23, 2006, p. 4.

30. For a hard-line newspaper view, see "The Nature of Political Crises and Iran's Nuclear Problem," *Jomhuri-ye Eslami* (Tehran), December 1, 2005, in BBC Monitoring, December 28, 2005.

31. Reformist Ahmad Shirzad presents a thoughtful discussion along these lines, noting that Iranians need to define "what is it that [they] require from the outside world and ... what sort of system and regime do [they] wish to be?" Quoted in "Iran Press Criticizes Government's Use of 'Threats' in Foreign Policy," *E'temad* (Tehran), December 25, 2005, in BBC Monitoring, January 5, 2006.

32. See "Critics of Nuclear Policy Must Be Allowed to Express Views," *Aftab-e Yazd*, December 3, 2005, in BBC Monitoring, December 14, 2005.

33. The conservatives believe that an enhanced nuclear capability would affect this regional role and that "the enemy would not like Iran to play such a role." See Hasan Rowhani, quoted in "Iran Needs to Counter 'Multi-Dimensional' Threat from West," *IRNA*, January 14, 2006. On the impact of an advanced nuclear program in the region, Rowhani comments: "They [the United States] believe that Iran's standing will change in the region if it acquires the capability to enrich uranium," something they wish to prevent. Quoted in "Iran's Regional Standing Is Source of Concern to USA—Former Security Chief," Iran Fars News Agency (Tehran), December 15, 2005, in BBC Monitoring, December 16, 2005.

34. For some, the interlude between the Iran–Iraq war and the current period has resulted in backsliding in foreign policy, which is seen as the renunciation of the export of the revolution. See Naser Bahramirad, "Foreign Policy: Active or Inactive?" *Keyhan*, December 18, 2005, in BBC Monitoring, December 21, 2005. For background on the new conservative government, see Ali Gheissari and Vali Nasr, "The Conservative Consolidation in Iran," *Survival*, vol. 47, no. 2, Summer 2005, pp.

175–90. Also Kazem Alamdari, "The Power Structure of the Islamic Republic of Iran," *Third World Quarterly*, vol. 26, no. 8, 2005, pp. 1285–1301. For the background to the Isargaran, the political party supporting Ahmadinejad, see William Abbas Sami'I, "The Changing Landscape of Party Politics in Iran—A Case Study," *Vaseteh: The Journal of the European Society for Iranian Studies*, vol.1, no.1, Winter 2005.

35. For press analysis sympathetic to this view, see "Iran Daily Supports Ahmadinejad's 'Active' Diplomacy," *Keyhan*, January 7, 2006, in BBC Monitoring, January 11, 2006; unattributed commentary. "We Have Preconditions," *Jomhuri-ye Eslami*, December 29, 2005, in BBC Monitoring, December 30, 2005; "Daily Says Iran 'Great Opportunity for Europe' in Nuclear Talks," *Tehran Times*, December 20, 2005, in BBC Monitoring, December 21, 2005.

36. Larijani made these comments to IRGC commanders. Quoted in "Larijani—Now Is the Time for Resistance," *Farhang-e Ashti*, November 30, 2005, in BBC Monitoring, December 12, 2005. On Iran's geopolitical position, see "Iran's Security Chief Explains Tehran's Nuclear Strategy in TV Interview," *Vision of IRI Network 2* (Tehran), January 1, 2006, in BBC Monitoring, January 3, 2006.

37. "US Firms Not Welcomed to Join Iran's Enrichment Plan—Larijani," Mehr News Agency, December 13, 2005, in BBC Monitoring, December 14, 2005.

38. Larijani in September 2005 press conference, quoted in Nazila Fathi and Michael Slackman, "Iran's President Rolls Back Clock," *International Herald Tribune*, December 21, 2005, p. 4.

39. Indicative of this was Larijani, who argued that Iran was the key to the area for Russia, which has other more important regional concerns than nuclear proliferation. See Ali Larijani, quoted in "Iran's Security Chief Explains Tehran's Nuclear Strategy in TV Interview," *Vision of IRI Network 2* (Tehran), January 1, 2006, in BBC Monitoring, January 3, 2006. Larijani was clearly and explicitly corrected by Russian Foreign Minister Sergey Lavrov, who pointedly rebutted this assertion, noting that for Russia non-proliferation took precedence over any bilateral considerations or economic advantages in relations with Iran. See *International Herald Tribune*, "EU Nations Want Iran Taken to the UN," January 13, 2006, pp.1–4.

40. "Iran's Rafsanjani Defends Nuclear 'Right,' Calls for Prudence," *Vision of IRI Network 1* (Tehran), January 11, 2006, in BBC Monitoring, January 12, 2006; and "New Government Depicts 'Harsh Image' of Iran—Rowhani," Fars News Agency (Tehran), November 15, 2005, in BBC Monitoring, November 17, 2005.

41. "Rafsanjani Warns US against Military Attack on Iran," *Voice of the IRI Network* (Tehran), September 30, 2005, in BBC Monitoring, October 1, 2005.

42. President Ahmadinejad is quoted as saying: "Some individuals are disgruntled because they can no longer gain access to the State Treasury. They therefore seek excuses by raising other issues [alleging] ... that the government is ignorant of conducting foreign policy." See "President Calls on 'Monopolizers of Power' to Step

Aside," *Voice of IRI Network* (Tehran), December 1, 2005, in BBC Monitoring, December 2, 2005. See also A. Savyon, "The Second 'Islamic Revolution': Power Struggle at the Top," *MEMRI*, no. 253, November 17, 2005.

43. See Michael Slackman, "In Iran, Dissenting Voices Rise on Its Leaders Nuclear Strategy," *International Herald Tribune*, March 16, 2006, p. 4; and Karl Vick, "In Iran, Even Some on the Right Warning against Extremes, Conservative Factions Fear Radicalism," *Washington Post*, March 27, 2006, p. A11.

44. For a useful if broad discussion, see Amir Ali Nourbaksh, "Iran's Foreign Policy and Its Key Decisionmakers," Tharwa Project, April 18, 2005, http://www.tharwaproject.com/English/index.php?option=com_keywords&task=view&id=2017&Itemid=0; and Mohsen Sazegara, "Iran: Toward a Fourth Republic?" Policy Watch no. 1001 (Washington, DC: Washington Institute for Near East Policy, 2005).

45. "Iranian Paper Views Delay to Nuclear Deal with Russia, 'Snub' to UK," *Iran* (Tehran), February 27, 2005, in BBC Monitoring, February 28, 2005; Hashemi Rafsanjani, quoted in "Ex-President Rafsanjani Says Iran Will Not Submit to Bullying on Nuclear Issue," *ISNA* (Tehran), September 15, 2004, in BBC Monitoring, September 16, 2004. One Iranian commentator said that "one must accept that the nuclear file is one that is entirely national and ultimately related to the country's national security." See "Iran Press: Commentary Says Iran's Nuclear File 'National Challenge,'" *Iran* (Tehran), April 6, 2005, in BBC Monitoring, April 14, 2005.

46. For example, negotiator Hossein Mousavian commented: "Now it is time [for Europe] to deliver something to Iranian public opinion and nation." Hossein Mousavian, interview by Najmjeh Bozorgmehr and Daniel Dombey, *Financial Times*, February 3, 2005, p. 10.

47. Hossein Mousavian, quoted in "Iranian Negotiator, Legislator Comment on Nuclear Dossier," *Aftab-e Yazd Website* (Tehran), April 13, 2005, in BBC Monitoring, April 14, 2005. An article in *Resalat* asserted that "Anyone who takes over in this election will not want to move against the peoples' interest and the people will not allow him to do so either." See "Iran Press: On Characteristics Required of Next President," *Resalat* (Tehran), May 22, 2005, p. 1, in BBC Monitoring, May 25, 2005.

48. See Foreign Minister Kharrazi's comment on May 4, 2005, in Dafna Linzer, "Iran Says Nuclear Plans on Hold: Leaders Are Frustrated, But Still Hope for Progress in Talks," *Washington Post*, May 5, 2005, p. A22. For a British diplomat's observation on how hard-line pressure translates into tough rhetoric in the negotiations, see Roger Wilkison, "EU Diplomats: Iran Risks Sanctions for Nuclear Activity," *Voice of America*, May 10, 2005, http://www.voanews.com/english/archive/2005-05/2005-05-10-voa34.cfm?CFID=46290374&CFTOKEN=56257987.

49. See Gareth Smyth, "Nuclear Dispute Boosts Critics of 'Great Satan' in Iran Poll," *Financial Times*, March 21, 2005, p. 7; and Gareth Smyth and Daniel Dombey, "EU3 Warns of 'Managed Crisis' over Iran Ambitions," *Financial Times*, May 1, 2005.

50. For Rowhani's take on the unbalanced nature of the commitments, see "Iran to Definitely Resume Part of Its Nuclear Activities in 'Near Future,'" *IRI News Network* (Tehran), May 12, 2005, in BBC Monitoring, May 14, 2005. On the costs of suspension and technical problems caused, see AEO head Reza Aghazadeh, quoted in "Iran's Atomic Energy Chief Says Suspension of Uranium Enrichment Problematic," *ISNA* (Tehran), December 12, 2003, in BBC Monitoring, December 12, 2003. On the retention of personnel indispensable for further progress in the nuclear area, see Reza Aghazadeh, "Iranian Officials Discuss Ways to Retain Nuclear Scientists," Sharq website (Tehran), December 16, 2004, in BBC Monitoring, December 20, 2004; and Mohammad Khatami, "President Khatami Says Iran Ready to Produce Fuel for Nuclear Plant," *Voice of IRI Network* (Tehran), March 31, 2005, in BBC Monitoring, April 1, 2005.

51. See the discussion of one nuclear expert, quoted in "Cessation of Iran's Enrichment Program Not an Option—Agency," *Baztab Website* (Tehran), March 30, 2005, in BBC Monitoring, April 1, 2005.

52. Hossein Shariatmadri is quoted as saying: "Whatever is going to happen after five years of suspension is going to happen now." And the right wing prefers to withdraw from the NPT altogether. See Scott Peterson, "Mixed Signals on Iran's Nuclear Program," *Christian Science Monitor*, June 14, 2005, http://www.csmonitor.com/2005/0614/p06s02-wome.html.

53. For a critique of Iran's dysfunctional rhetoric and negotiating style, see "Iran Reformist Criticizes Iran Officials for Policy toward EU," *Aftab-e Yazd* (Tehran), October 16, 2004, pp.1, 2, in BBC Monitoring, October 18, 2004; and "Daily Urges Iranian Officials to Make Prompt Nuclear Decision," *Aftab-e Yazd* (Tehran), February 21, 2005, in BBC Monitoring, February 22, 2005.

54. For a useful analysis, see Farideh Farhi, "Iran's Nuclear File: The Uncertain Endgame," *Middle East Report Online,* October 24, 2005, http://www.merip.org/mero/mero102405.html.

55. These revelations were picked up in the West. See Mousavian's comments about a "dual strategy" reported in "Iranian Ex-Envoy Says Country Used 'Dual Strategy' in Nuclear Talks with EU," *Die Welt*, Berlin, August 18, 2005, in BBC Monitoring, August 19, 2005; and Rowhani's statement about "cooperating to a minimum extent, in order to suspend our activities as little as possible." See Robert Nolan, "Iran and the EU-3," *Foreign Policy Association*, August 4, 2005, http://www.fpa.org/newsletter_info2583/newsletter_info_sub_list.htm?section=Iran%20and%20the%20EU-3.

56. For an exception, see Gareth Smyth, "Call for Openness over Nuclear Program," *Financial Times*, October 14, 2005, http://financialtimes.printthis.clickability.com/pt/cpt?action=cpt+%F+W.

57. For example, such technical fixes might include fuel guarantees, limited numbers of centrifuges in stages, or multinational schemes for enrichment. See

Brent Scowcroft and Daniel Poneman, "An Offer That Iran Cannot Refuse," *Financial Times*, March 9, 2005, p. 13; and Tim Guldiman and Bruno Pellaud, "A Plan to Bring about Nuclear Restraint in Iran," *Financial Times*, June 27, 2005, p. 15.

58. Gary Milhollin, testimony before Committee on Foreign Relations, U.S. Senate, May 19, 2005, http://www.iranwatch.org/Gary/sfr-milhollin-051905.htm. For more details on the intrusiveness of the inspections that would require "anyplace, anytime, anywhere" access, see http://www.iranwatch.org.

59. This proposal has floated around the negotiations and is well presented by Joseph Cirincione, interview by Bernard Gwertzman, Council on Foreign Relations, June 6, 2005, http://www.cfr.org.

60. U.S. President George W. Bush, speech delivered at the National Defense University (NDU), Washington, DC, February 11, 2004. Note, however, that the Bush approach is selective; it tolerates new enrichment by Brazil but not by Iran.

Chapter Three

1. I am indebted to Shai Feldman for emphasizing this.

2. This narcissism is visible in debates in Iran that often appear to reflect the belief that the whole world is concentrated on watching Iran and its development and to exaggerate the importance of Iran to others. President Ahmadinejad's speech to the United Nations in September 2005 seemed to be intended for a domestic audience and showed a misreading of what General Assembly speeches are about.

3. Notably, Iran's current urgent insistence on an enrichment capability for its power generation program is by no means a necessity, especially when the first reactor at Bushire is not yet operational. A second 40-megawatt heavy water reactor in Arak is "larger than needed for research but too small to make electricity and just right for producing bomb-quality plutonium." See Gary Milhollin, Director of the Wisconsin Project on Nuclear Arms Control, testimony before the Committee on Foreign Relations, U.S. Senate, May 19, 2005. See also the evidence compiled in Bureau of Verification and Compliance, "Adherence to and Compliance with Arms Control, Non-Proliferation and Disarmament Agreements and Commitments" (Washington, DC: U.S. State Department, 2005), pp. 72–80. Iran's insistence on the full fuel cycle makes little sense if it is intended to avoid dependence, for Iran will, in any case, need to import the raw uranium, which it does not possess in any quantity. The fact that the program was undeclared also suggests an illegal intent.

4. The IAEA has documented Iran's experiments with polonium, a specialized material that can serve as a neutron initiator in fission bombs. Iran is also known to have sought high-precision switches that can trigger a nuclear explosion.

5. Besides the questions relating to origin of the contamination of some sites and full history relating to P1 and P2 centrifuge technology, for the first time the IAEA noted unanswered questions about the "role of the military" in this peaceful program and documents "related to the fabrication of nuclear weapons components." See IAEA Director-General, "Implementation of the Nuclear Safeguards Agreement in the Islamic Republic of Iran," GOV/2006/15 (Vienna: IAEA, Board of Governors, February 27, 2006), paras. 18, 19, and 38.

6. Apparently it was the first time there was a bomb design available on the open market. See William J. Broad and David E. Sanger, "Unraveling Pakistan's Nuclear Web: Inquiry into Khan Hobbled by Discord and Concern over Ally," *International Herald Tribune*, December 27, 2004, p. 11. U.S. officials are all but certain that Iran received the same bomb designs as Libya: "We assume that the Iranians got what the Libyans got. Can we prove it? Not yet." David Sanger, "U.S. Demand Deepens Gulf with Iran over Nuclear Facilities," *New York Times*, http://nytimes.com/2005/05/03/international/middle east/03npt.html. Iranian leaders have carefully distinguished their purchases from that of Libya, saying that Iran sought only the parts but not the design for the production of bombs. "Had we attempted to develop nuclear arms, we would also have tried to attain the design for the bomb," stated Hasan Rowhani. Quoted in "Chief Negotiator Says Iran Has Not Imported Nuclear Parts," IRNA News Agency (Tehran), June 2, 2004, in BBC Monitoring, June 3, 2004. The clear implication is that if proof of Iran's acquisition of these bomb plans comes to light, it would constitute the smoking gun regarding Iran's weapons intentions.

There are many summaries of Iran's nuclear program apart from the eight IAEA reports (since February 2003). Seven of these reports can be found in the British Foreign Office document. Besides the IISS dossier, the most authoritative and comprehensive analyses include those by the Federation of Atomic Scientists (FAS) and Tony Cordesman (2004). For periodic assessments, see Sharon Squassoni, "Iran's Nuclear Program: Recent Developments," CRS Report for Congress (Washington, DC: Congressional Research Service, March 4, 2004); Esther Pan, "Iran: European Nuclear Negotiations" (New York: Council on Foreign Relations, April 14, 2005), http://www.cfr.org/publication/8075/iran.html. See also Ephraim Asculai, "Taking Stock of Iran's Nuclear Program," *Tel Aviv Notes,* JCSS no. 128, March 8, 2005. See also the interview with Iran's senior nuclear negotiator, Hasan Rowhani, who stated, "Technologically, [Iran has] obtained the nuclear fuel cycle." Rowhani said that Iran has the capacity, relying on its own uranium mine and resources, to turn the ore into yellowcake, to convert the yellowcake into UF4 and UF6, and to enrich the UF6 through centrifuges to a level of 3.5 percent. In the zirconium plant in Isfahan, Iran can turn the enriched uranium into tablets that will be used as fuel for reactors. Therefore, if Iran wants to produce fuel for a reactor, it has all the means, from the ore stage to turning the enriched material into tablets and inserting them into fuel rods. See MEMRI, TV Monitor Project, Clip no. 412, December 7, 2004, http://memritv.org/Transcript.asp?P1=412.

7. Sirus Naseri, Iranian nuclear negotiator, interview, quoted in "Iran to Put Forward Final Nuclear Proposal in Less than Three Months—Negotiator," *Vision of IRI Network 2* (Tehran), March 13, 2005, in BBC Monitoring, March 16, 2005.

8. U.S. intelligence on Iran's program is known to be deficient, "scandalously" so, according to one source. See the report on U.S. intelligence by Laurence Silberman and Charles Robb, "Data Is Lacking on Iran's Arms, U.S. Panel Says," *New York Times*, March 9, 2005, http://www.nytimes.com/2005/03/09/international /09weapons.html. Estimates, then, vary among analysts: see International Institute for Strategic Studies, *Iran's Strategic Weapons Programs: A Net Assessment* (London: Routledge, 2005); Vice Admiral Lowell Jacoby, Director of Defense Intelligence Agency, "Current and Projected National Security Threats to the U.S.," testimony before Senate Select Committee on Intelligence, February 16, 2005. For a later disputed estimate of a longer, ten-year period, see Dafna Linzer, "Iran Is Judged Ten Years from a Nuclear Bomb," *Washington Post*, August 2, 2005, p. A01; and Steven Weissman and Douglas Jehl, "Estimate Revised on When Iran Could Make a Nuclear Bomb," *New York Times*, August 3, 2005.

9. Tony Cordesman has said that "there is virtually no technical justification for building them unless you are going to put a nuclear warhead on them." Interview with Tony Cordesman, VOA News, May 20, 2005, http://www.voanews.com/english/2005-05-20-voa62.cfm. U.S. Secretary of State Colin Powell indicated that U.S. intelligence had information that Iran sought to adapt its missiles for the delivery of nuclear weapons (December 2004). U.S. sources indicate their interception under the Proliferation Security Initiative (PSI) of dual-use missile technology bound for Iran. Davis Sanger, "U.S. Shares Details on Efforts to Intercept Weapons Technology," *International Herald Tribune*, June 1, 2005, p. 4. President Bush alluded to a dozen interceptions of missile-related technology to Iran under the PSI. See President George W. Bush, speech delivered at National Endowment for Democracy, October 6, 2005, http://www.whitehouse.gov/news/releases/2005/10/20051006-3.html.

10. See the discussion in Shahram Chubin, "Whither Iran? Reform, Domestic Politics and National Security," Adelphi Paper no. 342 (London: Oxford University Press for IISS, 2002).

11. Defense Minister Ali Shamkhani, quoted in "Missile Technology Most Important Part of Iran's Military Deterrent—Minister," Mehr News Agency (Tehran), February 26, 2005, in BBC Monitoring, February 27, 2005. Sometimes missile technology is used as a metaphor. Shamkhani has suggested that Iran would mass produce missiles like a popular automobile (the Peykan) and that "the production of the Shihab-3 will never stop. There is [a] Shihab-3 missile embedded in every Iranian." Quoted in "Minister Says Iran Not Targeting U.S. Power Facilities," *ILNA* (Tehran), May 5, 2005, in BBC Monitoring, May 6, 2005.

12. Iran reported success in a test of a solid-fuel missile, which would increase their range and improve their shelf life. See "Iran Tests New Missile Using Solid-Fuel Technology—Agency," IRNA (Tehran), May 31, 2005, in BBC Monitoring, June 1, 2005. See also "Iran Reports Gain in Test of Missile Fuel," New York Times, June 1, 2005, http://www.nytimes.com/2005/06/01/international/middleeast/01iran.html.

13. Iran acknowledges possessing a maritime cruise missile program. See Robert Hewson, "Iran Ready to Field Cruise Missile," Janes Defence Weekly, February 25, 2004, p. 13.

14. See Chubin, "Whither Iran?" Iran also emphasizes short-range missiles such as anti-ship missiles for defense in the Gulf. Iran is reported to have purchased cruise missiles from Ukraine in 2004.

15. See International Herald Tribune, "Iranians Test Missile with Multiple War-heads," April 2006, p. 5; and "Iran Claims New Success with Underwater Missile," April 3, 2006, p. 10.

16. Iran has indulged in diplomatic ploys deflecting pressure away from its missile program by asking the UN Secretary-General for reports on "missiles in all their aspects" for two consecutive years. Iran has not joined the Hague Code of conduct regarding missiles. Foreign Minister Kamal Kharrazi justified Iran's need for missiles for defense purposes but added that "ours are not for first use." Quoted in "Iran Wants Sanctions Lifted before 'Rigorous' Inspections of Nuclear Sites," Star (Johannesburg), July 22, 2003, in BBC Monitoring, July 22, 2003.

17. Dov Raviv, father of the Israeli Arrow project, has suggested this response. Ha'aretz (Tel Aviv), June 4, 1998, in BBC ME/3246MED/7, June 6, 1998.

18. The U.S. government reportedly has documented evidence suggesting that Iran is attempting to develop a nuclear weapon payload for its medium-range Shi-hab-3 missile. The United States shared this information with the IAEA. See "U.S. Gives IAEA Info on Iranian Missile Capable of Carrying Nuclear Warhead," Wall Street Journal, July 27, 2005, p. A3. See also "Washington accuse L'Iran d'etudes sur un charge nucleaire pour missile," Le Monde, October 11, 2005, p. 6.

19. Nur Pir-Mozen, a Majles Deputy and nuclear specialist, observed that after many years and repeated questions about the technological situation and after the expenditure of millions of dollars, "we still do not know what has been going on in Bushire for the past thirty years." Quoted in "Majles Deputy Questions Spending on Nuclear Power Plant," Mardom-Salari (Tehran), October 5, 2005, p. 11, in BBC Monitoring, October 7, 2005.

20. Quoted in Judith Yaphe and Charles Lutes, "Reassessing the Implications of a Nuclear Iran," McNair Paper no. 69 (Washington, DC: National Defense University, 2005), p. 6.

21. See also Bill Sami'i, "The Military-Mullah Complex: The Militarization of Iranian Politics," Weekly Standard, May 14, 2005; and Mohsen Sazegara, "The New

Iranian Government: Resurrecting Past Errors," Policy Watch no. 1013 (Washington, DC: Washington Institute for Near East Policy, July 2005.)

22. Notably, they paraded captured British troops, who had allegedly strayed into Iranian territory in a provocative manner, blindfolded, reminiscent of the U.S. embassy hostages. Later they closed a new airport that they believed should not be under contract to a Turkish company that might have had ties with Israel.

23. For speculative comments on chain of command and "safety culture," see Gregory Giles, "The Islamic Republic of Iran and Nuclear, Biological and Chemical Weapons," in *Planning the Unthinkable*, ed. Peter Lavoy, Scott Sagan, and James Wirtz (Ithaca/London: Cornell University Press, 2000), pp. 98–103.

24. For a recent discussion, see Daniel Byman, "Confronting Syrian-Backed Terrorism," *Washington Quarterly*, vol. 28, no. 3, Summer 2005, pp. 99–113, esp.101–03, 108, 110–11.

25. Paul Bracken, "The Second Nuclear Age," *Foreign Affairs*, vol. 79, no. 1, January/February 2000.

26. See Sara Daly, John Parachini, and William Rosenau, "Aum Shinrikyo, Al Qaida, and the Kinshasa Reactor: Implications of Three Case Studies for Combating Nuclear Terrorism" (Santa Monica, CA: RAND Project Air Force, 2005).

27. See *The 9/11 Commission Report: Final Report of the National Commission on Terrorist Attacks upon the United States* (New York: W.W. Norton, 2004), p. 334.

28. Bush, speech to the National Endowment for Democracy, October 6, 2005, http://www.whitehouse.gov/news/releases/2005/10/20051006-3.html. Bush said that the United States would make no distinction between those who committed acts of terrorism and those who supported them, referring to Iran and Syria.

29. See, for example, Robert McMahon, "U.S. Says Iran 'Most Active' State Sponsor of Terrorism," RFE/RL, April 28, 2005, http://www.rferl.org/featuresarticleprint/2005/04af8904ce-0073-4cf4-bb19-aad24016373.

30. Senator Richard Lugar (R-IN), "Iran: Weapons Proliferation, Terrorism and Democracy," opening statement of Committee on Foreign Relations Hearing, Washington, DC, May 19, 2005, p. 1, http://foreign.senate.gov/testimony/2005/LugarStatement050519.pdf.

31. The quote from a Homeland Security report is found in Eric Lipton, "A Rosier View of Terror-List Nations," *International Herald Tribune*, April 1, 2005, p. 5.

32. For a discussion and citations, see Chubin, "Whither Iran?" For a similar view, see "Iran's Terrorist Sponsorship: Winding Down?" IISS: *Strategic Comments*, vol. 11, no. 2, March 2005.

33. Matthew Levitt, "Iranian State Sponsorship of Terror: Threatening U.S. Security, Global Stability and Regional Peace," testimony before Joint Hearing of Committee on International Relations, Subcommittee on the Middle East and Central Asia and Subcommittee on International Terrorism and Non-Proliferation, U.S. House of Representatives, February 16, 2005, http://www.washingtoninstitute.org/

html/pdf/Iran-Testimony-2-16-05.pdf. See also, Bill Sami'i, "A Look at Iran's Sponsorship of Terror Groups," http://www.rferl.org/featuresarticleprint/2005/01/347a2c5f-088a-408-a632-d5fc648046.

34. See *Economist*, "Lebanon: Time for Syria to Go," February 26, 2005, p. 10.

35. Velayati was personally indicted by a German court in the *Mykonos* case. *E'temad Website* (Tehran), May 1, 2005. Hezbollah official Seyyed Mohammad Bager Kharrazi, quoted in "Iran's Hezbollah Leader Warns to Set World Ablaze, No Place Safe for Americans," *Farhang-e Ashti*, January 31, 2005, in BBC Monitoring, February 1, 2005.

36. Allison Graham, *Nuclear Terrorism: The Ultimate Preventable Catastrophe* (New York: Times Books, 2004), p. 120.

37. See *9/11 Commission Report*, pp. 47–70, 240–1. See also *Economist*, "Still Haunting America," July 24, 2004, pp. 38–9.

38. Iranian officials argue that this was not their aim and that the decision to keep Al Qaeda members under house arrest and close surveillance in Iran was meant to keep them as hostages and a warning to Al Qaeda not to target Iranian cities. Author's interviews with Iranian officials, Geneva, May 2005. More plausible in my view is the explanation noted earlier of "keeping options open" for bargaining, together with the strong influence of hard-liners in the Security apparatus.

39. British allegations echo one by the United States a month earlier. See Christopher Adams and Roula Khalaf, "UK Accuses Iran over Iraqi Rebels," *Financial Times*, October 6, 2005, p. 5; and Alan Cowell, "Blair Suspects Iran Aids Insurgents," *International Herald Tribune*, October 7, 2005, p. 4.

40. See Judith Yaphe and Charles Lutes, "Reassessing the Implications of a Nuclear Iran," McNair Paper no. 69 (Washington, DC: National Defense University, 2005), p. 41.

41. See Chubin, "Whither Iran?" See also Paula DeSutter, *Denial and Jeopardy: Deterring Iranian Use of NBC Weapons* (Washington, DC: National Defense University, Center for Non-Proliferation Research, 1997), pp. 67–8. DeSutter suggests that a U.S. response should be to "deny Iran ambiguity"; see pages 85–6.

42. According to Porter Goss, "Iran continues to retain in secret important members of Al-Qai'da—the Management Council—causing further uncertainty about Iran's commitment to bring them to justice." Porter J. Goss, Director of Central Intelligence, "Global Intelligence Challenges 2005: Meeting Long-Term Challenges with a Long-Term Strategy," testimony before the Senate Select Committee on Intelligence, February 16, 2005, http://www.cia.gov/cia/public_affairs/speeches/2004/Goss_testimony_02162005.html.

43. See, for example, the excellent discussion between Scott Sagan and Ken Waltz, *The Spread of Nuclear Weapons: A Debate Renewed* (New York: W.W. Norton, 2003).

44. Pakistan's tacit support for Kashmiri terrorist attacks on India seems to have increased with nuclear weapons.

45. Giles, "Islamic Republic of Iran," p. 103. Giles contrasts the offensive view with that of civilians in Iran who see them as deterrents. The view of the IRGC as an aggressive element is supported by Paula DeSutter. See DeSutter, *Denial and Jeopardy*, pp. 19–24

46. For an example, see Chubin, "Whither Iran?" pp. 48–51. Another case occurred in 2002 when General Zolgadr of the Guards threatened to destabilize the Persian Gulf if the United States threatened Iran, only to be interrogated by reformist parliamentarians about the wisdom of threatening neighbors that Iran was seeking to cultivate as friends.

47. The comments were made by Ali Larijani, quoted in "Iran Accepts Negotiation Offers from Any Country, Top Nuclear Official," *IRNA* (Tehran), September 27, 2005, in BBC Monitoring, September 28, 2005; and "Nuclear Chief Says U.S. Dishonesty on Nuclear Issue Clear for Iran," *Siyasat-e Ruz* (Tehran), October 3, 2005, p. 1, in BBC Monitoring, September 10, 2005. They were echoed by AEO head Reza Aghazadeh, who threatened escalation in the region, warning that referral to the UNSC "initiates a chain of actions and reactions that escalate tension and adds volatility to an already vulnerable situation in the region." Quoted in "Iran's Aghazadeh says UN Referral Would Escalate Mideast Tensions," *IRNA* (Tehran), September 26, 2005, in BBC Monitoring, September 27, 2005.

48. Tony Cordesman makes the point directly, suggesting that Iran's conventional capabilities are "obsolescent." See Stefan Nicola, "Expert: Iran Nukes Replace Old Military," United Press International, May 20, 2005. In 1993, Iran's Defense Minister Akbar Torkan observed that Iran's defense budget of $850 million was one-twentieth of that of Saudi Arabia. See *Voice of the Islamic Republic of Iran* (Tehran), April 14, 1993, in BBC ME/1664A/8, April 16, 1993.

49. A question posed by a Western official vis-à-vis Iran in relation to this case. Quoted in Steve Coll, "Nuclear Crisis Extends Well Beyond Korea," *International Herald Tribune*, June 27, 1994, p. 1/4.

50. For sources specifically relevant, see Rob Litwak and Kathryn Weathersby, "The Kims Obsession: Archives Show Their Quest to Preserve the Regime," *Washington Post*, June 12, 2005, p. B01; Paul Bracken, "Nuclear Weapons and State Survival in North Korea," *Survival*, vol. 35, no. 3, Autumn 1993, pp. 137–153; Joseph Bermudez Jr., "The DPKR and Unconventional Weapons," in Lavoy, Sagan, and Wirtz, *Planning the Unthinkable*, pp. 183, 189–90. See also Andrew Mack, "North Korea Isn't Playing Games, It Wants the Bomb," *International Herald Tribune*, June 3, 1994 (not a bargaining chip but insurance for the regime). The South Korean Minister of Unification, Chung Dong Young, quoted Kim as saying: "If the regime security is guaranteed, there is no reason to possess a single nuclear weapon." See

Norimitsu Onishi, "Kim Jong Il Signals Readiness to Resume Nuclear Arms Talks," *International Herald Tribune*, June 18/19, 2005, p. 5.

51. For references, see Chubin, "Whither Iran?"

52. Farideh Farhi, "To Have or Not to Have? Iran's Domestic Debate on Nuclear Options," in *Iran's Nuclear Weapons Options: Issues* and Analysis, ed. Geoffrey Kemp (Washington, DC: Nixon Center, 2001).

53. See quote from an anonymous policy advisor to a senior cleric, in Richard Russell, "Iran in Iraq's Shadow: Dealing with Tehran's Nuclear Weapons Bid," *Parameters*, Autumn 2004, p. 3, http://carlisle-www.army.mil/usawc/Parameters/04autumn/russell.htm.

54. "Former Guards C-in-C Says Cooperation with EU Undermined Iran's 'Deterrent,'" *ISNA* (Tehran), November 24, 2004, in BBC Monitoring, November 25, 2004.

55. Amir Mohebbian of the *Resalat* newspaper, quoted in International Crisis Group, "Iran: Where Next in the Nuclear Standoff," *Middle East Briefing*, November 24, 2004, p. 10. This newspaper often refers to the existence of a "nuclear apartheid."

56. Iranians focus on Israel's nuclear capability but curiously do not note that the "massive imbalances in military capabilities" come not from nuclear weapons but disparities in conventional capabilities. See Ali Asghar Soltanieh, Director-General, Foreign Ministry, remarks given at Second Moscow International Non-Proliferation Conference, Moscow, September 20, 2003, http://www.ceip.org/files/projects/npp/resources/moscow2003/soltaniehremarks.htm.

57. Ali Khamenei, quoted in *Voice of IRI Network* (Tehran), August 6, 2003, in BBC Monitoring, August 8, 2003.

58. Rowhani also noted that while WMD had no place in defense doctrine, there is a place for such detailed discussions and that "these discussions have been held." Hasan Rowhani, quoted in "Iran's Top Security Official Warns U.S.A. against Attack," *Vision of IRI Network 2* (Tehran), February 7, 2005, in BBC Monitoring, February 9, 2005.

59. The principle that any directive can be reversed on the grounds of expediency or necessity (*maslahat*) undermines the strength of this argument. See Kamal Kharrazi, "Iran's Nuclear Program: We Are Not Building a Bomb," *International Herald Tribune*, February 5–6, 2005, p. 4. See also Foreign Ministry spokesman Hamid Reza Asefi, quoted in "Iranian Spokesman Says Use of Nuclear Weapons Religiously Forbidden," *Vision of IRI Network 1* (Tehran), September 12, 2004, in BBC Monitoring, September 13, 2004.

60. "Iranian Security Chief Interviewed by Al-Jazeera on Nuclear File, Iraq," *Al-Jazeera* TV (Doha), June 19, 2004, in BBC Monitoring, June 22, 2004. However, the argument does appear rather carefully crafted for his regional audience. General Shamkhani made a similar argument earlier: "The existence of nuclear weapons

will turn us into a threat that could be exploited in dangerous ways to harm our relations with the countries of the region," quoted in Takeyh, "Iran Builds a Bomb," p. 57.

61. "Iran: Rowhani Says Leader Opposed to Acquiring Nuclear Weapons," IRNA News Agency (Tehran), October 25, 2003, in BBC Monitoring, October 26, 2003.

62. "Nuclear Arms Detrimental to Iran's National Interest: Defence Minister," IRNA website (Tehran), February 7, 2005, in BBC Monitoring, February 8, 2005. Shamkhani added that Iran signed the NPT, respects the safeguards agreements, and wants a nuclear-free zone (NFZ) in the Middle East.

63. Ali Akbar Salehi, "Nuclear Weapons Will Not Bring Prestige to Iran, Top Official Says," *Iran Daily* (Tehran), June 9, 2004, in BBC Monitoring, June 10, 2004.

64. For a counterconventional and persuasive discussion, see Zeev Maoz, "The Mixed Blessing of Israel's Nuclear Policy," *International Security*, vol. 28, no. 2, Fall 2003, pp. 44–77.

65. "Hardline Daily Says Iran Must Complete Nuclear Plant," *Keyhan*, August 8, 2002, in BBC Monitoring, August 10, 2002; and "Iran: Editorial Says Nuclear Weapons Best Deterrence against Nuclear Powers," *Jomhuri-ye Eslami* (Tehran), November 8, 2003, in BBC Monitoring, November 10, 2003.

66. "A Short History of the Nuclear Bomb and Nuclear Parity," *Iran* (Tehran), December 13, 2004, in BBC Monitoring, December 30, 2004.

67. Nuclear weapons account for 10 percent of France's overall defense budget, and 20 percent of the equipment portion of the defense budget. Bruno Tertrais, "Case Study on France," paper presented to the workshop on "Governing Nuclear Weapons," Geneva Centre for the Democratic Control of Armed Forces (DCAF), Geneva, October 3, 2004.

68. See Hossein Mousavian, quoted in "Iran Security Official Says Nuclear Talks Eased Concern of Possible Conflict," *ISNA* (Tehran), December 21, 2004, in BBC Monitoring, December 24, 2004. For an example, see Sirus Naseri, "Iran Has Mastered the Fuel Cycle and This Cannot Be Turned Back under any Circumstances," Mehr News Agency (Tehran), November 9, 2004, in BBC Monitoring, November 10, 2004. Since the mid-1990s, the United States and Israel have exaggerated how advanced Iran's capabilities are in order to limit it before it reaches the point of no return. Iran has exaggerated its progress for reasons of pride, nationalism, and garnering domestic capital. Mousavian's comment appears apt because by talking up the issue, the time and space left for compromise are decreased and misused.

69. This is consistent with Iran's strategic culture and approach to negotiations. For a valuable discussion, see Shmuel Bar, "Iran: Cultural Values," p. 15.

70. See Hashemi Rafsanjani, quoted in Neil MacFarquahar, "For Many Iranians, Nuclear Power Is an Issue of Pride," *International Herald Tribune*, May 30, 2005, p. 7. Others disagree, arguing that most of the advantages of nuclear weapons come from having the capacity to produce them rather than their actual possession. See

Hamid Hadian, "Nuclear Weapons as the Central Focus of International Politics," *Diplomatic Hamshahri*, no. 20, September 2004.

71. For discussion, see Ayelet Savyon, "Iran Seeks EU Consent for Modelling Its Nuclear Program on the 'Japanese/German model': i.e., Nuclear Fuel Cycle Capabilities Three Months Short of the Bomb," Middle East Media Research Institute (MEMRI) no. 229, February 23, 2004, http://memri.org/bin/opener.cgi?Page=archives&ID=1A20905.

72. See also Ariel Levite, "Never Say Never Again: Nuclear Reversal Revisited," *International Security*, vol. 27, no. 3, Winter 2002/03, p. 69.

73. Mohammad Al Baradei, quoted in Steven Fidler, "Non-Proliferation Treaty, Testing Times: How the Grand Bargain of Nuclear Containment Is Breaking Down," *Financial Times*, May 23, 2005, p. 11; Carol Rodley, State Department's second top intelligence official, quoted in Douglas Jehl and Eric Schmitt, "Data Is Lacking on Iran's Arms, U.S. Panel Says," *New York Times*, March 9, 2005, http://www.nytimes.com/2005/03/09/international/09weapons.html?th=&pagewanted=p.

74. For an early discussion of the dangers within the NPT, see Avner Cohen and Joe Pilat, "Assessing Virtual Nuclear Arsenals," *Survival*, vol. 40, no. 1, Spring 1998, pp. 129–44. Michael Mazarr discusses how a nuclear option might be used for arms control purposes: "For most developed and a few developing states the question is not whether they could have nuclear weapons but how long it would take to deploy them. The key criterion becomes the cushion of time between a given stage of nuclear technology and a deployed nuclear force. Virtual arsenals would aim to create such a cushion for the nuclear weapon states and extend it for non-nuclear weapon states." Michael J. Mazarr, "Virtual Arsenals," *Survival,* vol. 37, no. 3, Autumn 1995, p. 14.

75. George Perkovich notes that this scenario, "a variant of the Japanese model is very difficult to counter, and could be a model for other states beyond Iran." See George Perkovich, testimony before the U.S. Senate Foreign Relations Committee, May 19, 2005, http://foreign.senate.gov/testimony/2005/PerkovichTestimony050519.pdf. For a generally sensible set of comments on Iran and nuclear weapons, see Christopher de Bellaigue, "Iran: Think Again," *Foreign Policy*, no. 148, May/June 2005, pp. 18–24.

Chapter Four

1. Shahram Chubin, "Does Iran Want Nuclear Weapons?" *Survival*, vol. 37, no. 1, Spring 1995.

2. In the autumn of 2003 (Tehran agreement) and again in the November 2004 Paris agreement, Iranian officials had to explain to their domestic audience the need

for prudent diplomacy to defuse pressures, suggesting that a domestic constituency existed for confronting the international community. Hossein Mousavian depicted the 2004 agreement as part of strategy of "preventing the formation of an international consensus against the Iranian nuclear program" (and possible referral to the UNSC). See "Iran Security Official Says Nuclear Talks Eased Concern of Possible Conflict," *ISNA* (Tehran), December 21, 2004, in BBC Monitoring, December 24, 2004.

3. On omissions, see interview with Ali Akbar Salehi, Iran's representative at the IAEA, quoted in "Iran's IAEA Envoy Insists Tehran Not Seeking to Become a Nuclear Power," *Der Spiegel*, September 15, 2003, in BBC Monitoring, September 25, 2003. Hashemi Rafsanjani has said that "it was possible that, at times, Iran has not reported its activities." Hashemi Rafsanjani, BBCTV interview, quoted in George Jahn, "Iran Admits Expanded Nuke Work," *CBS News*, June 15, 2005, http://www.cbsnews.com/stories/2005/06/15/world/printable702166.shtml. On U.S. sanctions as cause of nondeclaration, see Hasan Rowhani, quoted in "Security Chief Tells EU Iran Didn't Reveal Nuclear Information due to Sanctions," Iranian Labour News Agency (Tehran), November 17, 2003, in BBC Monitoring, November 17, 2003; and Hashemi Rafsanjani, quoted in "Iran: Rafsanjani Delivers Friday Prayers on Qods Day," *Voice of the IRI Network* (Tehran), November 21, 2003, in BBC Monitoring, November 21, 2003.

4. See Figure 2 on nuclear decision making.

5. Hasan Rowhani, quoted in "Iran's Nuclear Chief Denies Rumours of Resignation," *Sharq* website, July 14, 2005, in BBC Monitoring, July 15, 2005. At the time Supreme Leader Khamenei defended the agreement in similar words: "They [the United States] had come close to forming an international consensus against the Islamic republic on the issue of nuclear weapons ... Iran acted adroitly to clarify the situation." Quoted in "Iran's Khamenei Defends Decision on Nuclear Protocol," *Voice of IRI Network* (Tehran), November 2, 2003, in BBC Monitoring, November 4, 2003.

6. Mohsen Mirdamadi, Chairman of the National Security and Foreign Relations Committee of the Majles, quoted in "Prominent Reformist Says Iran Should Maintain US-EU Rift over Nuclear Programme," *ISNA* (Tehran), September 26, 2003, in BBC Monitoring, September 27, 2003.

7. Hasan Rowhani, "Iran's Security Chief Rejects IAEA Demand to Suspend Enrichment," *IRI News Network* (Tehran), September 19, 2004, in BBC Monitoring, September 20, 2004.

8. Negotiations helped create the atmosphere for long-term gas contracts with India, China, Pakistan, and the United Arab Emirates. See Hossein Mousavian, quoted in "EU Waiting for New Iranian Government to Proceed with Talks—Official," *IRNA* (Tehran), July 17, 2005, in BBC Monitoring, July 18, 2005.

9. Rowhani, "Iran's Nuclear Chief Denies Rumours."

10. Representative of this viewpoint is Mohsen Rezai, the Secretary of the Expediency Council, quoted in "Failure to Close Iran Nuclear File at IAEA Risks Paris Deal—Iran Official," *ISNA* (Tehran), November 21, 2004, in BBC Monitoring, November 24. 2004. For criticism of Europe as the mouthpiece of the United States and "Zionists," see "Iran Press: Editorial Says Europe 'Not to Be Trusted' in Nuclear Talks," *Jomhuriy-eh Eslami'*, July 18, 2005, in BBC Monitoring, July 20, 2005.

11. Ali Akbar Salehi, quoted in "Europe Should Understand That Its Security Is Closely Linked to Iran's Security," *IRNA*, March 9, 2005, in *MEMRI*, Inquiry and Analysis Series no. 218, April 7, 2005. Hasan Rowhani observed that if the negotiations failed "the region would come up against serious obstacles and regional security will be jeopardized." See Rowhani, quoted in IRNA, March 5, 2005, in *MEMRI*, Inquiry and Analysis Series no. 218, April 7, 2005.

12. See Roula Khalaf, Najmeh Bozorgmehr, and Gareth Smyth, "Interview with Hasan Rowhani," *Financial Times*, April 19, 2005.

13. As one Iranian negotiator noted, "The Europeans want to find a solution but their ability to manoeuvre in their political relationship with America is limited." See "Iran Press: Iranian Negotiator Says Nuclear Talks Reaching Dead-End," *Siyasat-e Ruz* (Tehran), May 26, 2005, in BBC Monitoring, May 30, 2005.

14. Rowhani noted, "The Americans say that we should force Iran to abandon the program. The Europeans say no, we should encourage Iran and gently convince it that it is to its benefit to abandon the program. The Russians too, may have an opinion similar to the Europeans." The bottom line, however, is that they all agree that Iran should not have this technology. Hasan Rowhani, quoted in "Iran's Nuclear Chief Denies Rumours of Resignation," *Sharq* website, July 14, 2005, in BBC Monitoring, July 15, 2005.

15. "Any Iranian government that wishes to stop uranium enrichment will fall," insisted Rowhani. Quoted in "Iranian Paper Views Delay to Nuclear Deal with Russia," *Iran* (Tehran), February 27, 2005, in BBC Monitoring, February 28, 2005. See also Reuters, "Iran Threatens to End Nuclear Talks if Its Agenda Is Not Accepted," *International Herald Tribune*, April 21, 2005, p. 4.

16. For a convenient source for all of these reports, see Secretary of State for Foreign and Commonwealth Affairs, *Iran's Nuclear Program: A Collection of Documents* (Norwich: HMSO, January 2005), http://www.globalsecurity.org/wmd/library/report/2005/cm6443.pdf.

17. AEO Head Reza Aghazadeh, quoted in "Iran: Atomic Energy Chief Says Test Production of Uranium Begins in 20 Days," *Vision of the IRI Network 1* (Tehran), March 28, 2004, in BBC Monitoring, March 29, 2004. For text of the Tehran agreement, see Secretary of State for Foreign and Commonwealth Affairs, *Iran's Nuclear Program*.

18. For text, see Secretary of State for Foreign and Commonwealth Affairs, *Iran's Nuclear Program*.

19. Hasan Rowhani, quoted in "Security Chief Says Iran Resuming Manufacture of Nuclear Components," *Vision of the IRI Network 1* (Tehran), June 27, 2004, in BBC Monitoring, June 27, 2004.

20. Hossein Mousavian, senior negotiator and IAEA delegate, quoted in "Nuclear Spokesman Says Resolution Not 'Major Threat' to Iran in Actuality," *IRI News Network* (Tehran), June 18, 2004, in BBC Monitoring, June 19, 2004.

21. For text, see Secretary of State for Foreign and Commonwealth Affairs, *Iran's Nuclear Program*.

22. The report, which is based on interviews with senior Iranian negotiators, is credible. See "Iran's Nukes Program Was Speeded Up," *Al-Jazeera*, December 12, 2004, http://www.aljazeera.com.

23. Foreign Ministry spokesman Hamid Reza Asefi, quoted in "Foreign Ministry Spokesman Says Iran Nuclear Crisis Over," *ISNA* (Tehran), December 10, 2004, in BBC Monitoring, December 12, 2004.

24. For this episode, see Hasan Rowhani's comments, quoted in "Foreign Minister Foresees Iran-EU Agreement on Nuclear Issue," *IRNA* (Tehran), May 10, 2005, in BBC Monitoring, May 11, 2005. Hamid Reza Asefi, quoted in "Iran Foreign Ministry Preparing Additional Bill," *IRNA* (Tehran), May 8, 2005, in BBC Monitoring, May 9, 2005; see also "Iran: Threats of SC over Nuclear Plans Are 'Propaganda,'" *Al-Jazeera.com*, May 11, 2005; Evelyn Leopold, "Iran to Tell U.N. Soon of Nuclear Work—Europe Envoy," *Reuters*, May 11, 2005, http://www.iranfocus.com/modules/news/article.php?storyid=2070.

25. Steven Weisman, "Atom Agency May Be Asked to Meet if Iran Resumes Uranium Work," *New York Times*, May 12, 2005, http://www.nytimes.com/2005/05/12/politics/12diplo.html?.

26. This raises interesting questions about Iran's strategic culture or myopia. There are parallels with North Korea. It has been suggested that North Korea has a distorted worldview and warped expectations about how countries will respond to its actions. See Daniel A. Pinkston and Phillip C Sanders, "Seeing North Korea Clearly," *Survival*, vol. 45, no. 3, Autumn 2003, p. 80. There are interesting parallels between North Korea's negotiating style for the Agreed Framework 1994 and that of Iran. See Joel Witt, Daniel Poneman, and Robert Galluci, *Going Critical: The First Nuclear Crisis* (Washington, DC: Brookings Institution, 2005), pp. 61, 75–6.

27. Gareth Smyth, "Interview with Hossein Mousavian," *Financial Times*, October 24, 2004; and Sirus Naseri, "Iran to Put Forward Final Nuclear Proposal in Less than Three Months—Negotiator," *Vision of IRI Network 2* (Tehran), March 13, 2005, in BBC Monitoring, March 16, 2005.

28. See "Iran Refuses to Show Centrifuge Machinery," *Vision of IRI Network 1* (Tehran), March 30, 2005, in BBC Monitoring, March 31, 2005.

29. Hashemi Rafsanjani, quoted in "(Corr) Rafsanjani Says Iran Will 'Definitely' Not Give Up Nuclear Technology," *Voice of the IRI Network* (Tehran), March 4, 2005, in BBC Monitoring, March 5, 2005.

30. Mohammad Al Baradei, quoted in "IAEA Chief Says Trust Would Improve if Iran Stopped Centrifuge Production," IRNA News Agency (Tehran), June 27, 2004, in BBC Monitoring, June 28, 2004.

31. Javier Solana, "New Challenges for NATO and the EU," speech delivered at the 41st Munich Conference on Security Policy, February 12, 2005.

32. In the words, respectively, of an unnamed British diplomat and Washington-based expert David Albright, quoted in Elaine Sciolino and David Sanger, "Pressed, Iran Admits It Discussed Nuclear Technology," *New York Times*, February 28, 2005, http://www.nytimes.com/2005/02/28/international/midleeast/28nuke.html?page-wanted; and Reuters, "IAEA Confirms Iran's Halt to Nuclear Activity," *ABC News Online*, June 11, 2005, http://www.abc.net.au/news/newsitems/200506/s1389877.htm.

33. "Trustfulness, sometimes bordering on naiveté, is not appropriate in relations with Iran." See Anton Khoplov, "Will the Iranian Atom Become a Persian Carpet for Russia?" *PIR Center: Arms Control and Security Letters*, no. 3 (159), May 2005; and *USA Today*, "Prod Putin on Freedoms, but Don't Isolate Key Ally," February 23, 2005. In reference to Iran, President Chirac told a gathering: "You can deal with the Sunnis but not with the Shi'ites." Quoted in Elaine Sciolino, "Chirac Holding to a Multipolar World," *International Herald Tribune*, February 9, 2005, p. 3. Reference to the Shiites may be to the practice of dissimulation (*taqiiyah*) authorized in extreme circumstances.

34. See the report of Iran IAEA delegation in response: "International Atomic Agency Delegation Will Visit Iran to Resolve Plutonium Issue," Mehr News Agency (Tehran), June 18, 2005, in BBC Monitoring, June 19, 2005.

35. Pierre Goldschmidt, IAEA Deputy Director-General for Safeguards, noted this in March 2005, and it was repeated by Director-General Al Baradei in June 2005. See "Iran Denies Monitors Access to Military Site," *International Herald Tribune*, March 2, 2005, p. 3.

36. Hasan Rowhani, quoted in "Hasan Rowhani Reacts to IAEA Resolution on Iran," *Vision of the IRI Network 1* (Tehran), March 13, 2004, in BBC Monitoring, March 13, 2004. This was repeated by Foreign Ministry spokesman Hamid Reza Asefi: "We would never allow anyone to talk to us using such language." Quoted in "Iran Says Wording of Resolution behind Delay in IAEA Visit," IRNA News Agency (Tehran), March 15, 2004, in BBC Monitoring, March 16, 2004.

37. Gareth Smyth and Guy Dinmore, "Iran Threatens Tough Measures in Event of Sanctions," *Financial Times*, August 9, 2004.

38. This is clearly the implication of the comments of two parliamentarians with expertise in the nuclear field. See "Iran's Majles Debates Suspension of Additional

Protocol," *Etemad* website, Tehran, 28 September 2005, in BBC Monitoring, September 30, 2005.

39. This is clearly put by Hasan Rowhani, quoted in "Iran's Nuclear Chief Denies Rumours of Resignation."

40. These divisions need not concern us here but they account for the ambivalence of some of Iran's statements, the grandstanding by its negotiators, and its setting and then ignoring deadlines.

41. See, for example, Najmeh Bozorgmehr, "Interview with Hossein Mousavian," *Financial Times*, February 3, 2005, p. 6. Also, Elaine Sciolino, "Iran Agrees to Continue Freeze on Nuclear Work," *International Herald Tribune*, 26 May 2005.

42. See former IAEA Representative Ali Akbar Salehi, quoted in "Ex-Envoy Says EU Should Meet Iran's Demands," *Mardom Salari* website (Tehran), December 13, 2004, in BBC Monitoring, December 14, 2004.

43. Reza Aghazadeh, quoted in "Iran May Negotiate Several Years," *Vision of IRI Network 1* (Tehran) in *Persian*, May 8, 2005, in BBC Monitoring, May 9, 2005. See also Aghazadeh's comment about Isfahan's 700 experts: "We cannot keep them idle for a long time. Nuclear technology is something that needs constant research and the knowledge needs to be completed." Quoted in "Iran Needs Nuclear Activity Resumption—Warning to EU," *Voice of IRI Network 2* (Tehran), May 12, 2005, in BBC Monitoring, May 14, 2005.

44. Rowhani noted that some European politicians "told [him] explicitly in Brussels that they are not only after resolving Iran's nuclear case peacefully but also making strategic relations with Iran." Hasan Rowhani, quoted in "Europe Is After Strategic Relations with Iran—Security Chief," *IRNA* (Tehran), March 5, 2005, in BBC Monitoring, March 6, 2005.

45. Rowhani, quoted in "Iran's Nuclear Chief Denies Rumours."

46. Hossein Mousavian has stated that "the European concern is that when Iran has the capability of enrichment, whenever it decides in the future it can divert ... Iran already has the capability. We have the minds, we have the yellowcake process [the process for converting uranium ore, or yellowcake, into uranium hexafluoride, the feeder material for enrichment]. We have centrifuges, scientists, sites." See Smyth, "Interview with Hossein Mousavian." Sirus Naseri also commented on the issue: "We have mastered the technology ... we have what is required for a fuel production program." Quoted in "Nuclear Negotiator Says Iran Ready for Agreement, Prepared for Confrontation," *Voice of the IRI Network* (Tehran), April 26, 2005, in BBC Monitoring, April 27, 2005. On invulnerability to military strikes that cannot destroy know-how, see Sirus Naseri, "Iran Says That Its Nuclear Skills Not for Sale," *Muslim News*, February 21, 2005, http://www.muslimnews.co.uk/news/print_version.php?article=8852. See also Deputy Head of the AEO Mohammad Saidi, who stated: "If an attack is made, Iran will be capable of reconstructing all its nuclear installations in a year (but would end inspections)." Quoted in "Iran Will Resume

Nuclear Fuel Production if Europe Breaches Commitments," Mehr News Agency (Tehran), January 6, 2005, in BBC Monitoring, January 8, 2005.

47. "If you take article IV out of the NPT, all the nonaligned countries will leave," commented Hasan Rowhani. Quoted in "Top Iranian Official Says 'No Discussion' of Ending Uranium Enrichment," *IRI News Network* (Tehran), March 5, 2005, in BBC Monitoring, March 7, 2005.

48. This was recognized by Iran's IAEA representative in 2003, who noted the good relations with the agency until 2002. Of a Board of Governors of 35, 18 were from Western countries or those inclined to the West, while the other half was from nonaligned states. But Salehi noted that "even many of them are inclined to support the West." Ali Akbar Salehi, quoted in "Envoy to IAEA Says Iran Enriching Uranium Takes 'Positive View' of NPT," *Iran* (Tehran), July 27, 2003, in BBC Monitoring, July 28, 2003.

49. This offer is sometimes half serious and for public relations reasons, as in the offer to the United States. Kevin Morrison, "Iran Offers to Let US Share Its Nuclear Program," *Financial Times*, March 16, 2005, p. 2.

50. Rowhani calls it the "biggest test for Europe," suggesting that "it would be a great failure on the part of Europe ... and multilateralism as a whole." Quoted in Roula Khalaf and Gareth Smyth, "Iran Turns Up Heat on Europe Ahead of Talks," *Financial Times*, April 19, 2005. Naseri echoes this line of thought, warning that "should Europe fail ... it may not be able to play a fundamental role in another political situation in the world." Sirus Naseri, quoted in "Iran to Put Forward Final Nuclear Proposal in Less than Three Months—Negotiator," *Vision of IRI Network 2* (Tehran), March 13, 2005, in BBC Monitoring, March 16, 2005.

51. See, respectively, Naseri, "Iran to Put Forward Final Nuclear Proposal"; and Rowhani, "Top Iranian Official Says 'No Discussion.'"

52. Rowhani, "Top Iranian Official Says 'No Discussion.'"

53. Rowhani, "Top Iranian Official Says 'No Discussion.'"

54. Rowhani noted that the United States "is trying to internationalize its sanctions on Iran and change its enmity toward Iran into an international one." Quoted in "Iran Ready to Repel Likely US Attack, Says Security Chief," *ISNA* (Tehran), January 27, 2005, in BBC Monitoring, January 30, 2005.

55. Hasan Rowhani, "Official Rebuffs US 'Hollow Threats,' Says Iranians Not Like Afghans or Iraqis," *ISNA* (Tehran), February 4, 2005, in BBC Monitoring, February 5, 2005; and "Iran's Nuclear Negotiator Says US Role in Talks Would Be 'Positive,'" *IRNA* (Tehran), February 25, 2005, in BBC Monitoring, February 26, 2005.

56. Interview with senior Iranian official dealing with this issue, Geneva, June 24, 2005.

57. Ali Akbar Velayati, Advisor to the Supreme Leader on International Affairs, quoted in "Iran in the Club of 10 Leading Nuclear States," *Sharq* website (Tehran), September 30, 2004, in BBC Monitoring, October 2, 2004. Rowhani saw two U.S.

aims: "to deny Iran access to peaceful technology" and "to prepare the ground for its other plans." Hasan Rowhani, quoted in "Iran's Security Chief Says Careful Planning Stopped Nuclear Dossier Reaching UN," Mehr News Agency (Tehran), January 27, 2005, in BBC Monitoring, January 28, 2005.

58. Supreme Leader Ayatollah Khamenei, quoted in "Iran's Supreme Leader Rejects US 'Lies,' Urges Continued Nuclear Work," *Vision of the IRI Network 1* (Tehran), March 21, 2005, in BBC Monitoring, March 22, 2005. This was echoed by presidential candidate Hojat-el Eslam Mehdi Karrubi, who saw concessions by Iran on the enrichment issue as leading to more U.S. pretexts—first terrorism and later human rights—that could be exploited by the regime's opposition abroad. Quoted in "Candidate in Iran Presidential Election Says US Hostile to Islamic World," *IRNA* (Tehran), June 8, 2005, in BBC Monitoring, June 9, 2005.

59. Salehi, "Envoy to IAEA Says Iran Enriching Uranium."

60. See Sirus Naseri, in Stolz, "L'AIEA reclame," p. 5.

61. Army Commander Major General Mohammed Salimi, quoted in "Iranian Army Commander Calls US, Israeli Threats Serious," *IRNA* (Tehran), March 15, 2005, in BBC Monitoring, March 16, 2005.

62. Khalaf, Bozorgmehr, and Smyth, "Interview Transcript: Hasan Rowhani." This sentiment is echoed by Foreign Minister Kharrazi. See "Iran Foreign Minister on Relations with US, EU, Election, Iraq," *ISNA* (Tehran), June 19, 2005, in BBC Monitoring, June 20, 2005. Iran's view was supported by Director-General Al Baradei. See Arnaud Leparmentier and Laurent Zecchini, "L'Iran doit avoir l'assurance qu'on ne songe pas a l'attaquer ou provoquer un changement de regime, " *Le Monde*, March 23, 2005, p. 7.

63. Apposite here is the proposition advanced in a recent study of British diplomacy that notes that "the cliché about rebuilding trust will not do: for trust is not a commodity. It cannot be built, or rebuilt. It can only be earned, given or frittered away. In the new world order we can do little better than rely on candour and openness." See Peter Aspden, "Colour of Culture No Longer Black or White," review of Mark Leonard and Martin Rose, "British Public Diplomacy in the Age of Schisms," *Financial Times*, March 19-20, 2005 (weekend edition), p. W6.

64. An unnamed senior Iranian official told a journalist, "The US is using the nuclear issue as a pretext for regime change. The issue is a diversion. The US wants to weaken Iran. Even if the nuclear issue was solved, they would want another thing and another thing." See Simon Tisdall, "Atomic Clock Ticks Down to Fallout with Iran," *Guardian*, March 18, 2005, http://www.guardian.co.uk/print/ 0,3858,5150908-103390,00.html.

65. "Former Nuclear Negotiator Quoted on Talks Background," *Etemad* website (Tehran) (in Persian), February 23, 2006, in BBC Monitoring, February 26, 2006. These excerpts are from the *Rahbod Quarterly: Journal of the Strategic Research Centre of the Assembly of Experts* based on a speech in Autumn 2005.

66. Iran reportedly threatened India with withdrawal of a major gas pipeline agreement if it voted against Iran in November at the IAEA. Joel Brinkley, "Congress Irate over Talks with India," *International Herald Tribune*, November 1, 2005, p. 4.

67. President Ahmadinejad referred to this offer of participation at the UN. Participation appears to mean, according to a senior nuclear official, "ownership supervision over Iran's nuclear installations which is a step higher than technical and legal supervision"—in effect, a confidence-building measure. Mohammad Saidi, quoted in "Comment Sees Possible Lose/Lose Outcome from Nuclear Impasse," *Etemad* website (Tehran), October 12, 2005, in BBC Monitoring, October 13, 2005. The foreign minister has talked of state-owned and private companies helping to develop Iran's nuclear program.

68. For an overview, see Associated Press, "Iran Tries to Burnish Image," *International Herald Tribune*, November 7, 2005, p. 4.

69. Respectively, on January 12 and 22, 2006.

70. See Carolo Hoyos and Dan Dombey, "Iran's Plan for Oil Cuts Is Snubbed by OPEC," *Financial Times*, January 31, 2006, p. 1; and Jan Mouawad, "OPEC Agrees to Maintain Current Production," *International Herald Tribune*, February 1, 2006, p. 13.

71. Hasan Rowhani, quoted in Gareth Smyth, "Iran Dashes Hopes for Russian Nuclear Deal," *Financial Times*, February 14, 2006, p. 4.

72. See Deputy Secretary of the SNSC Javad Vaidi's comments quoted in "Iranian Daily Calls on Government to Consider Russia's Proposal," *Iran* (Tehran), February 14, 2006, in BBC Monitoring, February 15, 2006.

73. President Ahmadinejad on February 11 and the Foreign Ministry spokesman on February 12, 2006. Whether this was inadvertent or an attempt to play "good cop, bad cop" is unclear. There were reports that Larijani gave the impression to Europeans in March of disassociating himself from the president. See Natalie Nougayrede and Laurent Zecchini, "Les negociateurs iraniens et europeens ne parvient pas a s'accorder sur le dossier nucleaire."

74. See "Iran Threatens Jump in Atom Work: A Final Proposal to Keep the UN at Bay," *International Herald Tribune*, March 6, 2006, p. 1/8; Nougayrede and Zecchini, "Les negociateurs iraniens et europeens ne parvient pas a s'accorder sur le dossier nucleaire," *Le Monde*, March 5-6, 2006, p. 4.

75. See, for example, Mohsen Rezai, who is typical in insisting that the issue is a legal one for the agency but that the United States and Europe seek to make it a "political" one. Quoted in "Expediency Council Secretary Says Tension between Iran and America Serious," *Etemad* website (Tehran), March 2, 2006, in BBC Monitoring, March 3, 2006.

76. Ali Hoseyni Tash, "Iran Negotiator Assesses Cost of Referral to Security Council," *Farhang-e Ashti* (Tehran), February 28, 2006, in BBC Monitoring, March 3, 2006.

77. See Gareth Smyth, "Iran Attempts to Backtrack from Oil Supply Threat," *Financial Times*, October 2, 2005; *Yahoo News*, "Iran Threatens to Resume Enrichment," September 26, 2005; *RFE/RL*, "Iran Threatens to Stop UN Nuclear Inspections," October 7, 2005; "Iran Threatens to Stop Abiding by Additional Protocol—Foreign Minister," *Voice of IRI Network* (Tehran), October 16, 2005, in BBC Monitoring, October 17, 2005; Reuters, "Iran Hints of Reductions of Oil Sales over Nuclear Dispute," *New York Times*, October 2, 2005; and Nazila Fathi, "In Shift, Iran Agrees to Resume Nuclear Talks," *New York Times*, October 13, 2005.

Chapter Five

1. Mohammad Al Baradei noted the risk that if referred to the UNSC, the council might not act and Iran might opt out of the NPT: "North Korea in many ways has revealed the limitations ... of the Security Council." See Louis Charbonneau, "El Baradei Wary of Taking Iran to the Security Council," *Reuters Foundation Alertnet*, July 8, 2004, http://www.alertnet.org/printable.htm?URL-the_news/newdesk/LO8157593.html. Even skeptics of the IAEA role acknowledge the uncertainty of a UNSC response given the record in Iraq and Korea. See Chen Zak, "Iran's Nuclear Policy and the IAEA: An Evaluation of Program 93+2," Military Research Papers no. 3 (Washington, DC: Washington Institute for Near East Policy, 2002), pp. 70–1. As Ephraim Asculai notes, if something is amiss regarding verification, the IAEA may, but is not obligated to, report it to the UNSC. Similarly, if a state withdraws from its safeguards agreement and declares an intention to withdraw from the treaty (under Article X), the Security Council is not required "to take any action or even debate the matter." Ephraim Asculai, "Rethinking the Nuclear Non-Proliferation Regime," Memorandum no. 70 (Tel Aviv: JCSS, June 2004), pp. 15, 18.

2. Louis Charbonneau, "Confrontation Won't Fix Iran Nuke Issue—El Baradei," Reuters, June 27, 2004.

3. See George Perkovich, "Bush's Nuclear Revolution: A Regime Change in Non-Proliferation," *Foreign Affairs*, vol. 82, no. 2, March/April 2003, pp. 2–8. For a defense of the Bush approach, see Lee Feinstein and Anne-Marie Slaughter, "A Duty to Prevent," *Foreign Affairs*, vol. 83, no.1, January/February 2004, pp. 143–4. The problem with this approach, focusing on weapons rather than states, is that its opening proposition is to treat North Korea as if it were Norway.

4. Condoleezza Rice, "The Promise of Democratic Peace," *Washington Post*, December 11, 2005, opinion-editorial.

5. President George W. Bush, address to American Legion, February 24, 2006. At a press conference earlier, Bush put it more simply: "I don't believe that non-transparent regimes that threaten the security of the world should be allowed to gain

the technologies necessary to make a (nuclear) weapon." See press conference, January 26, 2006, http://www.whitehouse.gov/news/releases/2006/01/20060126.html. See also Elaine Sciolino and David Sanger, "Iran Is Said to Start Enriching Fuel on a Very Small Scale," *New York Times*, February 25, 2006, p. A5. The distinction between types of regimes was emphasized in the contrasting approach of the United States toward India. As Under Secretary of State for Political Affairs Nicholas Burns noted, "The comparison between India and Iran is just ludicrous. India is a highly democratic, peaceful, stable state ... Iran is an autocratic state mistrusted by nearly all countries." Steven Weisman, "Dissenting on the Atom Deal," *New York Times*, March 3, 2006, p. A10.

6. See Condoleezza Rice, testimony before the Senate Foreign Relations Committee, February 14, 2006. See John O'Neill, "Rice Asks for Funds to Buoy Policy in Iran," *International Herald Tribune*, February 16, 2006, p. 4. U.S. Ambassador to Iraq Zalmay Khalilzad agrees that Iran is "an influential player seeking regional preeminence"(hegemony); see Associated Press, "U.S. Accuses Iranians of Aiding Iraqi Militia," *International Herald Tribune*, February 21, 2006, p. 6.

7. President George W. Bush, State of the Union address to Congress, Washington, DC, January 31, 2006.

8. For a skeptical view, see "Bush et l'Iran," *Le Monde*, March 8, 2006, p. 2.

9. Pakistan and China are not members of the PSI. See David Sanger, "U.S. Shares Details on Efforts to Intercept Weapons Technology," *International Herald Tribune*, June 1, 2005, p. 4.

10. See especially David Sanger, "Bush Seeks to Ban Some Nations from All Nuclear Activity," *New York Times*, March 15, 2005, http://www.nytimes.com/2005/03/15/politics15treaty.html?th=&pagewanted=print&po. Sanger reports that "so far the administration has not declared publicly that its larger goal beyond Iran is to remake a treaty whose intellectual roots date back to the Eisenhower administration, under the cold war banner of 'Atoms for Peace.'"

11. President George W. Bush, speech delivered at the National Defense University (NDU), Washington, DC, February 11, 2004.

12. David Sanger, "U.S. Demand Deepens Gulf with Iran over Nuclear Facilities," *New York Times*, May 3, 2005, http://www.nytimes.com/2005/05/03/international/middleeast/03npt.html?pagewanted.

13. Andrew Semmel, Principal Deputy Assistant Secretary, Bureau of Non-Proliferation, statement to NPT Review Conference, U.S. State Department press release, May 25, 2005. George Perkovich, Joseph Cirincione, Rose Gottemoeller, Jon B. Wolfsthal, and Jessica T. Mathews, *Universal Compliance: A Strategy for Nuclear Security* (Washington, DC: Carnegie Endowment, March 2005); Dafna Linzer, "Iran Plans Defense of Nuclear Program," *Washington Post*, May 2, 2005, p. A01.

14. Reports suggest that U.S. efforts to lobby the G-8 to agree to sanctions on Iran should the EU-3 offer to Iran be rejected by Tehran were unsuccessful. James

Harding and Hugh Williamson, "Bush to 'Think About' Europe's Iran Strategy," *Financial Times*, February 24, 2005, p. 1.

15. For text of statements at Evian and Sea Island G-8 meetings, see Secretary of State for Foreign and Commonwealth Affairs, *Iran's Nuclear Program: A Collection of Documents* (Norwich: HMSO, January 2005), http://www.globalsecurity.org/wmd/library/report/2005/cm6443.pdf. For the Gleneagles declaration, see *Payvand Iran News*, July 8, 2005, which called for Iran to cooperate fully with the IAEA and to ratify the Additional Protocol without delay.

16. For a useful summary of U.S. sanctions in place, see Kenneth Katzman, "Iran: U.S. Concerns and Policy Responses," Congressional Research Service no. RL32048, January 19, 2005. See also "U.S. Lawmakers Take Aim at Foreign Firms in Iran," *International Herald Tribune*, February 17, 2005, p. 13.

17. This followed a determination by Secretary Rice that Iran was acting to contribute to nuclear proliferation under U.S. legislation (PD 12938).

18. "Most analysts seem to agree that sanctions would have had a far greater effect on Iran if they were multilateral or international." See Katzman, "Iran: U.S. Concerns," p. CRS-26.

19. For this suggestion, see President George W. Bush, transcript of White House conference, quoted in *New York Times*, "For Bush, 'Results Mixed' on Iraqi Troops," December 20, 2004, http://www.nytimes.com/2004/12/20/politics/20web-ptext.html?pagewanted=1&ei=5070&en=ccdbfb92d6605f50&ex=1132203600&oref=login.

20. See Shahram Chubin and Robert Litwak, "Debating Iran's Nuclear Aspirations," *Washington Quarterly*, vol. 26, no. 4, Autumn 2003.

21. *International Herald Tribune*, "Back to Arms Control," January 20, 2003, editorial, p. 10.

22. Samantha Power, "Comment: Boltonism," *New Yorker*, March 21, 2005, p. 23.

23. See, especially, former official Flynt Leverett, who argues that ideologues in the administration did not use the opportunity to engage Iran. Flynt Leverett, interview with Bernard Gwertzman, Council on Foreign Relations, March 31, 2006, http://www.cfr.org/publication/10326/leverett.html. This is corroborated by James Risen, *State of War: The Secret History of the CIA and the Bush Administration* (London: Free Press, 2006), pp. 215–7. Guy Dinmore, "Iran Tells U.S. It Has Detained Terror Suspects, Al Qaida," *Financial Times*, May 23, 2003, p. 12; Robin Wright, "U.S. in 'Useful' Talks with Iran," *Los Angeles Times*, May 13, 2003. For a summary of past efforts along these lines, see Guy Dinmore, "Fears Grow of New Chapter in Story of Missed U.S.-Iran Opportunities," *Financial Times*, March 5, 2005, p. 3. Two prestigious institutes advocated engagement as a strategy: the Atlantic Institute and the Council on Foreign Relations. See, for example, http://www.cfr.org/pdf/Iran_TF.pdf.

24. Najmeh Bozorgmehr and Guy Dinmore, "Rafsanjani Offers Threats and Olive Branch," *Financial Times*, June 14, 2003, p. 7.

25. See reference in President Bush's 2005 State of the Union address: "And I say to the Iranian people: 'As you stand for your own liberty, America stands with you.'" On the State Department's human rights report, see Guy Dinmore, "Bush Targets 'Tyrants' in Human Rights Report," *Financial Times*, March 1, 2005, p. 4; on the elections, Caroline Daniel, "Bush Condemns Tehran's 'Rule of Suppression,'" *Financial Times*, June 17, 2005, p. 6; for Secretary Rice on Iran's "loathsome record," see Associated Press, "Rice Deflects Talk of Strike on Iran," *International Herald Tribune*, February 5, 2005, http://www.iht.com/bin/print_ipub.php?file=/articles/2005/02/04/news/.tehran.html.

26. Steven Weisman, "On Iran and Korea Few Options: U.S. Faces Prospect of Diplomacy Failing," *International Herald Tribune*, March 28, 2005, pp. 1, 4. Weisman notes that "conservatives in Congress are demanding that [the United States] promote dissident groups within Iran." Sonni Efron and Mark Mazzetti, "U.S. May Aid Iran Activists," *Los Angeles Times*, March 4, 2005, http://www.latimes.com/news/nationworld/world/la-fg-usiran4mar0407066840; and Guy Dinmore, "U.S. Offers Grants to Opponents of Iran's Clerics," *Financial Times*, May 6, 2005, p. 4.

27. See Guy Dinmore and Roula Khalaf, "U.S. Hawks Rooting for Hardline Candidate," *Financial Times*, June 24, 2005, p. 7; and "Iran Turns Right," *Financial Times*, June 27, 2005, editorial, p. 14.

28. Demonizing Iran is current practice. In the case of an Israeli lobby such as AIPAC, it serves a purpose; other cases, like that of Congressman Kurt Weldon and Kenneth Timmerman, appear more curious. See Guy Dinmore, "Books Add to Rightwing Campaign to Demonise Iran," *Financial Times*, July 8, 2005; and Guy Dinmore, "Iran's Nuclear Tactics Send Delegates into Interactive Dystopia," *Financial Times*, May 25, 2005, p. 4.

29. The phrase is attributed to Philip Stephens, "Bush Lacks a Plan to Back Up His Middle East Pledges," *Financial Times*, December 3, 2004, p. 13; see also *Financial Times*, "Try Diplomacy," February 11, 2005, editorial, p. 12.

30. See Brian Knowlton, "Two Key Senators Assail U.S. Policy on Korea," *International Herald Tribune*, June 15, 2005, p. 7. The second senator was Joseph Biden, who made the same criticism regarding Iran policy. See Senator Joseph Biden (D-Del.), "Iran's Weapons Proliferation," opening statement to U.S. Senate Committee on Foreign Relations Hearings, May 19, 2005. See also Guy Dinmore, "Critics Pour Water on U.S. Foreign Policy's Fiery Vision," *Financial Times*, February 21, 2005, p. 4.

31. See, especially, *Economist*, "Mr. Bush Goes to Belgium," February 19, 2005, pp. 9–10; see also *Financial Times*, "Rice Reaches Out to Europe," February 9, 2005, editorial, p. 12, which notes that "it is the very nature of the regime—its refusal to recognise Israel, or to respect human rights—that makes it antithetical to the U.S. vision of a Middle East remade." Among many references to the Bush administration perception, thus hesitancy, that engagement equals endorsement, see Javier

Solana, who stated: "President Bush has said very clearly they don't want to legiti-mate the regime. They cannot get engaged because it means legitimating them." See Judy Dempsey, "EU's Solana Remains Pessimistic," *International Herald Tribune*, February 21, 2005, pp. 1, 6.

32. See *Economist*, "Who Is John McCain?" June 18, 2005, p. 44; and Reuel Marc Gerecht, "Going Soft on Iran," *Weekly Standard*, March 8, 2004.

33. For a discussion, see Richard Haass, "Regime Change and Its Limits," *Foreign Affairs*, vol. 84, no. 4, July/August 2005, pp. 66–78. Haass, a former official, sees delay and drift in policy and argues that regime change is a complement to diplomacy and deterrence. He also notes that regime evolution through "opening up" (that is, engagement) is a more viable strategy, in effect endorsing the EU-3 approach.

34. Jim Dobbins, "In Iran, the U.S. Can't Stay on the Sidelines," *International Herald Tribune*, December 2, 2004, p. 8. His exact phrase was "Washington is no more than an excited bystander offering advice from a safe distance." For background, see also Geoffrey Kemp, *U.S. and Iran: The Nuclear Dilemma, Next Steps* (Washington, DC: Nixon Center, 2004)

35. Note that the distinction between "reporting" and "referral" of an issue to the Security Council is ambiguous and disputed. Reporting is simply a transmittal of an IAEA report, while a referral is transmittal of a report with the *expectation* of action. The UNSC can take note or endorse a report, make a hortatory appeal (call upon), condemn a policy, or move to mandatory measures requiring states to follow a certain course. In the case of Iran, both terms have been used loosely and interchangeably. The assumption is that initially, at least from mid-March 2006, the Security Council has simply been given a report. The Iranian government has noted that it makes no distinction between the terms in its evaluation of its own response.

36. See Robin Wright, "U.S. Wants Guarantees on Iran Effort," *Washington Post*, March 4, 2005. See also Guy Dinmore and Hubert Wetzel, "President Faces Tough Task Talking Congress Round to New Iran Stance," *Financial Times*, February 25, 2005, p. 4. For early advocacy of such an approach, see Robert Einhorn, "A Transatlantic Strategy on Iran's Nuclear Program," *Washington Quarterly*, vol. 27, no. 4, Autumn 2004, pp. 21–32.

37. In a statement to the IAEA, U.S. Ambassador Jackie Sanders put the U.S. (and allied) case clearly: "Given the history of Iran's clandestine nuclear activities and its documented efforts to deceive the IAEA and the international community, only the full cessation and dismantling of Iran's nuclear fissile material production can begin to give us any confidence that Iran is no longer pursuing nuclear weapons." Jackie W. Sanders, U.S. Ambassador to the Conference on Disarmament, "Iran Deceives International Nuclear Inspectors, U.S. Says," statement to the IAEA Board of Governors, Vienna, March 2, 2005, http://www.usembassy.it/file2005_03/alia/a5030204.htm. See also David Sanger and Steven Weisman, "U.S. and EU Forge

Joint Strategy on Iran Talks," *International Herald Tribune*, March 12-13, 2005, pp. 1, 6; Steven Weisman, "On Iran, Bush Weighs a Joint Strategy with the Europeans," *New York Times*, March 4, 2005; and Steven Weisman, "U.S. Reviewing European Proposal for Iran," *New York Times*, February 28, 2005.

38. Brian Knowlton, "U.S. Officials Cool on Iran's Hot Response," *International Herald Tribune*, March 14, 2005, p. 4. See also *Economist*, "A Grand Bargain with the Great Satan?" March 12, 2005, pp. 12–3; see Geoffrey Kemp, "Desperate Times, Half Measures," *National Interest*, Summer 2005, pp. 53–6.

39. The phrase "legitimate security concerns" is repeated in *Financial Times*, "Wanted: Iran Policy," January 28, 2005, editorial, p. 12; and *Financial Times*, "A Useful Pause in the Iran Talks," May 27, editorial, 2005, p. 12. The phrase referring to Europeans and China is from *Economist*, "Return of the Axis of Evil," May 14, 2005, pp. 9–10.

40. See Simon Tisdall, "Atomic Clock Ticks Down to Fallout with Iran," *Guardian*, March 18, 2005, http://www.guardian.co.uk/print/0,3858,5150908-103390,00.html. Tisdall quotes a diplomat as saying: "The Americans are trying to create an environment so that the U.S. can hit Iran and I don't think the Europeans would accept this." For less skepticism, see Philip Stephens, "Europe Cannot Retreat from the World," *Financial Times*, June 10, 2005, p. 13.

41. President Bush stated that "the international community must come together and make it very clear to Iran that we will not tolerate the construction of nuclear weapons." See President George W. Bush, statement at the White House, June 18, 2003. A more recent formulation by the president is that "the development of a nuclear weapon is unacceptable and the process which would enable Iran to develop a nuclear weapon is unacceptable." See Paula Wolfson, "Bush Calls for Tough Stand on Iran's Nuclear Program," Voice of America News, June 27, 2005, http://www.voanews.com/english/2005-06-27-voa41.cfm?renderfor print.

42. The Supplementary Act 12938 (I as amended) Presidential Directive blocks the assets of foreign governments and private companies and institutions having technical or financial cooperation with the Iranian AEO. For the latest definition of what is unacceptable; see "Les européens s'interrogent sur les intentions nucléaires du nouveau gouvernement iranien," *Le Monde*, June 29, 2005, p. 3.

43. After the successful vote to report Iran to the Security Council, which opened a new phase in diplomacy, Nicholas Burns acknowledged the change in U.S. policy: "We began supporting the European Union negotiating effort back on March 11th of 2005 and we patiently supported that set of negotiations all the way through until just this week." This included reaching out to Russia, India, China, and others. See Nicholas Burns, U.S. Under Secretary of State for Political Affairs, February 5, 2006, http://fpc.state.gov/fpc/60433.htm.

44. This estimate, however, might well be tainted. Dafna Linzer, "Iran Is Judged Ten Years from a Nuclear Bomb," *Washington Post*, August 2, 2005, p. A01; and

Steven Weisman and Douglas Jehl, "Estimate Revised on When Iran Could Make a Nuclear Bomb," *New York Times*, August 3, 2005. Before this National Intelligence Estimate (NIE), U.S. estimates, such as that by Defense Intelligence Agency Director Lowell Jacoby in February 2005, were "within five years." For a dissent from the ten-year estimate, see Ephraim Asculai, "Intelligence Assessment and the Point of No Return: Iran's Nuclear Program," *Tel Aviv Notes*, no.143, August 8, 2005. Perhaps the most reliable estimate put Iran, "if unobstructed," three to five years away; see David Albright and Corey Hinderstein, "The Clock Is Ticking" (Washington, DC: Institute for Science and International Security, March 27, 2006.

45. See Joel Brinkley, "U.S. Invested Political Capital against Iran," *International Herald Tribune*, September 28, 2005, p. 4; Guy Dinmore and Najmeh Bozorghmehr, "Rice Fails to Win Support for Iran Referral to Security Council," *Financial Times*, October 17, 2005, p. 4.

46. President George W. Bush, press conference, December 19, 2005, http://www.whitehouse.gov./news/releases/2005/12/print/2005/219-2html.

47. In Europe in February 2005, President Bush put it thus: "This notion that the United States is getting ready to attack Iran is simply ridiculous. Having said that, all options are on the table." Vice President Cheney repeated the formulation a year later. See Vice President Richard Cheney, remarks to the American Israel Public Affairs Committee, Washington, DC, March 7, 2006. Secretary of State Condoleezza Rice, while emphasizing the U.S. "commitment to the diplomatic approach," added: "People shouldn't want the President of the U.S. to take options off the table." *Times of India*, "US Warns Iran against Pulling Out of NPT," February 13, 2006, http://timesofindia.indiatimes.com/articleshow/1411960.cms. For a succinct and persuasive argument against the military option, see Joe Cirincione, *No Military Options* (Washington, DC: Carnegie Endowment, 2006), http://ww.carnegieendowment.org/publications/index.cfm?fa+print&id+17922.

48. According to an *LA Times*/Bloomberg poll, some 57 percent of Americans favor a strike if Iran persists in its program. Another poll gave the figure as 42 percent. See, respectively, Greg Miller, "57% Back a Hit on Iran if Defiance Persists," *Los Angeles Times*, January 27, 2006, http://www.latimes.com/news/printedition/asection/la-na-fornpoll27jan27,05918171.story?coll+la=news-a section; Claudia Dean, "Most Americans Back Sanctions on Iran," *Washington Post*, January 31, 2006, p. A13, http://www.washingtonpost.com/wp-dyn/content/article/2006/01/30/AR2006013001247.

49. For a view that sees the administration as overloaded and unable to take on much more, see Dennis Ross, "The Practical Realities of the Bush Foreign Policy in the Second Term," *Financial Times*, October 4, 2005, p. 15.

50. This "schizophrenic mission" is a perennial source of criticism; see, for example, Jane Martinson, "Nuclear Watchdog under Fire," *Financial Times*, September 19,

1995, p. 5. It is also accused of being an "unwitting enabler"; see Michael Levi, "Enabler," *New Republic*, October 6, 2003, pp. 17–8.

51. Chen Zak, "Iran's Nuclear Policy and the IAEA: An Evaluation of Program 93+2," Military Research Papers no. 3 (Washington, DC: Washington Institute for Near East Policy, 2002), pp. 67–8, 70–1.

52. Ephraim Asculai, "Rethinking the Nuclear Non-Proliferation Regime," Memorandum no. 70 (Tel Aviv: JCSS, June 2004), pp. 16–7, 33, 36, 41.

53. Asculai, "Rethinking," p. 37. Al Baradei observed: "Should a state with a fully developed fuel cycle capability decide, for whatever reason, to break away from its non-proliferation commitments, most experts believe it could produce nuclear weapons within a matter of months." Quoted in *Economist*, "By Invitation," October 18, 2003, p. 44.

54. For trenchant observations along these lines, see Asculai, "Rethinking"; and Chen Zak, "Iran's Nuclear Policy."

55. Asculai, "Rethinking," pp. 30, 37, 43–4. The U.S. government also took the position that the distinction is meaningless and the failure to declare should be put in the larger context of the covert program that it was intended to cover. Asculai sees this as part of the IAEA's tendency to trespass into the political rather than confining itself to the intended technical area.

56. Author interview with senior IAEA official, London, December 2005.

57. By late 2005, Al Baradei had made considerable headway on this proposal in getting major actors' support. See Guy Dinmore, "U.S. and Russia Back Establishment of International Fuel Bank," *Financial Times*, November 8, 2005, p. 4; Arnaud Leparmentier and Laurent Zecchini, "L'Iran doit avoir l'assurance qu'on ne songe pas a l'attaquer ou provoquer un changement de regime," *Le Monde*, March 23, 2005, p. 7; Mohammad Al Baradei, "Nuclear Non-Proliferation: Global Security in a Rapidly Changing World," speech delivered at the Carnegie International Non-Proliferation Conference, Washington, DC, June 21, 2004, http://www.ceip.org/files/projects/npp/resources/2004conference/speeches/elbaradei.doc; *Economist*, "By Invitation," October 18, 2003, p. 44; Al Baradei remarks on *Iran* website, Tehran, October 18,2003, in BBC Monitoring, October 21, 2003; and Al Baradei, "Seven Steps to Raise World Security," *Financial Times*, February 2, 2005, p. 13. See also various Al Baradei speeches at Carnegie, IISS, MIT, etc., all accessible on the IAEA website.

58. Al Baradei has said that "we can continue to act like a fire brigade but we need to look at the big picture." Interview with Roula Khalaf, "Insecurity Drives WMD Motivation," *Financial Times*, July 23, 2003, p. 3. Regarding the "iceberg," see Paul Kerr, "Tackling the Nuclear Dilemma: An Interview with IAEA Director General Mohamed El-Baradei," *Arms Control Today*, March 2005. The Director-General supports the European initiative that takes into account the broader issues in the nuclear, security, political, and economic "baskets" discussed in various committees.

59. See, respectively, "UN Nuclear Chief Presses Iran and North Korea," *International Herald Tribune*, November 2, 2004, p. 2; and Roula Khalaf, "UN Concern over Iran's N-Technology," *Financial Times*, December 9, 2004, http://news.ft.com/cms/s/6c3ca1f2-4a2a-11d9-b065-00000e2511c8.html.

60. Al Baradei used U.S. pressure to get enhanced access but resisted immediate referral because the agency wanted to get a better idea of the scope of the program. See Gillian Tett, "Alleged Noncompliance: Nuclear Watchdog Fails to Back U.S. Censure of Iran," *Financial Times*, June 19, 2003, p. 4.

61. IAEA Board of Governors, "Implementation of the NPT Safeguards Agreement in the Islamic Republic of Iran," GOV/2006/14, resolution adopted February 4, 2006.

62. Report of the Director-General, "Implementation of the NPT Safeguards Agreement in the Islamic Republic of Iran," GOV/2006/15, February 27, 2006. Earlier reports were made in 2004 and 2005, GOV/2004/83, paras. 106–114, and GOV/2005/67 paras. 42–52.

63. See Elaine Sciolino, "UN Agency Says It Got Few Answers from Iran on Nuclear Activity and Weapons," *New York Times*, February 28, 2006, p. A11.

64. "Al Barade'i: Ball Is in Iran Court," *IRNA* (Tehran), November 29, 2004, in BBC Monitoring, November 30, 2004.

65. Al Baradei, interview by Roula Khalaf; *Deutsche Welle*, "U.S., Europe Aligned on Iran Nuke Incentives," March 3, 2005, http://www.dw-world.de/dw/article/0,2144,1507134,00.html.

66. Al Baradei, interview by Paul Kerr, p. 10.

67. The technical assistance reportedly amounted to $1 billion a year. Ali Akbar Salehi, interview by the BBC, "Envoy to IAEA Says Iran Enriching Uranium Takes 'Positive View' of NPT," *Iran* (Tehran), July 27, 2003, in BBC Monitoring, July 28, 2003. The quote is from the Deputy Head of the AEO, Mohammad Saidi, in "Iran Says IAEA Report Had to Be Presented Prior to Board of Governors' Meeting," IRNA News Agency (Tehran), March 1, 2005, in BBC Monitoring, March 2, 2005.

68. Hasan Rowhani, quoted in "Iran: Rowhani Outlines Views on IAEA Resolution in News Conference," *ILNA* (Tehran), November 28, 2003, in BBC Monitoring, November 28, 2003.

69. See Mousavian's comment on Iran's aims in "IAEA Resolution Amendment Possible—Iranian Spokesman," *ISNA* (Tehran), June 15, 2004, in BBC Monitoring, June 16, 2004.

70. See Melissa Fleming, quoted in "IAEA Spokeswoman Welcomes Iran's Decision to Allow Inspection of Military Site," IRNA News Agency (Tehran), January 6, 2005, in BBC Monitoring, January 7, 2005.

71. This was Tehran's line initially in 2003 when it feared UNSC referral and speedily concluded the first agreement with the EU-3. The same tactic has recurred after every dispute arising from Iran's rather free interpretation of its commitments.

See Hasan Rowhani, quoted in "Chairman of Iran's Supreme National Security Council Welcomes IAEA Resolution," *Voice of IRI Network* (Tehran), November 26, 2003, in BBC Monitoring, November 26, 2003.

72. The source is Deputy Head of the SNSC for International Affairs Javad Va'idi. Quoted in "West Responsible for Adverse Atmosphere against Iran," *IRNA* (Tehran), February 14, 2006, in BBC Monitoring, February 15, 2006. The figure of 1,700 man/days of inspections is quoted as of March 2006 (2,000 by June 2006).

73. Mohammad Al Baradei, quoted in "UN Watchdog Calls on U.S. to Join Europe in Talks on Iran's Nuclear Issue," *IRNA* (Tehran), February 2, 2005, in BBC Monitoring, February 3, 2005.

74. President Putin urged Iran to stop enrichment activities and meet IAEA demands. *RFE/R Liberty*, September 25, 2003, http://www.rferl.org. Similarly, the NAM viewed Iran's signature of the AP as "positive" and encouraged Iran "to facilitate access to sites requested by the agency." See "Non-Aligned Movement Views Iran's Signing of NPT Additional Protocol as Positive," *IRNA* (Tehran), December 18, 2003, in BBC Monitoring, December 18, 2003; and "Text of Draft Resolution Proposed by the Non-Aligned on Iran's Nuclear Dossier," *IRNA* (Tehran), November 24, 2004, in BBC Monitoring, November 25, 2004.

75. For example, Al Baradei said, "I hope that in the discussions [between Iran and the EU-3] everyone puts their cards on the table. This is not just a technical issue, its a security issue," Al Baradei interview by Khalaf.

76. For the EU's WMD strategy, see "EU Strategy against Proliferation of Weapons of Mass Destruction (WMD)" (Brussels: EU, December 12, 2003), http://europa.euint/comm/external_relations/us/sum06_04/decl_wmd.pdf.

77. Gerard Quille, "Prospects for a Common Transatlantic Strategy to Deal with New Trends in Nuclear Proliferation," paper presented at Conference on Transatlantic Security and Nuclear Proliferation, Rome, June 2005, p. 6.

78. For an excellent summary of these negotiations, see Shannon Kile of SIPRI, "Status of IAEA Safeguards Inspections in Iran," background paper for Moscow Conference, October 3, 2005. See also Shannon Kile, ed., *Europe and Iran: Perspectives on Non-Proliferation* (Stockholm: Stockholm International Peace Research Institute, 2005), SIPRI Research Report no. 21; George Perkovich, *Toward Transatlantic Cooperation in Meeting the Iranian Nuclear Challenge*, Proliferation Papers (Paris: IFRI, 2005); Mark Leonard, *Can Your Diplomacy Stop Iran's Nuclear Program?* Working Paper, London: Center for European Reform, November 2005). Emily Landau and Ephraim Asculai, "Iran's Nuclear Program and Negotiations with EU-3," *Strategic Assessment*, vol. 8, no. 3, November 2005 pp.13–8. Other sources include Steve Evert, "Engaging Iran," Working Paper (London: Center for European Reform, March 2004); Sean Smeland, "Countering Iranian Nukes," *Non-Proliferation Review*, Spring 2004, pp. 40–72; *New York Times*, "Status of EU-Iran Nuclear Talks," May 16, 2005, http://www.nytimes.com/cfr/international/slot3_051605.html?pagewanted=

print. Paul Kerr, "Europeans: Iranians Honouring Agreement," *Arms Control Today*, March 2005, pp. 34–5.

79. Rowhani likened the United States to a Mercedes-Benz and the EU-3 to the locally built and inexpensive Paykan car: "There are those who ask us why we did not choose the bicycle because Paykans are useless, and we say to them that a Paykan is still superior to a bicycle. However, there are some who say a Mercedes-Benz would have been better, and we agree with them. But, at the same time, we tell them that we could not afford to buy a Mercedes." Hasan Rowhani, quoted in "Iran's Nuclear Chief Denies Rumours of Resignation," *Sharq* (Tehran), July 14, 2005, in BBC Monitoring, July 15, 2005.

80. See the report of Secretary Rice's visit to Paris where all these issues arose. Secretary Rice promoted Iran from "authoritarian" in 2004 to "totalitarian" in 2005 (due to faulty parliamentary elections) and responses of experts. See Elaine Sciolino, "'Madame Hawk' Ruffles Some Paris Feathers," *International Herald Tribune*, February 2, 2004, p. 2.

81. "For 26 years ... the ruling mullahs have compromised economics at home and abroad to fortify a clerical dictatorship." See Marc Ruehl Gerecht, "Europe Should Be Careful What It Wishes for in Iran," *Financial Times*, March 1, 2005, p. 13.

82. For example, as German Chancellor Schroeder has done. See Peter Spiegel and Daniel Dombey, "Beneath the Bonhomie in Munich, U.S. and EU Tensions Remain," *Financial Times*, February 14, 2005, p. 7.

83. See Francois Heisbourg, "A Common Iran Policy is Essential," *Financial Times*, February 9, 2005, p. 13.

84. Regarding the EU-3, one congressional source commented, "The fear is that there will be a windup but no pitch." On the other side, an EU diplomat stated: "A green light from the U.S. would add a lot of leverage to our capacity to negotiate with the Iranians." See Weisman, "U.S. Reviewing European Proposal for Iran."

85. I owe the phrase to Robert Litwak, see his "Non-Proliferation and the Dilemmas of Regime Change," *Survival*, vol. 45, no. 4, Winter 2003–2004, pp. 7–32.

86. Debates about whether unlimited suspension or indefinite suspension mean "permanent" or not, whether and when suspension becomes "cessation," whether "objective guarantees" are weaker or stronger than those in the AP, and how to assure that these and other guarantees are reciprocal (that is, guarantees on fuel deliveries for Iran and so on) need no further elaboration in the current discussion.

87. See Christopher Adams, Roula Khalaf, and Neil Buckley, "EU-3 to Offer Iran Help with Nuclear Power if It Agrees Not to Make Fuel," *Financial Times*, July 15, 2005, p. 7. In the discussions with the EU-3, there is the carrot of a possible long-term relationship with Europe. See Louis Michel, EU Commissioner for Development, quoted in "EU Seeks Long-Term Relationship with Iran—IRNA,"*IRNA* (Tehran), March 8, 2005, in BBC Monitoring, March 9, 2005.

88. *International Herald Tribune*, "Iran Threatens to Quit Nuclear Talks if Its Agenda Not Accepted," April 21, 2005, p. 4; see also Dafna Linzer, "Europeans Open Talks with Iran on Nuclear Program," *Washington Post*, May 25, 2005, p. A21; and *Arms Control Today*, "IAEA Criticizes Iran Cooperation," April 2005, pp. 34–5.

89. Farhan Bokhari and Roula Khalaf, "Pakistan Offers Nuclear Clues on Iran," *Financial Times*, March 26/27, 2005, p. 3; and Laurent Zecchini, "Les Européens font une concession sur le dossier Nucléaire Iranien," *Le Monde*, March 26, 2005, p. 3.

90. An unnamed EU diplomat, quoted in Roula Khalaf and Gareth Smyth, "EU Trios Relief over Tehran Nuclear Offer May Prove Short Lived," *Financial Times*, April 21, 2005, p. 6.

91. Gareth Smyth and Daniel Dombey, "EU-3 Warn of 'Managed Crisis' over Iran's Nuclear Ambitions," *Financial Times*, May 2, 2005, p. 8; Roula Khalaf, Gareth Smyth, and Najmeh Bozorgmehr, "Battle to Keep Iran Nuclear Talks Alive," *Financial Times*, May 13, 2005, p. 8.

92. The Russian proposal sought to take enrichment from Iran to Russia, which would then supply the product to Iran. It offered Iran a method of stepping back from insistence on having the fuel cycle on Iranian soil. Iran feigned interest in this proposal to buy time.

93. Daniel Dombey, "EU Gives Ahmadi-Nejad Toughest Warning Yet over Anti-Israel Remarks," *Financial Times*, December 19, 2005, p. 3; and Dan Bilefsky, "EU Warns Iran over Denial of Holocaust," *International Herald Tribune*, December 17/18, 2005, p. 3.

94. Scott McClellan, White House press briefing, January 10, 2006, http://www.whitehouse.gov/news/releases/2006/01/20060110-4.html.

95. British Foreign and Commonwealth Office (FCO), "E3-EU Statement on Iran" (London: FCO, January 12, 2006), http://www.fco.gov.uk/servlet/Front?pagename=OpenMarket/Xcelerate/ShowPage&c=Page&cid=1007029391629&a=KArticle&aid=1136903810989.

96. An EU spokeswoman, responding to Iranian criticism of EU-3 lethargy, stated the EU's goal: "The main challenge is to find what we call the objective guarantees that the Iranian program is of a peaceful nature.... The issue is not pace but substance." Quoted in "EU Rejects Iran's Call to Accelerate Nuclear Talks," *Al-Jazeera*, January 2, 2005, http://www.aljazeera.com/me.asp?service_ID=6912; Najmeh Bozorgmehr, "Interview with Hossein Mousavian," *Financial Times*, February 3, 2005, p. 6.

97. This is assuming that there is no parallel covert nuclear program in operation. One expert has observed that "if the Europeans' negotiations do nothing more than keep Iran from being overt in deployment and testing, they have accomplished a great deal." Tony Cordesman, quoted in Stefan Nicols, "Expert: Iran Nukes Replace Old Military," United Press International, May 20, 2005.

98. See Strobe Talbott, *The Russia Hand: A Memoir of Presidential Diplomacy* (New York: Random House, 2002).

99. Estimates on the number of technicians trained in Russia vary but one estimate suggests there were some 300 technicians trained over a period of five years (between 1999 and 2004). See "Nuclear Executive Describes Training for Iranians in Russia," ITAR-TASS News Agency (Moscow), June 9, 2004, in BBC Monitoring, June 10, 2004. The Rosatom website (www.minatom.ru) says that 620 specialists were trained as of December 23, 2004, and two more groups are to be trained at Novovoronezh in 2005, making for a total of 707 for Bushire. The figure of 700 Iranian experts trained at Novovoronezh is confirmed by Russian news agency ITAR-TASS. See "Iranian Engineers Complete Training at Russian Nuclear Power Centre," ITAR-TASS, December 20, 2005, in BBC Monitoring, December 21, 2005. For background of Russia's cooperation with Iran, see Robert Einhorn and Gary Samore, "Ending Russian Assistance to Iran's Nuclear Bomb," *Survival*, vol. 44, no. 2, Summer 2002, pp. 51–70.

100. Quoted in Michael Wines, "Russia to Resume Arms Sales to Iran," *International Herald Tribune*, March 13, 2001.

101. Russian President Putin, quoted in *International Herald Tribune*, "Russia and Iran Affirm Ties," May 18, 2004, p. 3.

102. See Vladimir Orlov and Alexander Vinnikov, "The Great Guessing Game: Russia and the Iranian Nuclear Issue," *Washington Quarterly*, vol. 28, no. 2, Spring 2005, pp. 49–66.

103. Putin has said that "a country like Iran and the Iranian people must not be humiliated." See President Vladimir Putin, interview by Israeli Television Channel One, April 20, 2005, http://www.kremlin.ru/eng/text/speeches/2005/04/201149_type82916_87008_shtml.

104. Putin noted: "Our level of understanding (with the EU) on the Iranian problem is rather high ... we follow one indisputable principle—the non-proliferation of nuclear weapons." Quoted in "Putin Says Russia, EU Share Stance on Iran Nuclear Issue," ITAR-TASS (Moscow), March 18, 2005, in BBC Monitoring, March 20, 2005; see also Foreign Minister Sergey Lavrov, "Russia Hails Coordination with Europe over Iran as 'Important,'" RIA News Agency (Moscow), February 28, 2005, in BBC Monitoring, March 2, 2005; and Katrin Benhold, "Russia Backs Initiative from Europe on Iran," *International Herald Tribune*, January 22–23, 2005, p. 5.

105. Quoted in "Putin Says Iran Does Not Need Nuclear Weapons," *IRNA* (Tehran), September 26, 2004, in BBC Monitoring, September 28, 2004. See also "Iran Must Prove It Has No Nuclear Weapons—Putin," ITAR-TASS (Moscow), September 24, 2004, in BBC Monitoring, September 25, 2004. Putin has said that Russia is "categorically opposed to enlarging the club of nuclear states, including the addition of Iran." Quoted in Richard Bernstein, "Looking More Closely at the Message of Sochi," *International Herald Tribune*, September 3, 2004, p. 2.

106. *Los Angeles Times*, "On Visit Putin Criticizes Iran's Nuclear Program," April 29, 2005, http://latimes.com/news/nationworld/world/la-fq-briefs29.1apr291, 25355554,prnt. See also "Russia Advises Iran against Creating Its Own Nuclear Fuel Cycle," ITAR-TASS (Moscow), February 28, 2005, in BBC Monitoring, March 1, 2005; "Russian Atomic Energy Chief Details Plans for Nuclear Cooperation with Iran," *Vremya Novostey* (Moscow), May 12, 2005, in BBC Monitoring, May 18, 2005

107. The agreement was finally concluded on February 27, 2005. See Paul Kerr, "Iran, Russia Reach Nuclear Agreement," *Arms Control Today*, April 2005, pp. 35–6; Brian Knowlton, "Russia Will Give Iran Fuel for Reactor," *International Herald Tribune*, February 28, 2005, pp. 1/8.

108. At the Sea Island G-8 summit, Putin committed Russia to halt nuclear cooperation if Iran refused to be transparent and cooperate with the IAEA. Transcript of press conference following the G-8 Summit, Sea Island, GA, June 11, 2004, http://www.kremlin.ru/eng/text/speeches/2004/06/11/1401_72690.shtml. An Iranian negotiator subsequently said: "Our talks with the Europeans were reaching a standstill and the Russians sent a message to us, saying that if we reached a standstill, they would stop cooperating with us." Hossein Mousavian, quoted on *ISNA* website (Tehran), December 21, 2004, in BBC Monitoring, December 24, 2004.

109. David Sanger, "Russia Won't Abandon Reactor Pact with Iran," *International Herald Tribune*, September 29, 2003, p. 3; "Iran Unhappy with Russia's Proposed Time-Scale for Nuclear Plant," *IRNA* (Tehran), February 27, 2005, in BBC Monitoring, February 28, 2005; Reuters, "Russia Delays Nuke Fuel Shipments to Iran—Source," *New York Times*, April 11, 2005.

110. Some analysts consider Russia part of the problem rather than solution. See Valerie Lincy and Gary Milhollin, "Russia's Sweetheart Deal for Iran," *International Herald Tribune*, February 2, 2006, p. 8. Others see a Russian interest in "controlled tensions" that increase Russia's leverage. See *Economist*, "A Colder Coming We Have of It," January 21, 2006, p. 29.

111. The Russian arms deal comprised 30 Tor-M1 air defense missile systems valued at between $700 million and $1.4 billion. See "Russia to Supply Surface-to-Air Missile Systems to Iran," Interfax–AVN military news agency (Moscow), December 2, 2005, in BBC Monitoring, December 3, 2005; and "Russia to Fulfil Its Contract to Supply Air Defence Systems to Iran," ITAR-TASS (Moscow), February 9, 2006, in BBC Monitoring, February 10, 2006. For Russian efforts to slow down the momentum for sanctions, see Putin's comments warning against "abrupt erroneous steps." Elaine Sciolino and Alan Cowell, "Putin 'Close' to Iran Critics, but Warns on Errors," *International Herald Tribune*, January 17, 2006, pp. 1–8. This is echoed by his Foreign Minister Sergey Lavrov in "Russian Minister Counsels Extreme Caution in Handling Iranian Dispute," *RIA Novosti* (Moscow), January 17, 2006, in BBC Monitoring, January 18, 2006. Russia's caution led to slowing the move to sanctions. Steve Weisman reports that "the West's incremental approach is

a response to Russian and Chinese reluctance to press for immediate sanctions." See his article "West Tells Russia It Won't Press to Penalize Iran Now," *New York Times*, January 19, 2006, http://www.nytimes.com/2006/01/19/politics/19diplo.html?page-wanted print.

112. "Russian Defence Minister Hopes Iran Problem Will Not Turn into Armed Conflict," ITAR-TASS (Moscow), January 9, 2006, in BBC Monitoring, January 10, 2006.

113. The violation was underlined by Russian representative Grigoriy Berden-nikov at the IAEA. See "Russian Representative Says Iran Violated Agreement with IAEA," *RTR* Russia TV (Moscow), February 2, 2006, in BBC Monitoring, February 3, 2006. Foreign Minister Lavrov insisted on an indefinite freeze on enrichment as a precondition for talks (not enforced) as indicative of Moscow's desire to show its toughness. See Associated Press, "Russia Offers Terms to Iran," *International Herald Tribune*, February 16, 2006. p. 5.

114. Rosatom chief Sergey Kiriyenko, quoted in "Russian Official Clarifies Pro-posals to Resolve Iran Nuclear Problem," ITAR-TASS (Moscow), January 25, 2006, in BBC Monitoring, January 26, 2006.

Chapter Six

1. Significantly, Ali Larijani has recently called Iraq, where the Shiites are in the ascendancy, "a natural ally." Quoted in "Iran's Security Chief Says Iraq Is Natural Ally," *IRNA* (Tehran), January 22, 2006, in BBC Monitoring, January 23, 2006.

2. The phrase is attributed to Hossein Agha; see his interview in, "Ariel Sharon aura, peu fait, peu promis, mais énormément réalisé," *Le Monde*, January 15-16, 2006, p. 14.

3. Ali Larijani met Muqtada Al Sadr and pledged Iran's support for him, while Muqtada offered "Islamic support" for Iran if it were attacked. See "Iraq's Moqtada Sadr Offers 'Islamic' Iran Support in Case of Attack," *Keyhan* (Tehran), January 23, 2006, in BBC Monitoring, January 25, 2006.

4. Russia has sought to balance strategic and commercial relations with Iran with its commitment to non-proliferation. Russia has argued on practical grounds that Iran, with only one reactor operating in the near future, should find it uneconom-ical to seek the full fuel cycle at this stage.

5. Some arms and technology issues are crucial in the current crisis over the nuclear program, notably 30 Tor-M1 air defense missiles. See "Russia to Supply Surface-to-Air Missile Systems to Iran," *Interfax-AVN* military news agency (Moscow), December 2, 2005, in BBC Monitoring, December 3, 2005; Alexandr

Kolesnichenko, "Iran: War Is Postponed," *Argumenty i Fakty* (Moscow), December 20, 2005, in BBC Monitoring, December 23, 2005.

6. Reza Djalili uses the phrase in his excellent article, 'Le Paradoxe Iranien," *Enjeux Diplomatiques et Strategiques*, 2005, p.158.

7. Shahram Chubin, "Whither Iran? Reform, Domestic Politics and National Security," Adelphi Paper no. 342 (London: Oxford University Press for IISS, 2002).

8. This statement was made by a moderate leader, Hasan Rowhani, in a report before his resignation as Secretary of the Supreme National Security Council. See "Iran's Chief Negotiator Presents Khatami with Report on Nuclear Activities," *ISNA* (Tehran), July 31, 2005, in BBC Monitoring, August 3, 2005.

9. See the comments of the Commander in Chief of the Revolutionary Guards Corps (IRGC), General Yahya Safavi, quoted in "Commander-in-Chief Criticizes US; Details Naval Preparedness," *Keyhan* (Tehran), June 8, 2005, in BBC Monitoring, June 11, 2005. See also "Iran Press: Bush Using Military Bases for 'Long-Term Control' of Iraq, Region," *Keyhan* (Tehran), August 14, 2005, in BBC Monitoring, August 17, 2005.

10. See, for example, Rami Khouri, "Monitor Iran's Centrifuges and Its Honor," *Daily Star* (Beirut), August 10, 2005, http://www.dailystar.comlb/printable.asp?art_ID=17482&cat_ID=5.

11. Belatedly, the Arab states have stirred themselves to offset Iran's influence in Iraq. See Roula Khalaf, "Arab Countries Look to Play a Role Countering Iranian Influence in Iraq," *Financial Times*, October 15-16, 2005, p. 5.

12. The phrase is from Ali Shamkhani, quoted in "Iran Undisputable Regional Power—Defence Minister," *IRNA* (Tehran), August 29, 2004, in BBC Monitoring, August 29, 2004.

13. Supreme Leader Khamenei's advisor Ali Akbar Velayati and many others have echoed this theme. See, for example, "Leader's Advisor Says Enrichment 'Imperative' for Iran's Progress," *Resalat* (Tehran), October 30, 2004, in BBC Monitoring, November 3, 2004.

14. Najmeh Bozorgmehr, "Interview with Hossein Mousavian," *Financial Times*, February 3, 2005, p. 6.

15. See comments by Shamkhani on "deterrence," quoted in Yossi Melman, "Russia Joins International Community, Calls on Iran to Cease Enriching Uranium," *Ha'aretz,* August 9, 2005, http://www.haaretz.com/hasen/objects/pages/PrintArticleEn.jtml?itemNo60=610492; "Others Will Have to Accept Iran as a Regional Power—Defence Minister," Fars News Agency (Tehran), August 13, 2005, in BBC Monitoring, August 14, 2005; "Defence Minister Says Iran Has Nuclear 'Counter-Attack' Capability," *ISNA* (Tehran), December 18, 2004, in BBC Monitoring, December 21, 2004. See also "Iran Seeks Regional Non-Aggression Pact: Defence Minister," *Tehran Times*, December 2, 2004, http://www.tehrantimes.com/Description.asp?12/2/2004&Cat=2&Num=7.

16. "Iran Election Program: Larijani Says US 'Propaganda,' Policy Different," *IRNA* (Tehran), June 3, 2005, in BBC Monitoring, June 7, 2005. On Iran's new foreign policy see "Larijani Who Could Become Iran's Next Foreign Minister Explains His Principles," *ILNA* (Tehran), July 22, 2005, in BBC Monitoring, July 23, 2005.

17. See Muwaffaq al-Rubay'i, "Iran, Iraq Assert Security Depends on Regional States," Mehr News Agency (Tehran), November 16, 2005, in BBC Monitoring, November 17, 2005.

18. "Iran Negotiator Says President to Propose New Nuclear Solution," *IRNA* (Tehran), August 26, 2005, in BBC Monitoring, August 27, 2005. Larijani repeated the threat when the reality of sanctions came closer, saying that "if these countries use all their means to put Iran under pressure, Iran will use its potential in the region." Roula Khalaf and Gareth Smyth, "Russia and China Put Pressure on Iran," *Financial Times*, February 1, 2006, p. 5.

19. See Thomas Fuller, "Iran Rejects UN Nuclear Concerns as 'Absurd,'" *International Herald Tribune*, August 12, 2005, p. 3.

20. "Iran's Rowhani Wraps Up Five Nation Tour," *IRNA* (Tehran), June 15, 2005, in BBC Monitoring, June 16, 2005. (Clearly, Pakistani participation would dilute Iran's influence.)

21. The Saudi King Abdullah noted that the war in Iraq had "served Iran's interests." Quoted in "Saudi King on Efforts to End Syrian Crisis, Terrorism in Iraq," *Al-Hayat* (London), November 27, 2005, in BBC Monitoring, November 28, 2005. For Saudi security perceptions in this context, see Flynt Leverett, "Prince Turki Comes to Washington," *International Herald Tribune*, July 27, 2005, p. 6. Another concern was indicated by a newspaper; see "Saudi Paper says Ahmadinejad's 'Religious Fervour' Might Influence Iraq," *Saudi Gazette* (Jeddah), June 26, 2005, in BBC Monitoring, June 28, 2005.

22. See Abdulaziz Sager, "For Saudi Arabia and Iran, Searching for Security Is a Priority," *Daily Star* (Beirut), June 13, 2005, http://www.dailystar.comlb/printable.asp?art_ID=15853&cat_ID=5.

23. President Ahmadinejad expressed this rationale in New York in 2005. It is a very different argument from the usual one that the Palestinians have been dispossessed by the Israeli interlopers and that it is the duty of every Muslim to support the Palestinians and not recognize Israel. See Corinne Lesnes, "Le President Ahmadinejad defend devant l'ONU le droit au nucleaire et attaque les 'puissants,'" *Le Monde*, September 20, 2005, p. 5.

24. Kharrazi called Sistani's role in Iraq "very valuable." Quoted in "Iranian Minister Says Ayatollah Al-Sistani's Role 'Very Valuable' in Iraq," *IRNA* (Tehran), May 20, 2005, in BBC Monitoring, May 21, 2005. Kharrazi observed that the U.S. presence would end "sooner or later," but Iran was Iraq's permanent neighbor. Quoted in "Iran Press: Editorial Praises Declaration by Minister Visiting Iraq," *Sharq* (Tehran), May 22, 2005, in BBC Monitoring, May 25, 2005. For an excellent discussion, see Geof-

frey Kemp, "Iran and Iraq: The Shi'a Connection, Soft Power and the Nuclear Factor," USIP Special Report no. 156 (Washington, DC: U.S. Institute of Peace, November 2005).

25. Hashemi Rafsanjani, quoted in "Senior Cleric Says Iraqi Elections a Victory," *Voice of IRI Network* (Tehran), December 16, 2005, in BBC Monitoring, December 17, 2005.

26. See Gareth Smyth, "Iran Agrees to Extend Iraq $1bn Credit," *Financial Times*, July 21, 2005, p. 7. More broadly, see Seymour Hersh, "Get Out the Vote," *New Yorker*, July 25, 2005, pp. 52–7; International Crisis Group (ICG), "Iran in Iraq: How Much Influence?" ICG report no. 38 (London: ICG, March 21, 2005); Peter Galbraith, "Iraq: Bush's Islamic Republic," *New York Review of Books*, August 11, 2005, pp. 6–9; and Abbas William Sami'i, "The Nearest and Dearest Enemy: Iran after the Iraq War," *MERIA*, vol. 9, no. 3, September 2005.

27. Hashemi Rafsanjani stated: "You see, now the Americans have become bogged down in Iraq. They are suffocating." Quoted in "Iran's Rafsanjani Criticizes US on UN Iraq Role," *Voice of the IRI* (Tehran), September 12, 2003, in BBC Monitoring, September 13, 2003. Revolutionary Guards Commander General Yahya Rahim Safavi referred to the "swamp" in which the United States finds itself in Iraq, claiming that the United States seeks to "stay in Iraq and ... create disagreements between the Shi'ites and Sunnis." Quoted in "Iran Press: Guards Commander Says USA Will Not Create Problems for Iran," *Siyasat–e Ruz* (Tehran), May 21, 2005, in BBC Monitoring, May 29, 2005.

28. The United States sees "continuing troubling indications of Iranian interference in Iraqi internal affairs." R. Nicholas Burns, Under Secretary of State for Political Affairs, "US Policy Toward Iran," testimony before the Senate Foreign Relations Committee, May 19, 2005, p. 7. National Security Advisor Steve Hadley also expressed concern about Iran's attempts to increase its influence in Iraq. See Brian Knowlton, "US Warns N. Korea on Atomic Test," *International Herald Tribune*, May 16, 2005, p. 4. See also, "Iraqi Papers Attack Iranian 'Mullahs' for Meddling in Iraq's Affairs," *Al Furat* (Baghdad and Paris), May 14, 2005, in BBC Monitoring, May 20, 2005.

29. See, notably, Rafsanjani's admonition to the United States to recognize Iran's right to nuclear technology, to accept that the revolution is permanent, and to adopt a policy of compromise. Quoted in "Iranians Shall Benefit from All Gains of Nuclear Science Soon: Rafsanjani," *IRI News Network* (Tehran), February 11, 2005, in BBC Monitoring, February 12, 2005. While running for president, he noted that Iran was in a position to influence regional issues like Iraq and Afghanistan "very well": "We can prevent extremism in the region ... and help in the restoration of peace and calm in the region.... if the Americans do not abuse public rights and entrust regional affairs to the people themselves." See "Iran's Rafsanjani Says Continuation of Iran-

EU3 Dialogue 'Best Option,'" *IRNA* (Tehran), May 11, 2005, in BBC Monitoring, May 12, 2005.

30. Senator Joseph Biden Jr. (D-Del.), "Iran: Weapons Proliferation, Terrorism and Democracy," opening statement to the U.S. Senate Committee on Foreign Relations, May 19, 2005, p. 2. The U.S. suggestion in November that Ambassador Khalilzad was ready to engage Iran on Iraq was met by a rejection from Iran.

31. Peter Spiegel, "Roadside Bombs in Iraq Still Taking Heavy Toll on US Forces," *Financial Times*, August 19, 2005, p. 3; and Mouna Naim, "Les Accusations d'ingerence en Irak s'aggravent contre l'Iran," *Le Monde*, August 20, 2005, p. 3.

32. U.S. intentions regarding future bases in Iraq remain cloudy. See Gary Hart, "End This Evasion on Permanent Army Bases in Iraq," *Financial Times*, January 4, 2006, p.13.

33. The arguments in favor of forward defense and regime change led, easily enough, to the proposition that the lack of democracy was the principal cause of terrorism and extremism and that forcible intervention could bring about a stable democratic system. See Adam Roberts, "The 'War on Terror' in Historical Perspective," *Survival*, vol. 47, no. 2, Summer 2005, p. 119. See also Senator John McCain (R-AZ), "Security in the Middle East: New Challenges for NATO and the EU," speech delivered at Munich Security Conference, Munich, February 12, 2005, http://www.securityconference.de/konferenzen/rede.php?menu_2005=&menu_kon feren. Secretary of State Rice stated that "in the Middle East, President Bush has broken with six decades of excusing and accommodating the lack of freedom in the hope of purchasing stability at the price of liberty. The stakes could not be higher. As long as the broader Middle East remains a region of tyranny and despair and anger [it] will produce extremists and movements that threaten the safety of Americans and their friends." Condoleezza Rice, confirmation hearing before the Senate Foreign Relations Committee, January 18, 2005.

34. For a thorough and excellent discussion of U.S. policy since September 2001, see Robert Litwak, *Regime Change: Through the Prism of 9/11* (Baltimore, MD: Johns Hopkins University Press, forthcoming 2006).

35. While in Europe, President Bush called reports of a military attack on Iran "simply ridiculous," adding "having said that all options are on the table." See Elisabeth Bumiller, "Bush May Weigh the Use of Incentives to Dissuade Iran," *New York Times*, February 24, 2005.

36. For indications that the United States is considering the military option, see Seymour Hersh, "The Coming Wars," *New Yorker*, January 2–31, 2005. Of a voluminous literature, see especially Ephraim Kam, "Curbing the Iranian Military Threat: The Military Option," *Strategic Assessment*, vol. 7, no. 3, December 2004; Richard Betts, "The Osirak Fallacy," *National Interest*, no. 83, Spring 2006, pp.22–5. Iran has moved to put some of its facilities underground. See "Iran Is Said to Build Atom Storage Tunnels," *International Herald Tribune*, March 4, 2005, p. 3. For U.S. overstretch,

see Thom Shanker, "Pentagon Says Iraq Effort Limits Ability to Fight Other Conflicts," *New York Times*, May 3, 2005, http://www.nytimes.com/2005/05/03/politics/03military.html?th=&emc=th&pagewante.

37. Richard Clarke, "More Reasons to Invade Iran than Iraq," Reuters, http://asia.reuters.com/newsArticle.jtml?type=topNews&storyID=5372497. See *Daily Princetonian*, "Blix Criticizes Bush Non-Proliferation Policies," March 9, 2005, http://www.dailyprincetonian.com/archives/2005/03/09/news/12303.shtml?type=printable.

38. For a report critical of U.S. intelligence, see Judge Laurence H. Silberman and Senator Charles S. Robb, *Commission on the Intelligence Capabilities of the United States Regarding Weapons of Mass Destruction* (Washington, DC: White House, March 31, 2005). For press reports on parts related to Iran, see especially Douglas Jehl and Eric Schmitt, "Data Lacking on Iran's Arms, US Panel Says," *New York Times*, March 9, 2005; and David Sanger and Scott Shane, "Panel Report Assails CIA for Failure on Iraq Weapons," *New York Times*, March 29, 2005; Andrew Tully, "US/Iran: Former Weapons Inspector Says US Must Avoid Mistakes of Iraq," Radio Free Europe and Radio Liberty, February 8, 2005, http://www.rferl.org/featuresarticle/2005/02/A5423980-B287-4DB9-811E-9D84DDE5D06B.html; and Joseph Nye, "Heed Iraq Lessons to Avoid Disaster in Iran," *Financial Times*, March 31, 2005, p. 15. For original Secretary of State Rice quote, see Associated Press (Paris), http://www.mytellus.com/news/article.do?viewType=print&articleID=1890267.

39. On complication, see Ali Shamkhani, quoted in Ray Takeyh, "Deterring Iran," *Baltimore Sun*, June 22, 2003, http://www.baltimoresun.com/bal-op.irannukes22jun22,0,7381263.story. On deterrent, see Ali Shamkhani, quoted in "Iran Says Self-Sufficient in Producing Solid Fuel," *IRI News Network* (Tehran), July 28, 2005, in BBC Monitoring, July 29, 2005. Shamkhani is also quoted as saying, "I believe that the power of our regional influence stretches from Quds [Jerusalem] to Kandahar, and nobody can deny our power." Quoted in "Defence Minister Says Iran Has Nuclear 'Counter-Attack' Capability," *ISNA* (Tehran), December 18, 2004, in BBC Monitoring, December 21, 2004. The press has been more blatant: "Columnist Says Nuclear Fuel Cycle Needed for Strategic Superiority," *Keyhan* (Tehran), August 4, 2005, in BBC Monitoring, August 7, 2005.

40. Burns, "US Policy toward Iran."

41. Burns, "US Policy toward Iran."

42. For example, George Perkovich, Joseph Cirincione, Rose Gottemoeller, Jon B. Wolfsthal, and Jessica T. Matthews, *Universal Compliance: A Strategy for Nuclear Security* (Washington, DC: Carnegie Endowment, March 2005), p. 169. See also Senator Richard G. Lugar (R-IN), *The Lugar Survey on Proliferation Threats and Responses* (Washington, DC: U.S. Senate, June 2005), p. 30, which reported that Iran and North Korea were listed by experts as the second most important priority in proliferation after loose nukes in the former Soviet Union.

43. See Associated Press, "US Official Rips into Iran's Nuclear Ambitions," *MSNBC*, January 30, 2005, http://www.msnbc.com,/id/6887724/print/1/display-mode/1098. A Homeland Security report argued, "Only Iran appears to have the possible motivation to use terrorist groups, in addition to its state agents, to plot against the US homeland." Eric Lipton, "A Rosier View of Terrorist-List Nations," *International Herald Tribune*, April 1, 2005, p. 1.

44. President Bush's speech, quoted in Scott D. Sagan and Kenneth N. Waltz, *The Spread of Nuclear Weapons* (New York: W.W. Norton, 2002), pp. 144–53, 201.

45. Burns, "US Policy toward Iran."

46. President George W. Bush, speech delivered at the National Defense University (NDU), Washington, DC, February 11, 2004.

47. John R. Bolton, Under Secretary of State for Arms Control and International Security, testimony before the House International Relations Subcommittee on the Middle East and Central Asia, June 24, 2004.

48. This is the theme of several of Bracken's works. See Paul Bracken, "The Second Nuclear Age," *Foreign Affairs*, vol. 79, no. 1, January/February 2000, pp. 146–56.

49. See Christopher Adams and Hugh Williamson, "Rice Uses Europe Trip to Get Tough with Iran," *Financial Times*, February 5-6, 2005, p. 4; Burns, "US Policy toward Iran"; and General John Abizaid, Head of US Central Command, quoted in "US Commander Warns Iran Nukes May Invite Attack by Other Regional Power," March 2, 2005, http://news.yahoo.comnews?tmpl=story&cid=1521&u=/afp/20050302/pl_afp/usiranabi. President Bill Clinton observed that if Iran developed nuclear weapons, it would find it tough to use them. Naomi Koppel, "Clinton Urges Diplomacy for Iran," *CBSNews.com*, January 27, 2005, http://www.cbsnews.com/stories/2004/01/23/world/printable595350.shtml.

50. One could argue that the Iranian leadership's use of the nuclear issue, including its brinksmanship, for domestic benefits is a model. See Bennett Remberg, "A Way to Break the Nuclear Impasse," *International Herald Tribune*, March 24, 2005, p. 7.

51. For a suggestion of a possible strategy, see George Perkovich, *Iran Is Not an Island: A Strategy to Mobilize the Neighbors*, Policy Brief no. 34 (Washington, DC: Carnegie Endowment, February 2005).

52. Amelia Gentleman, "Rice Tells India about US Worries on Iran Deal," *International Herald Tribune*, March 17, 2005, p. 2. The United States apparently is not interested in assessing whether a major Iranian investment could give it an incentive to maintain regional security. See also Philip Bowring, "How America's Interests Collide in Asia," *International Herald Tribune*, March 22, 2005, p. 8.

53. Among other sources for background discussion about the regional repercussions of an Iranian nuclear capability, see Richard Russell, "A Saudi Nuclear Option?" *Survival*, vol. 43, no. 2, Summer 2001, pp. 69–79; Kathleen McInnis,

"Extended Deterrence: The US Credibility Gap in the Middle East," *Washington Quarterly*, vol. 28, no. 3, Summer 2005, pp. 169–86, together with Thomas W. Lippman, "Saudi Arabia: The Calculations of Uncertainty," pp. 111-44; Ellen Laipson, "Syria: Can the Myth Be Maintained without Nukes?" pp. 83-110; Leon Fuerth, "Turkey: Nuclear Choices amongst Dangerous Neighbors," all in *The Nuclear Tipping Point: Why States Reconsider Their Nuclear Choices*, ed. Campbell, Einhorn, and Reiss. See also Ian Lesser, "Turkey, Iran and Nuclear Risks," pp. 89–112; Wyn Q. Bowen and Joanna Kidd, "The Nuclear Capabilities and Ambitions of Iran's Neighbors," pp. 51–88, both chapters in *Getting Ready for a Nuclear-Ready Iran*, ed. Henry Sokolski and Patrick Clawson (Washington, DC: Strategic Studies Institute of the U.S. Army War College, 2005). In addition, see George Perkovich and Silvia Manzanero, "The Global Consequences of Iran's Acquisition of Nuclear Weapons," draft, Carnegie Endowment, Washington, DC, April 2004; and Robert Einhorn, "Egypt: Frustrated but Still on a Non-Nuclear Course," in *The Nuclear Tipping Point: Why States Reconsider Their Nuclear Choices*, ed. Campbell, Einhorn, and Reiss, pp. 48–82; Mustafa Alani, "Probable Attitudes of the GCC States toward the Scenario of a Military Action against Iran's Nuclear Facilities," *Policy Analysis* (Dubai: Gulf Research Center, November 2004); as well as Henry Sokolski and Patrick Clawson, eds., *Checking Iran's Nuclear Ambitions* (Washington, DC: Strategic Studies Institute, 2004).

54. "Editor Says Neighbours Fearful of Iran's Drive to Acquire Nuclear Weapon," *Al Sharq Al Awsat* (London), October 8, 2003, in BBC Monitoring, October 10, 2003. The same newspaper noted that "Iran is not a peaceful country" and it "continues to occupy Arab land," leading it to argue for regional cooperation and arms control. See "Gulf Fears Being Scorched by Iran's Nuclear Activities," *Al Sharq Al Awsat* (London), June 12, 2005, in BBC Monitoring, June 15, 2005.

55. Mustafa Alani, "Probable Attitudes of the GCC States toward the Scenario of a Military Action against Iran's Nuclear Facilities," Gulf Research Center Report on GCC Attitudes toward Iran's Nuclear Program, *Policy Analysis* (Dubai: Gulf Research Center, November 2004).

56. For a GCC official's critique of Iran's nuclear program, see Anwar al-Khatib, "Al Attiyah: Iran's Possession of Nuclear Weapons Causing Apprehensions in the GCC States," *Al-Rayah*, November 28, 2005, in BBC Monitoring, November 30, 2005; "Editorial Says Gulf Summit Signifies Tougher Stand against Iran" [text of editorial headlined "Important Gulf Summit by Any Yardstick], *Al Quds al-Arabi* website (London), December 20, 2005, in BBC Monitoring, December 21, 2005. "Gulf States Declare Iran's Nuclear Program 'Worrisome,'" *Al-Jazeera* satellite TV, December 18, 2005, in BBC Monitoring, December 19, 2005. See also Simon Henderson, "The Elephant in the Gulf: Arab States and Iran's Nuclear Program," *Policywatch*, no. 1065 (Washington, DC: Washington Institute for Near East Policy, December 21, 2005); Emily Landau, "Taking a Stand on a Nuclear Iran: Voices from the Persian

Gulf," *Tel Aviv Notes*, no.157 (Tel Aviv: Jaffee Center for Strategic Studies, January 16, 2006).

57. "Saudi Crown Prince on Iranian Nuclear Plans, Terrorism," *SPA* (Riyadh), December 25, 2005, in BBC Monitoring, December 26, 2005; in a London interview, Foreign Minister Saud al-Faisal asked of Iran: "Where are they going to use these weapons? If they hit Israel, they are going to kill Palestinians. If they miss Israel, they are going to hit Saudi Arabia or Jordan. Where is the gain in that?" See Frank Gardner, "Iran Nuclear Bid Fault of West," *BBC*, January 16, 2006, http://news.bbc.co.uk/1/hi/world/middle_east/4615832.stm); and text of report by Iranian news agency, "Saudi FM says West Partly to Blame for Nuclear Stand-off with Iran," *IRNA* website (Tehran), January 16, 2006, in BBC Monitoring, January 17, 2006; "Saudi FM Opposes Iranian Attempts to Build Nukes," *Jerusalem Post* online, January 16, 2006.

58. For a brief discussion, see Henry Sokolski, "Defusing the Mullah's Bomb," *Policy Review*, August 3, 2005, http://www.frontpagemag.com/Articles/Printable.asp?ID=18994.

59. For full references, see Chubin, "Whither Iran?"

60. See Pramit Mitra, "India's International Oil Ties Risk US Displeasure," *International Herald Tribune*, April 7, 2005, p. 6.

61. This was implicit in Hashemi Rafsanjani's controversial comments on this issue. See "Rafsanjani Warns of High Cost of US Support for Israel," *Voice of IRI Network* (Tehran), December 14, 2001, in BBC Monitoring, December 15, 2001.

Conclusion

1. Iranian Supreme Leader Ali Khamenei has said that Iran is "strongly opposing [U.S.] domineering policies in the region," and that the United States is "building an empire. They want domination over the whole world. America has plans for the Middle East, the Persian Gulf, and North Africa." Quoted, respectively, in "Iranian Leader Says International Relations Should Not Be Selective," *Voice of IRI* (Tehran), October 21, 2005, in BBC Monitoring, October 22, 2005; and "Regimes Destroyed by Nations' Resistance Not Nuclear Weapons—Iran's Leader," *Voice of IRI* (Tehran), October 30, 2005, in BBC Monitoring, November 1, 2005.

2. See, for example, "Dangers the Outsiders Pose to the Region," *Keyhan*, November 8, 2005, in BBC Monitoring, November 9, 2005.

3. Iranian First Vice President Parviz Davudi noted that "Russia and China are 'priority' countries for Iran's policy," quoted in "Iranian Vice-President Says Russia, China Policy Priorities," *ITAR-TASS* News Agency (Moscow), October 26, 2005, in BBC Monitoring, October 28, 2005.

4. President Mahmoud Ahmadinejad, quoted in "Iranian President Addresses Parliament, Says Wants Justice in Foreign Policy," *IRI News Network* (Tehran), August 21, 2005, in BBC Monitoring, August 22, 2005.

5. Ali Larijani, quoted in Mehr News Agency (Tehran), "Iranian Nuclear Chief Says No Alternative but to Resist Pressure by Big Powers," September 28, 2005.

6. Ali Larijani has resorted to a favorite Iranian tactic, linking Iran's security to regional security and implicitly threatening to destabilize the region if threatened. Associated Press, "Iran Envoy Insists on Pursuit of Enrichment," *International Herald Tribune*, August 27, 2005. For earlier examples, see regional chapter above and Shahram Chubin, "Whither Iran? Reform, Domestic Politics and National Security," Adelphi Paper no. 342 (London: Oxford University Press for IISS, 2002).

7. See "Iran Guards Chief (General Yahya Rahim-Safavi) Says 'Political Pressure Will Prompt Strong Reaction,'" *IRNA* (Tehran), September 23, 2005, in BBC Monitoring, September 24, 2005.

8. Ambiguous or incoherent, Iran seeks at once a stabilized Iraq and an Iraq free of foreign forces. Whether the two are compatible is not self-evident.

9. Saudi Arabia canceled a visit of the Iranian foreign minister to the kingdom in October to express disagreement over Iran's interference in Iraq. See "Middle East Split over Iraq," *Al-Jazeera*, October 5, 2005. See also "Turkish Columnist Notes Iran's Growing Influence in the Region," and Nasuhi Gungor, "Iran Raises the Bar," *Istanbul Milli Gazette*, October 31, 2005, in BBC Monitoring, November 3, 2005; Sami Kohen, "Iran's President's Remarks on Israel Signal 'New Danger'—Turkish Paper," *Milliyet* website, November 1, 2005, in BBC Monitoring, November 3, 2005.

10. Ephraim Sneh, "Between North Korea and Iran," *Jerusalem Post*, September 22, 2005.

11. Anatol Lieven, "Lessons of Iraq: If You Can't Lick 'em, Try Diplomacy," *International Herald Tribune*, September 10-11, 2005, p. 6; see also Anatol Lieven, "Engage Muslim Support or Lose the War," *Financial Times*, July 14, 2005, p. 15.

12. Iranian families "are interested in first and foremost in how to ensure their livelihood." See "Daily Criticises Iranian Government for Causing World Tension," *Mardom -Salari* (Tehran), October 30, 2005, in BBC Monitoring, November 1, 2005. Afshin Molavi writes, "Most Iranians concern themselves far more with the price of meat and onions than with the Arab-Israeli peace process or uranium enrichment." See *International Herald Tribune*, "No Time to Abandon Our Natural Allies," November 4, 2005, p. 6.

13. See Jessica T. Mathews, "Speak to Iran in One Voice," *International Herald Tribune*, March 22, 2006, p. 8; and George Perkovich, testimony before the House Armed Services Committee, February 1, 2006.

Glossary

Al Qaeda

Islamist terrorist group headed by Osama bin Laden, responsible for the attacks on the United States on September 11, 2001. Umbrella organization for terrorist groups worldwide.

Aum Shinrikyo

Japanese religious sect (Hindu and Buddhist mix), responsible for sarin gas attack in Tokyo subway system in 1995.

AQ Khan network

Network engaged in the proliferation of nuclear information.

Badr Brigade

Armed wing of the Supreme Council for the Islamic Republic of Iraq (SCIRI).

Basij

A paramilitary organ affiliated to IRGC, lightly armed, numerous, and dispersed throughout country, intended to deal with civil unrest.

Guardian Council

Consisting of clerics and lawyers, whose task is to interpret new laws passed by parliament and determine if they are consistent with Islamic law or the constitution. Although it is not a legislative body, it has veto power over the Iranian parliament.

Hamas

Palestinian Islamist (Sunni) paramilitary organization and political party.

Hezbollah	Islamist (Shiite) political party, founded to oppose Israeli insertions into southern Lebanon.
IRGC	Islamic Revolutionary Guards Corps (aka Pasdaran). The parallel military organization set up by revolutionary Iran to assure internal or domestic security primarily. They control the missile program and sensitive WMD sites.
Islamic Jihad	Syrian-based Islamist group, responsible for 1983 U.S. Embassy bombing in Lebanon.
Karine A	Freighter intercepted by Israeli Defense Force in December 2001, which was carrying weapons loaded in Iran and destined for Palestinian areas.
Keyhan newspaper	Most conservative Iranian newspaper, under direct supervision of the Office of the Supreme Leader.
Majles	Iranian parliament.
Taliban	Fundamentalist Islamist group, who sheltered Al Qaeda during their five-year reign in Afghanistan.

People

Mahmoud **Ahmadinejad**	Succeeded Mohammed Khatami when elected President of Iran August 2005. Former Mayor of Tehran. Considered to be a religious conservative.
Mohammad **Al Baradei**	Director-General of the International Atomic Energy Agency since 1997. Recipient of the Nobel Peace Prize for 2005.
John R. **Bolton**	U.S. ambassador to the UN since August 2005.
Saddam **Hussein**	Former president of Iraq. Accessed power through the secular Baath Party, assuming the position of president of Iraq in 1979.
Ibrahim Al-**Jafaari**	Prime Minister of Iraq January 2005–May 2006.

AQ **Khan**	Abdul Qadeer Khan, "Godfather" of Pakistan's nuclear weapons program.
Ayatollah **Khamenei**	Seyyed Ali Hosseini Khamenei, Supreme Leader of Iran.
Kamal **Kharrazi**	Iranian Minister of Foreign Affairs from August 20, 1997, to August 24, 2005. Iranian representative at the UN from 1989 to 1997.
Kim Jong-Il	Chairman of the National Defense Committee and General Secretary of the Korean Workers' Party. North Korea's leader since 1994.
Ali **Larijani**	Conservative Iranian politician. Replaced Hasan Rowhani in August 2005 as the Secretary of the Supreme National Security Council. President of Islamic Republic of Iran Broadcasting (IRIB) from 1994 to 2004. Placed sixth in Iranian presidential elections of 2005.
Mostafa **Moin**	Iranian reformist presidential candidate in 2005 elections. Supported by the Islamic Iran Participation Front.
Hossein **Mousavian**	Former senior Iranian nuclear negotiator.
Sirus **Naseri**	Senior nuclear negotiator (until August 2005).
Mohammad Bager **Qalibaf**	Former head of police, resigned in order to run for president in 2005 elections, succeeded Ahmadinejad as mayor of Tehran.
Hashemi **Rafsanjani**	Chairman of the Expediency Discernment Council of Iran. Former president of Iran from 1989 to 1997. Lost election for a third term to Mahmoud Ahmadinejad in 2005 elections.
Mohsen **Rezai**	Former Guards Commander (IRGC) from 1981 to 1997. Secretary of Expediency Council.
Hasan **Rowhani** Hojjat-el-Eslam	Former Secretary of the SNSC acting as chief negotiator with the EU-3 over Iranian nuclear program.
Yahya Rahim **Safavi**	Revolutionary Guards Commander.
Mohammed Reza **Shah** Pahlavi	Shah of Iran from 1941 to 1979.
Admiral Ali **Shamkhani**	Iranian Defense Minister replaced by Brigadier General **Mustafa Mohammad Najjar.**

Hossein **Shariatmadri**	Editor of hard-line *Keyhan* newspaper. Representative of Supreme Leader Khamenei.
Javier **Solana**	High Representative for the Common Foreign and Security Policy, Secretary-General of the Council of the European Union.
Grand Ayatollah Ali **Sistani**	Senior Shiite cleric in Iraq.
Ali Akbar **Velayati**	Former foreign minister. Advisor on international affairs to Supreme Leader Khamenei.

Places

Arak	Heavy water production plant.
Natanz (near Isfahan)	Uranium enrichment facility.
Bushire	Site of nearly completed reactor on the Persian Gulf.
Lavizan/Parchin	Sites and barracks with some nuclear-related activity.

Index

About the Author

Shahram Chubin is Director of Studies at the Geneva Centre for Security Policy. He was a visiting scholar at the Carnegie Endowment for International Peace in 1994 and served as Director of Regional Security Studies at the International Institute for Strategic Studies in London.

Carnegie Endowment
for International Peace

The Carnegie Endowment for International Peace is a private, nonprofit organization dedicated to advancing cooperation between nations and promoting active international engagement by the United States. Founded in 1910, Carnegie is nonpartisan and dedicated to achieving practical results.

Through research, publishing, convening and, on occasion, creating new institutions and international networks, Endowment associates shape fresh policy approaches. Their interests span geographic regions and the relations between governments, business, international organizations, and civil society, focusing on the economic, political, and technological forces driving global change. Through its Carnegie Moscow Center, the Endowment helps to develop a tradition of public policy analysis in the states of the former Soviet Union and to improve relations between Russia and the United States. The Endowment publishes *Foreign Policy*, one of the world's leading journals of international politics and economics, which reaches readers in more than 120 countries and in several languages.